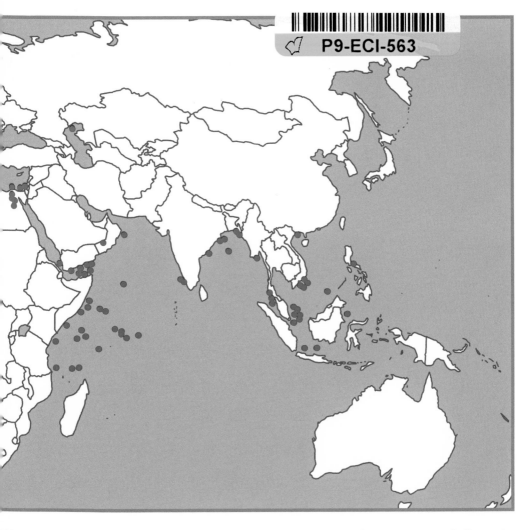

2005	Attack on the American cruise vessel *Seabourne Spirit* by Somali pirates	**2008**	Planned al Qaeda operation against Caribbean cruise ships uncovered by British Intelligence MI6
2007	Hijacking of the North Korean cargo vessel MV *Dai Hong Dan* by Somali pirates	**2009**	Hijacking of the MV *Maersk Alabama* by Somali pirates and subsequent rescue of Capt. Richard Phillips by the US Navy
2007	Hijacking of the tanker *Nepline Delima* by Indonesian pirates in the Malacca Strait	**2009**	Attempted attack on Suez Canal infrastructure by al Qaeda
2008	Hijacking of the French luxury yacht *Le Ponant* by Somali pirates	**2009**	Attack on the Italian cruise ship MSC *Melody* by Somali pirates
2008	Hijacking of the Ukrainian arms vessel MV *Faina* by Somali pirates	**2009**	Capture of the British yacht *Lynn Rival* by Somali pirates; owners and crew held for ransom
2008	Hijacking of the Saudi supertanker MV *Sirius Star* by Somali pirates off the coast of Kenya	**2010**	Attack on the USS *Nicholas*, an Oliver Hazard Perry class frigate, by Somali pirates
2008	Attack on the American cruise ship MS *Nautica* by Somali pirates	**2010**	Capture of the South Korean supertanker *Samho Dream* by Somali pirates

THE WORLD FOR
RANSOM

THE WORLD FOR RANSOM

PIRACY IS TERRORISM, TERRORISM IS PIRACY

D. R. BURGESS

 Prometheus Books

59 John Glenn Drive
Amherst, New York 14228–2119

Published 2010 by Prometheus Books

Inquiries should be addressed to
Prometheus Books
59 John Glenn Drive
Amherst, New York 14228–2119
VOICE: 716–691–0133
FAX: 716–691–0137
WWW.PROMETHEUSBOOKS.COM

14 13 12 11 10   5 4 3 2 1

Library of Congress Cataloging-in-Publication Data

Burgess, D. R., 1977–
    The world for ransom : piracy is terrorism, terrorism is piracy /
by D. R. Burgess.
        p. cm.
    Includes bibliographical references and index.
    ISBN 978–1–61614–173–8 (cloth : acid-free paper)
    1. Piracy—History—21st century. 2. Terrorism—History—21st century.
I. Title.

G535.B86 2010
364.16'4—dc22

                                                    2010003617

Printed in the United States of America on acid-free paper

8/11

CONTENTS

PART 2: TERRORISM IS PIRACY

DEDICATION

On July 31, 2002, a bomb detonated in the Frank Sinatra cafeteria at the University of Jerusalem. Nine persons, all students, some American, were killed. The story made the usual round of headlines, the usual images flickered momentarily on television screens: young women clutching blood-soaked scarves to their faces, medics bending over gurneys. One image in particular appeared in all the newspapers. It was an aerial shot, taken from a helicopter, showing a line of corpses wrapped in black plastic. Nothing could be seen of the figures except bare legs emerging from beneath the tarp.

One of them was my friend David Gritz. He had arrived in Jerusalem just two weeks before, the recipient of a prestigious fellowship to examine Arab-Israeli relations and philosophy. David was a brilliant student, whom nothing would deter from seeking the truth. His parents were adamantly opposed to his leaving, especially as tensions between Israel and Hamas had grown in recent days. I, too, counseled him strongly against the trip. But I was in New York, and he was in Paris. In the last days before he departed I volunteered to fly there myself and discourage him, without success. In his last e-mail, David wrote to me, "I hope you don't intend this to be a last visit to a future corpse!"

When someone is taken suddenly, we hear the same pane-gyrics of loss: "a gentle soul," "kind-hearted," "a great friend." It angered me to hear these words about David Gritz. He was all those things, but so very much more. He was a genius whose intellect was just beginning to be recognized. His theories on Arab-Israeli relations were revolutionary, far in advance of his years, bespeaking a great career to come. He was also pro-foundly spiritual. His faith was neither Jewish nor Christian nor any denomination, but rather a constant search for the good and the divine that transcends religions and binds them. But what I remember most about David was his almost preternat-ural ability to experience life. He was never bored or out of sorts. He lived through each day in a constant state of expecta-tion and curiosity: for places, for experiences, for people. My one consolation for his early loss is that he lived a full lifetime in twenty-four years.

This book is dedicated to the memory of David Gritz, in the hope that his may be among the last sacrifices to the barbaric maw of terrorism.

ACKNOWLEDGMENTS

A project of this kind requires not one but many leaps of faith, and I am forever grateful to those who believed in it and in me. First I must acknowledge my friend and mentor Professor Peter Burns, for his encouragement and advice. Thanks also to my editor, Steven L. Mitchell, and my fantastic agent Kimberley Cameron, for their confidence and assistance in making this book a reality.

I must also thank my parents, Doug and Shannon Burgess, who were there at the dining room table when we first spoke of piracy and terrorism and whose counsel has sustained me ever since.

Finally, my biggest thanks go to A. Q. Bui, who has endured both project and author with unfailing good humor and grace.

FOREWORD

OCTOBER 7, 1985

The ship had left Alexandria that morning. Nearly all her passengers were ashore, exploring the pyramids on day tours to Cairo and Saqqara. Those who remained were mostly too old or infirm to make the journey. It was an autumn cruise in the Mediterranean, not known for attracting swinging youth. The ship was old herself, thirty-five years, an age when most cruise liners were already being cut to ribbons in the scrapyards of Kaosung or Alang. No one knew quite why this ship had been spared. Fires had plagued her throughout her long career, even as recently as her last refit. It was then that she received a new sports deck and a new name: *Achille Lauro*.[1]

Sixty-nine passengers remained on board as the *Achille Lauro* steamed slowly from Alexandria to Port Said, at the mouth of the Suez Canal. Most were in the dining room; lunch was being served. At 1:30 p.m. four men carrying automatic weapons burst through the dining room door and fired several rounds into the ceiling. The passengers, those who were mobile, fell to the floor. The men shouted something unintelligible and herded the remainder of the passengers into the center of the room. One Austrian woman tried to run for the door but was struck across the face and pulled back to join the others.[2]

Capt. Gerardo de Rosa was in his cabin. An officer burst through the door and told him that hijackers had stormed the ship and were firing at passengers. De Rosa made for the stern, where the dining room was located, but even as he approached, the *Achille Lauro*'s loudspeakers blared and an anxious voice summoned him to the bridge. He obeyed and was met with two Arab men pointing automatic rifles at his chest. They ordered him to alter the ship's course and make for Tartus, Syria, some three hundred miles to the northeast.

For the next twenty-four hours the *Achille Lauro* made her way through the Mediterranean Sea in total radio silence. Passengers returning from their excursions to Port Said were told by local agents that the ship had been detained due to unusually heavy traffic in the Suez. Only in the late afternoon did the Lauro Company finally admit the truth: the *Achille Lauro* was captured, her destination unknown.

She arrived in Tartus at 11:00 a.m. the following day. It was then that radio silence was broken, as the hijackers made their demands. They were, they said, members of the Palestinian Liberation Front, a splinter sect of the PLO. The four men demanded the release of some fifty Palestinians held by Israel, including Samir al-Qantari, one of the most notorious terrorists of the age. If al-Qantari and the others were not released, the men promised, they would begin executing passengers at 3:00 p.m. sharp.[3]

As the hour approached and no answer was forthcoming, the hijackers met in the dining room and decided whom they would kill by rifling through the passports of the remaining passengers. The man they chose was Leon Klinghoffer, a sixty-nine-year-old American Jew from New York who had recently suffered a stroke and was wheelchair-bound. Youssef Majed Molqi, the leader of the hijackers, ordered a Portuguese waiter to push Klinghoffer's wheelchair out onto the open deck, away from the rest of the passengers. The other hijackers were instructed to tell the rest that Klinghoffer was ill and being escorted to the infirmary. Once on the deck, Molqi aimed a pistol at Klinghoffer and shot him twice, once in the head and once in the chest. The body slumped forward and fell out of the wheelchair. Molqi ordered the waiter and another crew member to throw Klinghoffer's corpse over the side. With some difficulty they did so, and then Molqi ordered the wheelchair thrown overboard as well. This was done in full view of the Syrian authorities on shore at Tartus.[4]

The American people had suffered an early casualty in a conflict that would one day be dubbed the "war on terror." But President Reagan, speaking to the airwaves one week after the *Achille Lauro* hostages were released, adopted a more familiar term. The hijacking was, he said, "an act of piracy."[5]

*   *   *

The outrage over the *Achille Lauro* affair gradually subsided, and today it is almost forgotten. The supervening horror of September 11, 2001, seemingly banished all prior acts of terrorism from the American consciousness, replacing them with the stark image of the World Trade Center consumed in flames. For eight years potentates have spoken blithely of a war on terror, with no clear indication of what such a war entails. Is it simply a war against Osama bin Laden and al Qaeda? Or all terrorist groups? Or just those which threaten the United States? As early as June 2004, President George W. Bush declared that "like the Second World War, our present conflict began with a ruthless surprise attack on the United States. We will not forget that treachery," he went on, "and we will accept nothing less than total victory over the enemy."[6]

Such ringing declarations left many mystified. What was the definition of "total victory" against an enemy that had no territorial boundaries, no standing army, no recognized government? Wars were understood to be either interstate or intrastate—that is, between two nations or civil war. The war on terror, a war between state and nonstate actors, had no obvious precedent.[7]

The failure to define "our present conflict" has proved crippling. The United States has engaged in illegal captures around the world, held suspects without charge in detention facilities, vastly abridged the constitutional liberties of its citizens, and still we are no closer to "winning" the war on terror. It continues to be a war without definition, fought with no rules governing its conduct and no prospect of closure, much less success.

But Reagan was more right than he knew. The history of piracy and the history of terrorism have long moved in tandem. Even in the last century, jurists began to speak of "maritime terrorism," just as they defined hijacking an airliner as "aerial piracy."[8] Today, with incidents of piracy on the rise throughout the world, many with connections to terrorist groups like al Qaeda, the two are more closely linked than ever.

This book will explore those linkages. If two crimes share both a history and a legal definition, then they are not two crimes but one. Terrorists can be given the same legal status that pirates have held for two thousand years: *hostis humani generi,* "enemies of the human race." With definition come the means, legal and actual, to capture terrorists and bring them to justice. We will explore those means and how the United States can employ the law to accomplish what eight years of military endeavor have so far failed to do: strike international terrorist organizations at their roots.

The war on terror is unique in our time, a state versus nonstate conflict where traditional rules of engagement and yardsticks of success are obsolete. It will require unique and unconventional means to achieve success. The first task, which has yet to be done, is defining the nature of that war itself. While no book can present a clear path to victory, I hope with this one to show that the war on terror, while extraordinary, is not without precedent. A precedent exists in piracy, and with it several centuries of law and history that reveal how a global scourge can be fought and conquered.

NOTES

1. Jack Gottschalk and Brian Flanagan, *Jolly Roger with an Uzi* (Annapolis, MD: Naval Institute Press, 2000), p. 36.

2. Michael K. Bohn, *The* Achille Lauro *Hijacking: Lessons in the Politics and Prejudice of Terrorism* (Washington, DC: Brassey's, 2004), pp. 1–5.

3. George Constantinople, "Toward a New Definition of Piracy: The *Achille Lauro* Incident," *Virginia Journal of International Law* 26 (1986): 749.

4. Antonio Cassesse, *Terrorism, Politics and Law: The* Achille Lauro *Affair* (New York: Polity Press, 1989).

5. Gerardo P. McKinley, "The *Achille Lauro* Affair—Implications for International Law," *Tennessee Law Review* 53 (1985): 690.

6. Comments available at http://www.whitehouse.gov/news/releases/2004/06/print/20040602.html.

7. See Brian Jenkins, "Future Trends in International Terrorism," in *Violence at Sea: A Review of Terrorism, Acts of War and Piracy, and Countermeasures to Prevent Terrorism*, ed. Brian A. H. Parritt (Paris: ICC Publishing, 1986), pp. 41–42.

8. Convention for the Suppression of Unlawful Acts against the Safety of Maritime Navigation, March 10, 1988, 1678 U.N.T.S. 221.

Introduction

BEYOND THE LAW

In October 2008, I sat in the darkened Roundabout Theatre on West Forty-seventh Street. The play was Robert Bolt's brilliant *A Man for All Seasons*, currently enjoying a second Broadway revival. The scene was one in which English jurist and martyr Sir Thomas More is confronted by his son-in-law, William Roper. Incensed at More's apparent passivity in the face of an unjust law, Roper declares, "I would tear down every law in England to get at the devil!" There is a collective breath in the audience, a few nods, radiating approval of a young man's passion for justice. One can almost hear the sympathetic susurration of torn playbooks.

But then More answers him: "And when the law was down and the devil turned round on you, where will you hide, Roper, the laws all being flat? This country's planted thick with laws from coast to coast—man's laws, not God's—and if you cut them down. . . . d'you really think you could stand upright in the winds that blow then? Yes, I give the devil the benefit of law—*for my own safety's sake!*"

More's warning has never been more apt. For nine years after the attacks of September 11, 2001, the United States in its

17

war on terror has lain the law flat to get at the devil. President George W. Bush pithily summed up this policy with the phrase, "You are either with us or with the terrorists."[1] Yet the lines of demarcation are difficult to place. Terrorism in the twenty-first century has a quicksilver, elusive quality of definition. President Bush repeatedly conflated the war on terror with American involvement in Iraq, despite the tenuous—perhaps nonexistent—linkage between the two. This gave ironic weight to the hackneyed adage long cited by insurgents and their supporters, that "one man's terrorist is another man's freedom fighter." Unfortunately they are right: the term *terrorist* has been so widely bandied about as an epithet that it lost whatever meaning it once had.[2]

The Bush administration has ended, yet the murkiness it engendered still remains. There is still no conclusive definition in American law for the crime of organized terrorism, at home or abroad. Since 2001 we have been fighting in a "war on terror" that no one has successfully explained. Who are these enemies? How can we defeat them? How do we know if we are winning? How will we know if we have won?

At this moment both the United States and its nemeses pursue each other across a vast chessboard of states with no international covenants governing their actions. Such a situation has not been present for centuries, and the opportunities for abuse and barbarism are rampant. The United States has held several hundred persons captive at Guantanamo Bay, Cuba, and engaged the full weight of its secret services in a covert and silent manhunt. It has tortured prisoners and suspended habeas corpus. Al Qaeda and other terrorist organizations, meanwhile, continue to plan and execute their crimes beyond the jurisdiction of the United States, its allies, the International Criminal Court (ICC), or any international judicial bodies.[3]

It is not only our own nation that has neglected to define its battle against organized terrorism. The rest of world has done so as well. Terrorists are still perceived by many as revolutionaries, with no distinction drawn between individual insurgent groups within states and multinational terrorist organizations like al Qaeda. There is a world of difference. The latter are highly structured, well funded, and cellular, with bases and agents throughout the world. In legal terms, they are powerful nonstate actors whose strength is derived from the very properties that distinguish them from states: lack of territorial boundaries, lack of recognized government, and lack of international recognition.

Yet international law falls well behind in addressing this new reality, written instead for a world in which terrorism existed only on the lunatic fringe of society and the greatest enemy to the nation-state came from another state.[4] A single perpetrator of a terrorist act may be brought to justice, but the organization itself remains beyond the law. Thus the twenty-first-century war on terror is being waged—by both states and terrorists—in a vacuum.

Some might say this is not a bad thing. Without the gridiron of legal responsibility, all is permissible. Rendition, torture, indefinite imprisonment: as the United States pursues its war, the question is no longer what laws it must obey but whether it need obey any at all. The myriad uncertainties of a post-9/11 world have made us doubt what we once held inviolable. Threats that seemed remote in Yemen and Nigeria suddenly became paramount in the American consciousness.

Our response was chilling. America, under President George W. Bush, embarked on a campaign to root out terrorism at its source, beginning with states known or suspected to have harbored terrorists. It captured men and women and held them prisoner in camps outside of American legal jurisdiction. It engaged in acts of brutality, humiliation, and outright torture against those it believed—rightly or wrongly—participated in terrorist crimes.

This disregard of human rights was matched on a larger scale by indifference or hostility to international agreements. The United States, which in 1998 had helped create the International Criminal Court, abruptly withdrew its support and participation when the specter was raised that the American military might fall, like everyone else, within its jurisdiction.[5] With the United States determined to act aggressively to protect itself from future attack, deference to the law was a luxury many felt they could no longer afford.

So we laid the law flat to get at the devil. But now the devil has turned around on us. The war on terror has become perpetual. It cannot end, nor can it be won, because it lacks all the normal qualities associated with traditional conflict. Ours is a war waged not against states, but against terrorist cells existing in almost every nation, including our own. Terrorists may be of any nationality, and may be found anywhere on earth. Their cellular structure gives them an inestimable advantage over the states they target. Ephemeral and ubiquitous, terrorist organizations can never truly be defeated as long as they find safe havens in which to plan their attacks and train their recruits. These bases exist in states that, while potentially hostile to our own, are not at war with us. But if we enter their borders and capture their citizens, as we have done, we commit an act of war against them. Renditions are *causus belli*, grounds for war. Hence the United States' righteous efforts to defend itself from attack have become covert, illegal, and ineffectual. We may temporarily prevent another 9/11, but as long as hostile states feel justified in harboring terrorists, the threat will never cease.

The history of the last nine years is a somber one, but our attempts to act with impunity around the world have now brought us to a cold truth: rule of law is more important than the threat, however great, to the nation-state. This is so because the rule of law *is* the nation-state: law is the matrix for society, and the government's source of legitimacy. International law translates this relationship from "citizen-to-government" to "state-to-state," providing a code of diplomatic conduct that ensures the continued survival of the international community from lawless war and universal destruction. Organized international terrorism challenges the very heart of these relationships.

That challenge remains, but we are no longer blind to it. The United States has now begun reckoning with its ongoing war on terror. Guantanamo will be closed, and the Supreme Court has upheld the rights of its detainees to a fair trial. A new administration is uniquely positioned to undertake the arduous, long-delayed task of fashioning a law for terrorism, at home and around the world. The crucial first step is defining the crime.

But that first step has, so far, eluded us. A war on terror is a war against an idea, a concept. We cannot wage war against an idea. Terrorism will always exist, and has existed in some form since time immemorial. Whether a lone assassin lobs a bomb into Czar Alexander's theater box or detonates it on an airplane full of passengers, the directed use of violence to achieve political consciousness is an indelible part of human history.[6] What we can eradicate, however, is not the idea but its most pernicious outgrowth: the international terrorist organization. Unlike individuals, these organizations exist only because there is a lack of political consensus to see them destroyed. That lack of consensus exists because no one has yet defined the crime of terrorism.

There have been attempts. But the terrorist's unique hybrid status—neither ordinary criminal nor military combatant—has so far made such efforts futile. Domestic criminal law deals only with specific crimes (homicide, theft, destruction of property) any of which might be present in an act of terror, but has no law for the crime of *belonging* to a terrorist organization. Most jurists recognize that terrorist acts transcend the scope of ordinary law. Yet if domestic criminal law cannot cope with international terrorism, what can?

One possible solution that the Bush administration tinkered with was treating terrorists as enemy combatants. Yet this raised a host of different problems.[7] Combatants fall under the laws of war. The Geneva Convention and other treaties and covenants delineate the capture and treatment of prisoners, and more recent laws promulgated after the Second World War also deal with crimes against humanity and war crimes. The difficulty, however, is that terrorists are not soldiers. A soldier is an extension of his or her state and is answerable to the military codes of that state. Likewise, when soldiers engage in war, they do so at the behest of their nations, and thus they share liability for their actions with the state that commands them.

Terrorists do not act on any state's command; if they do, they are not terrorists but extensions of that state's militia. A terrorist organization may receive funds or protection from a state, but that does not make it that state's creature. Al Qaeda, for example, while linked financially with certain countries, does not exist to do their bidding. It is precisely their independence from state control that makes these organizations so dangerous: all the usual pressures—diplomatic, financial, military—that one nation may use to compel another cannot be used against organizations like al Qaeda. If terrorists are combatants, then terrorist organizations must be defined as belligerent states, giving them precisely the recognition they crave and do not deserve.

But if international terrorists are neither ordinary criminals nor enemy combatants, what are they? There is an answer. Old, dusty, anachronistic perhaps, but eminently workable and entirely accurate.

They are pirates.

This book will prove that a precedent for terrorism exists in piracy—that they are, in fact, the same crime. Once we have a precedent, we have a law: terrorists will borrow not only pirates' unique status as enemies of the human race (about which more later) but also the equally unique measures accorded to states to hunt them down.

Piracy is no longer the faded sepia image of Captain Kidd and buried treasure. Recent events in Somalia have put it center stage once again, and introduced the twenty-first century to a new set of stereotypes. The Zodiac boat and rocket launcher have displaced parrots and planks. That is as it should be; piracy never disappeared. It diminished and relocated to more distant waters, but not since the first traders embarked on the first sea voyages has the earth been entirely free of piracy. What the Somali pirates accomplished was to remind us how a tiny band of brigands, if properly placed, can hold the world for ransom. One need only conjure up the image of the one-hundred-thousand-ton supertanker *Sirius Star* drifting helpless, held captive by a group of men that would not fill one of its lifeboats, to find a telling metaphor for the effects of organized terrorism on the nation-state.

But the case for linking piracy and terrorism goes much deeper than shared imagery. For over two thousand years pirates have held a unique status in the law as international criminals, malevolent satellites to the law of nations. Pirates are not enemies of one state or group of states but of all states; accordingly, every state shares in the obligation to capture and destroy them. Equating terrorists with pirates recognizes their level of organization and potential threat without granting them the legitimacy reserved for soldiers and belligerent states. From this threat comes the ancient doctrine of universal jurisdiction: pirates may be captured wherever they are found, by anyone who finds them. If the same rule were extended to terrorists, the United States could defend entry and capture within the borders of uncooperative states by citing its right under piracy law, correctly claiming that such entry does not violate state sovereignty. Nor would states be able to defend offering protection to known terrorists on the grounds that they are freedom fighters.

This would seem, at first glance, to be merely yet another legal excuse for the United States to justify rendition. But the beauty of the law is that works both ways. If the United States gives a legal definition to terrorism, it is obligated to prove that the suspects it captures fit that definition. This, as I have suggested, is precisely what the Bush administration declined to do. The law is a helix of obligation and right, bestowing on the state the prerogative to enforce its codes, provided that it defines them justly and works within their strictures. A new law on terrorism, based on piracy, will give the United States and other states the unquestioned right to seize terrorists wherever they may be found, but it will enjoin them to prove their case afterward. That, in short, is the difference between anarchy and law.

To prove that piracy and terrorism are the same crime, they must share three elements familiar to criminal lawyers everywhere: the *mens rea*, or mental state of the criminal; the *actus reus*, or actions constituting the crime; and the *locus in quo*, the place where the crime occurred. The task of the following chapters is to prove that the *mens rea*, *actus reus*, and *locus in quo* of piracy and terrorism are the same. The first step is looking at the history of piracy. Can we draw a link between Blackbeard or the Barbary corsairs and al Qaeda?

The next step is to look at the law. How did nations define pirates, and what measures did they take to extirpate them? Is there a correlation between the "war against the world" that Daniel Defoe spoke of in 1722 and our own "war on terror"? Has piracy changed over the years? And, if so, has it begun to look more or less like terrorism?

Then we will turn to consider piracy as it exists today. Is it mere "sea robbery," as one judge defined it, or is it more complicated? What are the links between pirate bands and terrorist organizations? The explosion of piracy off the Somali coast was the direct result of a combination of factors all leading back to a root cause: the ongoing war on terror. We will consider how piracy evolved from mere sea robbery into the hybrid crime that exists today, which I have termed *piraterrorism*.

Then we will look at the problems facing today's navies as they try to combat the pirate menace. In a remarkably brief span of time, piracy has gone from a peripheral annoyance to a crucial threat to world commerce. It has overstrained the abilities of the United States and other nations to respond to it, at a time when their militaries are already stretched thin. Most of all, the second pirate "golden age" must be placed within a larger framework of a global war on terror to understand its true significance. But by melding the problems of piracy and terrorism, we are also presented with the solution: universal jurisdiction for both crimes.

With the precedent and the modern-day examples settled, we will try to construct a model law for terrorism based on piracy. Once this is done, we will see how it holds up in the context of actual terrorist attacks. Can these be called piratical? If so, how should we prosecute them?

Finally, we will look at how a law for terrorism may transform the hunt for al Qaeda and other terrorist organizations. This transformation cannot be overstated. Piracy cuts the Gordian knot of definition that has brought the prosecution of terrorist crimes to an impasse, providing both a precedent and a legal framework for future trials. It facilitates the capture of suspected terrorists around the world. Most important, it sets the parameters to understand the war on terror and the means to resolve it—a resolution that begins with the recognition that terrorism, like piracy, is a threat not just to one state or people, but the human race entire.

Recall that More spoke of "man's laws, not God's" keeping order against the devil's wind. That is the task of terrorism law: to affect a bulwark against the anarchy inherent in a conflict without territorial boundaries, obvious contestants, or legal parameters. It is a task that can be met only by giving terrorists their correct legal status as pirates, enemies of the human race.

NOTES

1. D. T. Max, "The Making of the Speech," *New York Times*, October 7, 2001, p. 32.

2. See Jennifer Trahan, "Terrorism Conventions: Existing Gaps and Different Approaches," *New England International and Comparative Law Annual* 8 (2002): 215–43; J. Bowyer Bell, "Revolutionary Organizations," *International Terrorism & World Security* 21 (1976): 78.

3. Paisley Dobbs, "Three Years in Operation, Guantanamo Remains," *Boston Globe*, January 10, 2005.

4. Yonah Alexander, "Terrorism: A Definitional Focus," *Terrorism and the Law* 3 (2001): 35.

5. See Alfred Rubin, "Legal Response to Terror: An International Criminal Court?" *Harvard International Law Journal* 43, no. 1 (Winter 2002).

6. Michael Rossetti, "Terrorism as a Violation of the Law of Nations after *Kadic v. Karadzic*," *St. John's Journal of Legal Commentary* 12 (1997): 565.

7. See Jonathan Mahler, *The Challenge:* Hamdan v. Rumsfeld *and the Fight over Presidential Power* (New York: Farrar, Strauss & Giroux, 2008).

Part 1
PIRACY IS TERRORISM

Chapter 1
"AT WAR WITH ALL THE WORLD"

The Republic was under siege.[1]

Reports filtered in from provincial governors, each more harrowing than the last. They told of entire fleets sunk within sight of shore, their hulls doused with hot pitch and set alight, until the horizon glowed orange. Captains returning to the city spoke of roving bands that appeared suddenly in the night, stormed aboard their vessels, and cut the throats of their crews. In Ostia empty barges sat in desolate rows along the docks, waiting for shipments that would not come. Broken and discarded amphorae, clay jars that should have been filled with wine, honey, or oil, were dry.

The lifeblood of Roman commerce had dried up also. There would be no Grecian wine, no Syrian wool, no African wood. The Egyptian trade was the hardest hit of all. From there came the wheat, papyrus, and building stone that served as the foundation for Rome's dazzling architecture. Not a single Egyptian shipment had arrived for weeks.

Many in the Curia felt this loss keenly. With paper in short supply, scribes were reduced to recording their oratory on wax tablets, the same ones Roman children scrawled their first letters upon. Food tasted bland; the spice merchants were out of stock. Worse still, wives complained that Arabian perfumes could no longer be found, not even on the black market. Rome was beginning to smell.

Dire as this all was, it was nothing compared to the political firestorm developing in the Senate. A young, brash general by the name of Gnaeus Pompeius had offered to solve Rome's pirate problem once and for all, if only they would give him command of the fleet and unlimited power to devise whatever tactical solutions he saw fit. It was a dangerous proposal: Pompeius, or Pompey, was an ambitious man. His successes on the battlefield in Hispania had made him a popular hero; the citizens displayed their affection by electing him consul.

Some in the Senate believed that the pirate menace was nothing more than a pretext for Pompey to claim another triumph and thus position himself for his ultimate goal: dictatorship of Rome. Surely, they argued, the state was great enough to deal with a small band of brigands. Not so, others said. Look at the condition of our docks, our fleets. Look at our reputation abroad. The Republic is being made to look ridiculous.

The argument had reached stalemate in the Curia when one senator rose to speak. Marcus Tullius Cicero was a young man, still in his thirties, but his reputation as an orator of consummate skill was already known. One year earlier he had been elected *aedile,* the youngest ever awarded that high office. The other senators paused to listen.

He rose, he said, in defense of Pompey, and to illuminate the Senate on the menace confronting it. The danger to Rome was no pretext. Piracy was much more than a threat to trade, he told them, and pirates themselves were much worse than robbers. Small in numbers they may be, but the effects of their actions were vastly disproportionate to their size. "We are faced," Cicero told the Senate, "with a war that is ancient, widespread, and shameful." Warming to his theme, he went on: "What province is free of pirates? What cargo is safe? . . . Should I talk of those illustrious cities, Cnidus, Colophon, or Samos, and many more captured by pirates, when you know your own port city fell to pirates? . . . Or should I even mention the misfortune and devastation of Ostia when you were all eyewitnesses to the capture and destruction of a fleet under the command of the consul elected by you, the Roman people?"[2]

A threat to trade was a threat to Rome's very existence, for the Republic's stature hinged on its ability to maintain its seas, keep contact with its satellites, secure its trade routes, and protect its allies. Piracy threatened all of these objectives. "I say to you," Cicero thundered, "that you could not even reach your allies by sea, since your army dared not sail the seas from Brundisium [for fear of pirates] except in dead of winter." Pirates were not common criminals, for no ordinary criminal could pose such a dire menace to the state as a whole. They were a scourge that must be eradicated, by whatever means necessary.

The Senate gave Pompey his command. Under his successful leadership the pirates were driven from the seas, and the first legal definition of piracy was inscribed in Roman law. Pirates were *hostis humani generi*, enemies of the human race. They remain so by law today.[3]

*   *   *

I have chosen to contentiously title this part "Piracy Is Terrorism," just as the second on modern terrorist law is titled "Terrorism Is Piracy." This is not to invite charges of Cartesian circularity, but rather to emphasize a critical point of this book: in its acts and motivations, in almost every known manifestation throughout its history, piracy shares crucial similarities with modern international terrorism. Chief among these is the concept of state versus nonstate warfare, so-called private war, whereby bands of brigands divorce themselves from their nation-state and launch attacks against it or other states. In the case of piracy, the states responded forcefully, and in the pirate wars from Republican Rome to the nineteenth century we find a crucial precedent for understanding and waging our own fight against terrorism.

Before that argument can be made, however, we must first separate the reality of piracy from the carefully constructed myth that has obscured its significance as a precedent and rendered the pirates themselves as jolly, comical figures whose only significance is offering an outlet for adolescent fantasies. Much work has recently been done to debunk romanticized images of piracy, with mixed success. While scores of historians have repeatedly emphasized that most pirates were neither romantic nor attractive, Hollywood and the publishing world continue to generate reams of drivel reinforcing the stereotype—eye-patch, parrot, and all. When I first began arguing for a link between the two crimes, piracy and terrorism, in 2003, I found to my dismay that my most ardent supporters were those who were eager to, as one phrased it, "make Bin Laden walk the plank." When my articles hit the Internet, responses came back from otherwise well-known and reputable blog sites with titles like "Argghhhh Qaeda" and "Rum, Osama, and the Lash."

The sea change, if one might call it that, came in 2008, when the long-festering problem of Somali piracy exploded across the headlines. Suddenly piracy was no longer amusing. An unintended but welcomed consequence of piracy's sudden reemergence in our century is that its contemporary iteration is stark and unsentimental—just as it was, in truth, in 1700.

While the Johnny Depp/Long John Silver/Captain Blood effigy can now be easily dispensed, other myths of piracy are harder to break. The most common of these, and the most common objection to comparing piracy to terrorism, is that piracy is all about robbery. Many notable jurists also share this view, and it has become almost a mantra for those seeking to limit the definition of piracy in our own century. Most, however, do not realize that they are actually echoing the words of a seventeenth-century English judge. At the trial of a pirate crew at the Old Bailey in 1696, Justice Charles Hedges declared, "Now Piracy is only a Sea term for Robbery, Piracy being a Robbery committed within the Jurisdiction of the Admiralty; if any man be assaulted within that Jurisdiction, and his Ship or Goods violently taken away without a Legal Authority, this is Robbery and Piracy."[4] But Hedges had his own reasons for limiting the definition thus, as we shall see.

In fact, piracy has never been only sea robbery. In the Roman example outlined above, piracy was a private war that threatened the very foundation of the Republic. Whatever the motivations of the pirates themselves, states have long defined the crime of piracy as a form of quasi war against the nation-state. This is the reason for piracy's status as a crime of universal jurisdiction, meaning pirates may be captured wherever they are found, by anyone who finds them. Their extranationality, coupled with the disproportionate threat their actions posed to trade, alliances, and empire, have given pirates a unique hybrid status in the law: neither ordinary criminals nor recognized military combatants, but a combination of the two. It is precisely this status that I argue should be awarded to twenty-first-century terror organizations.

The purpose of this chapter is to trace the thread of the pirates' war against states, and the corresponding growth of international custom, law, and military practice in response. Far from sea robbery, piracy represented a fundamental challenge not only to states but to the idea of statehood itself. Pirates defied and threatened the mores of societies, their laws and social hierarchies, their trade and relations with foreign powers, their colonies, their militaries, and their sovereignty. As a war against all the world, fought with every means of intimidation and depredation, piracy was the first and only example of such a conflict until our own war on terror.

ENEMIES OF THE HUMAN RACE: PIRACY IN THE ANCIENT WORLD

Since the first traders left with ships filled with casks of wine and grain, pirates have waited offshore. Thucydides writes of the Cretan ruler Minos's attempts to "clear the Aegean" of pirates who lurked in the myriad shoals and islets surrounding the city-state, "in order that his revenues might come in." Plutarch credited a similar endeavor to that industrious Hellenic hero, Jason of the Argonauts.[5] Sometimes the pirates were even bolder. The first recorded example of a pirate raid occurred during the reign of Ramses III (1198–1167 BCE) when Egypt found itself overrun with Libyan pirates emerging from boats and sacking cities along the Nile delta.

Yet, like bacteria, piracy flourished best in neglect. The pattern of its history, from the ancient Rhodians to the Barbary corsairs of the nineteenth century, is a wave chart of surge and decline, determined by the relative vigor of the nation-states in condoning, ignoring, employing, or stamping out the pirates. The very first records of piracy are, in fact, records of a state's attempts to destroy them. Even as the early city-states were forging trade relations with one another, renegade pirates threatened those relationships and occasionally even brought the states to the brink of war.[6] What one finds is that paradox persists until the nineteenth century: while piracy as a profession never entirely vanishes, pirates themselves dispersed, disbanded, and disappeared at the first sign of an aggressive state response. Like Minos, the Athenian ruler Pericles undertook the task of policing the Aegean in 470 BCE. In the intervening time the Dolopes of Scyros and the Thracian Chersonese, two tribes of sea marauders, had returned in force. Pericles invited delegates from all over the Greek world to meet in Athens and formulate a plan of attack— an early example of international cooperation to stamp out piracy—and sought the alliance of the warlike Spartans. So successful was this policy that Thucydides would write that during Pericles' later reign the only region where it was still necessary to carry arms at sea was north of the Corinthian Gulf, hundreds of miles from where the Thracian pirates once flourished.

Yet, as would happen again and again in the coming centuries, war and destabilization undermined the temporary reprieve and piracy returned. The Peloponnesian War decimated the Athenian navy, and no ships were left to police the sea. This task fell to Rhodes, which inherited Athens's title as primary city-state of the Aegean. Rhodians were free traders in the most draconian sense: any threat to Rhodian trade was tantamount to an act of war. As trade and foreign relations were intricately interwoven, Rhodes followed Pericles' example and entered into numerous agreements with neighboring city-states to protect their ships and root out the pirates. One such treaty, between Rhodes and the Cretan city of Hierpytna, still survives. It is astonishingly detailed, declaring that if pirates enter Cretan waters, Rhodes pledges its navy to stamp them out. Hierpytna in turn agrees to assist the Rhodian navy. Captured pirates and their vessels would be given to Rhodes as spoils of war, and any captured booty divided equally between the two cities.

And what of the pirates themselves? Most congregated into settlements: some joined by shared tribal bonds, others by shared profession. A few gathered around charismatic leaders, as with the pirate Pentathlus in the Lipari Islands. Those heterogeneous communities not bound by tribal or ethnic linkages quickly developed their own set of rules and mores, which one historian described as "a communistic organization, eminently suited to a piratical community of this type, and imitated to some extent after many years [specifically, in the 1690s] in the colony of pirates in Madagascar."[7] It is an interesting connection, for it reveals that even in the Hellenic period pirates already had begun to view themselves—and were viewed by others—as standing apart from, and in opposition to, established communities. Freed from the laws and social hierarchies of their city-states, they made their own. The Roman historian Livy writes of one such "pirate colony" where members were evenly allocated to the fleet and the fields, with all land held in common and all plunder divided equally among the freemen. It was precisely this sort of activity that eighteenth-century authors writing of their own pirates dubbed "a world turned upside down" and decried as challenging the very foundations of organized society.

This view of pirates as outliers matured yet further in Republican Rome. "There was," one jurist has written, "an implication of impropriety to that way of life. It had nothing to do with political motivation or criminality . . . [but] instead with the place of an antiquated way of life in a new commercial and political order."[8] But the Cilician pirates who threatened Rome were more than a peripheral annoyance. Nestled in the southern slopes of the Taurus mountain range, where the mountains reached the sea at Cilicia Tracheia, Cilician bands had developed over centuries into tightly knit familial units that passed the seamanship and skills of piracy from father to son, much as the Barbary corsairs in a later era. For many years—indeed, a shockingly long period—the Cilicians flourished with little or no retaliation from Rome. It was not until 102 BCE that the Senate commissioned one of its own, Marcus Antonius (grandfather of Cleopatra's lover, Mark Antony), to stamp them out. His force was small and untested, and evidence suggests the pirates repelled him easily. Several decades later another Roman nobleman, Lucullus, took up the task. By now the Cilician pirates had allied themselves with the powerful Mithradates, transforming Rome's private war into a genuine conflict. Lucullus met the combined navies of the Cilicians and Mithradates and, in a series of pitched engagements, defeated both handily. Lucullus returned to Rome and was instantly awarded a triumph.

The immediate result of Lucullus's victory was to reestablish Roman dominance of the sea, but it did little to ameliorate piracy. It may, in fact, have accomplished the inverse. Much as it would after the Anglo-Spanish wars of the sixteenth century, piracy adapted and transformed to meet a new reality. Rome's dominance over the region, won by near-constant wars of conquest, had engendered an ever-widening class of subjugated peoples: refugees and outliers who lay on the wrong side (metaphorically and sometimes actually) of the burgeoning empire. New villages and towns sprang up along the coasts, populated by a heterogeneous mix of the displaced and destitute. Naturally, many took to piracy—as both a means of employment and a means of revenge. This infusion of new blood revitalized the Cilician pirates. Nor were their new recruits merely the dregs. "No doubt," one historian writes, "the refugees provided them [the Cilicians] with many of their boldest leaders, men who knew the more distant coasts and could lead profitable raids."[9]

As the character of the pirates changed, so too did their relationship with Rome. The early Cilicians maintained a healthy respect and fear of the Republic and were careful to treat Roman prisoners with dignity. The new generation, fueled by the hatred of the dispossessed, knew no such restraint. Proud, insular Romans regarded their citizenship as a talisman against all evil, and if captured by pirates would frequently declare, "I am a Roman citizen!" At this, the pirates were expected to drop their swords. Now, when an unfortunate Roman fell into the pirates' clutches, a curious game was played out. At the words, "I am a Roman citizen," the pirates instantly fell to their knees and begged pardon. Naturally, they said, no Roman could be held captive against his will. The citizen was free to go. In fact, the pirate chief went on, as if struck by the sudden idea, you can walk all the way back to Rome from here. Then the pirates would dress the captive in his boots and toga and force him down a ladder into the Aegean, where they left him.[10]

One of the more notable captives of the Cilician pirates was a young nobleman by the name of Julius Caesar. Oppressed by the heat of the city, Caesar had escaped and sought the relative cool of the nearby hills. There the pirates seized him and carried him by sea to their camp in the Taurus mountains. The young man was dressed in fine clothes and jewelry, so the pirates determined his ransom at some twenty talents. Caesar laughed and told them that for a personage of his importance they should ask at least fifty. For the thirty-eight days of his captivity, Caesar became a great favorite of the pirates, competing in their games and even reciting poetry of his own composition. If they failed to attend him, he promised they would all be crucified after his release, then laughed heartily at his own joke.

The ransom was paid, and Julius Caesar was bid farewell with many tears and promises of eternal friendship. Not long afterward he returned to the camp with a brigade of soldiers and captured the whole band. Against the wishes of the local governor, Caesar ordered the men crucified—just as he had once laughingly threatened. The governor protested that such men were captives of war and entitled to better treatment, but Caesar demurred. Only when every one of the pirates had been duly crucified did he remember his promise of mercy, whereupon he had their throats slit.

These actions may have seemed barbaric even to Romans, for many years later Cicero felt compelled to write in Caesar's defense. It was no dishonor to execute the pirates, he said, for they were not soldiers but criminals. Likewise, no oaths taken before them had any weight—they had relinquished such prerogatives by becoming pirates in the first place. Cicero's defense was thus one of the earliest articulations of the concept of piracy as a distinct crime, and pirates themselves as *hostis humani generi*.

Julius Caesar's antics were colorful, but they did not address the greater problem. Piracy had brought Roman trade to a virtual standstill, and in the state's evolution from a small republic to a burgeoning empire made regular trade essential. The Senate's response was singularly unimaginative: in 74 BCE it commissioned the son of Marcus Antonius (and father of Mark Antony), praetor Marcus Antonius Creticus, to finish the work of his father. But this Antonius, described by Plutarch as "generous but weak," fared no better. Utterly humiliated by the Cilicians in battle, he was forced to conclude a peace treaty so anathema to Roman interests that the Senate denounced both it and him. Meanwhile, the situation had deteriorated yet further. Not long after Antonius's return, two Roman praetors were captured with their retinues and carried off into slavery, port cities were devastated by pirate raids, and Roman women were taken into bondage—among them the sister of the disgraced Marcus Antonius. In 73 BCE came the ultimate indignity:

pirates raided the critical Roman port of Ostia, lifeline to the city itself, and burned the consular fleet at anchor there.

This provoked the political crisis outlined earlier, and Pompey's solution was both novel and effective. He divided his command into thirteen legates, each patrolling a different zone of the Mediterranean. One hundred twenty thousand men were under his command, including twenty-five commanders and four thousand mounted cavalry. In addition to a formidable armada of some two hundred seventy ships, a war chest of six thousand talents (roughly six hundred million US dollars) was given him, with instructions to disperse as he saw fit. Most important, however, was the status awarded Pompey himself. The previous commissions for Marcus Antonius *père et fils* gave them the titular rank of general. Pompey's commission, as the Roman historian Plutarch makes clear, was neither a generalship nor an admiralty "but an out-and-out monarchy and unbridled power over all men."[11] Little wonder his rivals were worried. Pompey's authority now extended throughout the whole of the Aegean islands, Crete, and Asia Minor. Given that this power extended from the sea to the shore, rather than vice versa, Pompey was actually less a king than a Neptune, with sea armies massed on the horizon.

The nature of Pompey's "monarchy" reveals much about how Rome regarded the pirate menace. Never before had a commission of this sort been awarded: even when marching against Rome's most formidable enemies—Carthage, for example—generals remained generals. Likewise, ordinary criminals merited no such concerted effort nor special status for their pursuers. What the Senate appears to have recognized is that piracy was a hybrid: a war without defined parameters, waged not against a single entity but a hydra of multiple units. It would not be enough to engage one enemy at one place, for others would yet remain. In short, Republican Rome encountered a menace startlingly like that currently confronting the United States: bands of brigands organized in cells throughout the world, coordinating independent attacks yet coalescing into a single, unparalleled threat to the security of the nation.

The only solution was to confront and annihilate the enemy everywhere at once. Consequently, Pompey dispersed his fleet throughout the Aegean, while he himself traveled from one district to another. The results were stunning. Each commander engaged the pirates in his own territory, and when the pirates fled one zone of battle they invariably fell into another. Pompey moved systematically, removing their safe havens, closing off sea lanes, driving them further and further into the tiny wedge of sea around Cilicia itself. Once there, as Plutarch writes, Pompey delivered the coup de grâce:

> The most numerous and powerful [of the pirates] had bestowed their families and treasures and useless folk in forts and strong citadels near the Taurus mountains, while they themselves manned their ships and awaited Pompey's attack near the promontory of Coracesium in Cilicia. Here they were defeated in battle and then besieged. . . . The men themselves, who were more than 20,000 in number, [Pompey] did not once think to put to death but determined to transfer the men from sea to land. . . . Some of them, therefore, were received and incorporated into the small and half-deserted cities of Cilicia.[12]

Pompey's mercy was also shrewd politics. Unlike his subordinate Metellus, who delighted in wiping out entire pirate villages in Crete, Pompey understood that cruelty shown to pirates invariably led to more outrage against the Republic and, thus, more piracy. If the root of piracy lay in discontent, he reasoned, let the men be contented. Also, by placing them in villages well inland and instructing them on how to "till the ground," Pompey effected a change in hearts and minds that insured no future pirate wars could spring from the ashes of the last. "What an incredible man!" Cicero enthused, in a speech at the Curia. "What heaven-sent courage and ability! You, Senators, who just a brief moment before saw an enemy fleet at the mouth of the Tiber, now do not even hear rumors of a pirate in the ocean outside our sea."[13]

Pompey's success not only left a valuable precedent for future pirate wars but also gave the international community its first recorded pirate law. Although Cicero is commonly credited with coining the phrase *hostis humani generi* as a definition of pirates, it was in fact an English jurist who interpreted Cicero's commentary thus. What Cicero actually wrote was: "*Nam pirata non est ex perduellium numero definitus, sed communis hostis omnium; cum hoc nec fides debet nec ius iurandum esse commune.*" ("For a pirate is not included in the list of lawful enemies, but is the common enemy of all; among pirates and other men there ought be neither mutual faith nor binding oath.")[14]

The events surrounding this testimonial are significant. It comes not from Cicero's early speeches to the Senate, but from *De Officiis*, his last book, written when Cicero was well into his sixties. By that time, the political circumstances surrounding the crime of piracy had drastically altered. When Cicero gave his first address on the subject, the threat to Rome came from without: bands of marauding Cilicians drawing their numbers from throughout the Mediterranean world. Now, however, the threat came from within Rome itself. The third and most famous Marcus Antonius, better known as Mark Antony, had employed the Cilician pirates as hired mercenaries in his war against Caesar's assassins, Brutus and Cassius. It was in this context that Cicero penned his famous definition of piracy. No friend of Antony's, he deemed the use of pirates in war as akin to sponsoring criminals. Yet beyond the obvious dig at his political rival, there is an added layer of subtlety to Cicero's definition. By distinguishing pirates from "lawful enemies" (aka enemy soldiers) and taking the further step of declaring that they were incapable of being bound to any oath, Cicero in effect created a separate and entirely unique species of criminal: neither recognized combatant nor ordinary miscreant, but one who has so utterly severed his ties with state and society that he is, in a legal sense, no longer even human. It was this concept—the pirate as a malevolent satellite to both society and its laws—that would eventually find full expression in the doctrine of universal jurisdiction.

Cicero's opposition to Antony ultimately cost him his life (indeed, Antony's wife Fulvia is alleged to have skewered the deceased orator's tongue with hair pins, to silence it forever), and the body of his legal writings lay dormant for over a decade. During that turbulent time Antony joined Cleopatra of Egypt and declared war on his erstwhile ally, Octavius. Contrary to Cicero's condemnation of the practice, both sides employed pirates freely. After Antony's defeat at the Battle of Actium, however, Octavius turned ruthlessly on both his and Antony's sea mercenaries: among his first acts as Emperor Augustus was a ruthless pogrom against all pirates within striking distance of Rome. He reinstituted Pompey's system of patrols and financed the construction of a new fleet to police the coasts and sea lanes. It was the greatest systematic antipiracy undertaking yet, and piracy virtually disappeared from the Mediterranean for three hundred years.[15]

The reestablishment of order under Augustus had the ironic effect (given Cicero's antipathy to Octavius) of seeing many of Cicero's legal treatises become codified in Roman law. Among these was his definition of pirates as "the common enemy of all." Imperial jurists followed Cicero's precedent in distinguishing pirates (*pirata*) from both robbers (*praedones*) and common brigands (*latrones*). Pomponius, writing in the time of Hadrian, defines pirates in starkly military terms as "those . . . enemies who declare war against us, or against whom we publicly declare war; others are robbers or brigands."[16] A century later, under the emperor Severus, another jurist makes precisely the same distinction: "Enemies are those against whom the Roman people have publicly declared war, or who themselves have declared war against the Roman people; others are called robbers or brigands."[17] It was clear that pirates fell into the former rather than the latter category.

The Roman definition of piracy as private war and pirates themselves as common enemies of all mankind would shape the dialogue of piracy law for centuries to come. It also provided a crucial precedent: the first state versus nonstate conflict codified in law. Pirates were defined as a breed apart, lacking the recognition accorded to lawful enemies, yet whose actions transcended ordinary criminality. Rome recognized this distinction both in its actions—giving Pompey the title of monarch of the Aegean, for example—and in its laws. In contrast to the common misconception today of pirates as robbers, Rome clearly distinguished between ordinary thieves and pirates, whose depredations against trade carried far greater consequences. Moreover, Roman law acknowledged that a pirate carried his status wherever he went, even ashore. Raids on Ostia and other cities were termed, by Cicero and his successors, acts of piracy, even though they did not occur on the high seas. Thus the Roman precedent not only provides the positive concept of piracy as private war but also neatly disposes of two fallacies: that piracy is merely sea robbery, and that it can only occur at sea. This precedent will be of critical importance as we attempt to define the crime of international organized terrorism.

LOST AND FOUND: PIRACY AND THE LAW FROM THE MIDDLE AGES TO THE RENAISSANCE

While it is no longer fashionable to speak of the Middle Ages as "the Dark Ages," there is no question that much was lost or forgotten during this time, including the carefully constructed edifice of Roman law and precedent. Yet, ironically, the war that Roman jurists identified between pirates and city-states was never more apparent.

With the empire in disarray, no navy remained to guard the seas. It was during this era that Muslim corsairs established bases in North Africa and the European continent that they would hold, to a greater or lesser degree, for the next one thousand years. By the eighth century CE, however, the threat from the sea no longer centered exclusively on the Mediterranean and Aegean. The so-called age of the Vikings began haltingly, with isolated raids within Scandinavia and its environs. As shipbuilding technology improved, however, the Vikings ventured further southward, striking at targets in present-day England and France. Their success is almost unfathomable. In 836, Viking raids extended up the river Thames to London; by 840, following the fragmentation of France after the death of its king, Louis the Pious, Vikings attacked and razed Bordeaux, Perigueux, Limoges, Angouleme, Toulouse, Angers, Tours, and Orleans. One year later a Viking fleet of six hundred ships sacked Hamburg and defeated the Frankish king, Charles the Bald. In less than a decade the Vikings had spread across Western Europe, leaving a trail of devastation in their wake.

The sheer success of these raids has led some historians to question whether Vikings can even be considered pirates at all. This is reminiscent of Sir Walter Raleigh's offhand assertion in 1585: "Did you ever know of any that were pirates for millions?" he scoffed. "Only they [who] work for small things are pirates."[18] Yet while their numbers and organization were far greater than their Cilician predecessors, it would be difficult to define the Vikings as anything else. The word *Viking* itself meant "sea warrior," and that was precisely how they saw themselves. A Viking raid was scarcely distinguishable from the Cilician attacks on Ostia and other Roman ports, albeit carried out on a much larger scale and with a great deal more brutality.

In fact, it was under the Vikings that pirates finally began to earn their title as enemies of the human race. They attacked indiscriminately, canvassing a much wider area than any pirate in history. The methods they developed for intimidating and subduing their victims would resonate throughout the centuries with other pirate raids in other hemispheres. It was the Vikings who first instituted the practice of leaving one or a handful of villagers alive after the destruction of a town, forcing them to watch the execution of their neighbors. These survivors then became, in effect, roving ambassadors, spreading tales of the Vikings' ferocity to other cities.

For the first time in the history of piracy, terror became a weapon in itself. The Vikings relied on their own reputation for savagery to grease the treads of their advance. Towns warned of imminent Viking raids either fled, leaving behind their goods and treasures, or raised enormous bribes to stay the hand of the invaders. Often, and with increasing frequency, Viking raiders seized entire cities without any bloodshed whatsoever. On the rare occasion when a town or city did resist, the Vikings seized the opportunity for a monitory lesson. Entire populations were hanged in rows, within sight of their burning homes. Soon, as one historian notes, "legend and reality intertwined,"[19] and local resistance crumbled before the invaders. It is for this reason—the deliberate use of terror to achieve private ends—that some have termed the Vikings "the first terrorists."

Centuries earlier Cicero had warned of the destabilizing effects of unrestrained piracy on the sovereignty of states. Now the Western world witnessed it firsthand. Kingdoms fragmented and governments collapsed, each township withdrawing into itself. The nation-building efforts of Charlemagne (768–814), which saw over thirty principalities united under a single crown, were undone in less than a decade. As Alfred Bradford writes: "In the Frankish lands, secular government broke down, and so did the governing authority of the church. Locals areas looked after themselves. Towns raised fortifications and organized local defense; local lords recruited followers, built castles, and sought local dominance and independence."[20]

While Viking dominance of Western Europe was relatively brief, the horrors they inflicted remained seared on both memory and landscape. Much of Europe's intricate system of castles and other fortifications, for example, is owed to the constant fear of Viking raids. The legacy of the Vikings on piracy law is less obvious, but equally important. After their decline, piracy—like so much of European culture and practice—became localized. Pirates of the Middle Ages lacked the ambition of the Vikings: for the most part, they scoured the areas close to home, then returned at nightfall like fishermen with their daily catch. Coastal areas and narrow straits, rivers, and channels became pirate havens.

The localization of piracy, however, did not diminish its

effects. While coastal cities no longer feared pirate raids (with a few notable exceptions) the expansion of international trade from 1300 on found a corresponding menace in piracy. Yet lacking the organized navies of their Roman and Rhodian forebears, states had fewer options for curtailing the pirates who cruised their waters. Like piracy itself, antipiracy was a local affair. In the 1340s the English towns of Hastings, Romney, Dover, Hythe, and Sandwich—the "Cinque Ports"—banded together to hire a fleet and police the English Channel. Likewise the Hanseatic League, a trading organization formed in 1241 between the continental cities of Hamburg, Lubeck, and others, began hiring dubious mariners to protect their ships. Yet this attempt to send a thief to catch a thief was, for both the Cinque Ports and the Hanseatic League, disastrous. The pirate-hunters soon realized the opportunities presented to them, and became pirates themselves.

For several hundred years, before the establishment of formidable navies, pirates dominated the trade routes of Europe. Nor was the problem confined there. The Strait of Babs-al-Mandab, connecting the Red and Arabian seas, and the Strait of Hormuz, between the Persian Gulf and the Gulf of Oman, were almost too dangerous to pass. The same was true of the Malacca Straits, a hotbed of piracy even today, where in the Middle Ages Malay pirates scoured one side and Dyaks the other. In the Far East, the Ming emperors waged intermittent war with the Wo-k'you, pirate bands composed of renegade Chinese and Japanese mariners.[21] Kings T'aejo and T'aejong of the Yi dynasty in Korea (1392–1418) pursued a different approach. They offered pardons to the Waco pirates who surrendered themselves and their vessels, while ruthlessly pursuing those who did not.[22] This use of clemency, coupled with force, would be the model for the English pirate wars throughout the seventeenth and eighteenth centuries.

The evolution of piracy throughout the Middle Ages saw the practice gradually moving away from the seaport raids, barbarity, and political instability of the Viking era (and, further back, the Cilicians) to something that resembled sea robbery.

Therefore it is all the more extraordinary—and significant—that jurists seeking to define the crime in the early Renaissance resolutely distinguished between piracy and ordinary robbery and rendered it even more an offense to the law of nations than it had been in Roman times.

Their decision can only be understood in context. The Renaissance, as its name implies, was a time of rediscovery: most particularly the art, culture, and laws of ancient Rome and Greece. The many relics resuscitated included Cicero's *De Legibus* and *De Officiis*, as well as surviving records of his speeches at the Curia. After centuries of unfettered piracy, it was with great eagerness that late Medieval and early Renaissance scholars seized upon the definition of pirates as a separate breed of international criminals who must be rooted out wherever they are found. Moreover, the concept that pirates posed a fundamental threat to the order of states must also have been reinforced by the memory of the Vikings, whose depredations against coastal towns had wrought instability and collapse for much of the Western world.

Consequently, the new generation of jurists not only revivified the Roman definition, they expanded it. Piero Belli's (1327–1400) seminal work on the laws of war contains what may be the first expression of the doctrine of universal jurisdiction. Claming that while custom requires states to formally declare war against one another, he cautions: "it is customary to make an exception in the case of pirates, since they are both technically and in fact already at war; for people whose hand is against every man should expect a like return from all men, and it should be permissible for any one to attack them."[23]

Renaissance jurists and philosophers, fascinated by holistic structures in science, religion, and statecraft, began to grope toward the concept of a universal law that bound all nations together. Such a law, if it existed, must be founded upon a shared understanding of good and evil: which behaviors to praise, which to condemn. Piracy, as the only international crime, quickly moved to the center of this new philosophy. If certain crimes were universally abhorred, then all states were equally responsible for capturing and prosecuting the criminals, wherever they might be found. Much later, Cesare Beccharia articulated this concept: "There are also those who think that an act of cruelty committed, for example, at Constantinople may be punished at Paris for this abstract reason, that he who offends humanity should have enemies in all mankind, and be the object of universal execration."[24]

The notion of a shared responsibility among states to pursue and capture international criminals had profound implications. Previously, international law was little more than a collection of treaties between individual states, or combinations formed for trade or mutual security. In the fifteenth and sixteenth centuries, however, the concept of a community of states emerged. And, as M. Cherif Bassiouni writes, "because the right of freedom of navigation on the high seas was applicable universally, it followed that an infringement on that right by pirates would be universally punished. This doctrine became the foundation of the modern theory of universal jurisdiction."[25]

What this meant in practice was that pirates, unique among all criminals, could be seized anywhere they were found, by anyone who found them. Not only was this "permissible," as Belli had written, it was (by the sixteenth century) obligatory. All principalities, victims or not, shared equal responsibility. *Aut dedere aut judicare*—"either prosecute or extradite"—became the norm.

Why was piracy singled out, when later judges and scholars would dismiss it as mere robbery? The answer lies in the understanding of pirates as perpetually at war with all states. The parameters of this war, however, were a matter of scholarly debate. In 1570 Italian jurist Alberigo Gentili declared: "Pirates are common enemies, and they are attacked with impunity by all, because they are without the pale of the law. They are scorners of the law of nations; hence they can find no protection in that law. They ought to be crushed by us, and by all men. This is warfare shared by all nations."[26]

While acknowledging the war between pirates and states, this sweeping declaration apparently absolves the state of obeying any laws of war regarding them. It is thus akin to Cicero's statement that one need not keep oaths made to pirates, a link that Gentili makes clear when he states later that "Cicero says the laws of war cannot apply to them [pirates]." Yet the amount of prerogative given to states in distinguishing pirates from "legitimate" enemies raises its own concerns. Much like the United States applying the blanket term *terrorists* indiscriminately to all manner of insurgents, rebels, and even recognized states (and, conversely, nations like Iran and Syria labeling al Qaeda operatives as freedom fighters), Gentili was criticized for giving sovereigns carte blanche to turn anything and anyone into a "pirate": "No degree of political organization or goal," Alfred Rubin writes, "could make a 'rebel' into a lawful combatant. . . . Moreover, each sovereign would seem to be awarded the legal power . . . to determine what legal regime would be applied to any struggle between the 'sovereign' and an enemy of uncertain status."[27] The problem facing jurists of the Renaissance was thus astonishingly akin to that facing our present government: how to distinguish international criminals from legitimate insurgents, and how to prevent states from declaring one as the other for their own political advantage.

The lacunae of definition was resolved, to some extent, a century later by the Dutch philosopher Hugo Grotius. By the time of writing (1625) a second form of piracy had taken precedence: privateering. States now regularly commissioned private vessels to harass enemy trade, only to be accused (rightly) of pirate brokering. Clearly there needed to be some method of distinguishing between pirates, privateers, rebels, armies, and ordinary criminals. Grotius provided one: pirates were only those who banded together *for criminal purpose*. This distinguished them from both rebel armies that committed illegal acts and, additionally, states that used privateers. Neither rebels nor states relinquished their status, under law, by employing pirates; pirates, however, did relinquish status *qua* pirates when thus employed and became, under the laws of war, military combatants and agents of the state.

Grotius's logic has critical relevance today. By distinguishing piracy from other forms of state-sponsored activity, Grotius preserved the conception of pirates as enemies of all, rather than tools of the state. States and rebel armies might employ privateers, but pirates were defined by existing independent of political entities. This did not mean, however, that pirates with avowedly political motives were anything other than pirates. On the contrary, the definition centers on the *acts* that constitute piracy, not the motives. Traditionally, under most systems of law, the only defense for the charge of piracy was a commission proving that the defendant acted on the orders of a state. That commission, as a legal imprimatur, changed the pirate's status to privateer, and thus an extension of the state itself.

I would argue that this distinction between pirate and privateer may help us resolve our own current difficulties in distinguishing terrorists from insurgents. Some scholars and even prominent political figures maintain that terrorist organizations are political by virtue of the fact that they profess political motives, some of which may be shared by states or insurgent groups. But the raison d'etre of a terrorist organization is different. The organization exists not to form or replace a government, but to perform such acts of violence and depredation as will further that or other aims. Terrorist objectives may be political, but are not exclusively so. Consequently, Grotius's definition of pirates as banding together "for criminal purpose" is a critical parallel, for it is the acts that define terrorist organizations like al Qaeda, not the motives behind them. These acts are undeniably criminal.

PIRACY AS STATE-SPONSORED TERRORISM

As we have seen, piracy and privateering are two very different animals. Yet while the definition of pirates as a band existing outside the laws and parameters of states is crucial for understanding terrorism today, it is important to note the additional parallel of privateering. Today the United States and other nations struggle with the vexing problem of distinguishing between terrorist organizations, insurgent groups, and state militia. States often declare dissident elements within their own borders as "terrorists,"[28] and aside from the many specious claims, there are several examples where this is veritable. Moreover, groups like al Qaeda have recently shown a willingness to aid insurgent groups within states, blurring the line between them.

The problem is worsened by the fact that certain rogue states have persistently aided international terrorist groups in numerous ways. Such aid might take the form of a simple cash subsidy, or weapons, or safe haven for training camps. The question for our government, then, is this: are state-sponsored terrorist organizations still independent entities, and when does such an organization become a de facto organ of the state?

The question is much older than most people realize. As early as the thirteenth century, King Edward I of England granted "commissions of reprisal" to mariners willing to seek out and destroy England's enemies. The commissions entitled captains to seize any merchantman flying the enemy's colors. A portion of the captured wealth went into the Crown's coffers, and the first admiralty prize courts appeared.

Piracy's advantages for states became most apparent in England's wars with Spain in the late sixteenth century. Queen Elizabeth I of England viewed pirates as an essential adjunct to the Royal Navy and was lavish in granting them commissions, aka *licentia marcandi*, "letters of marque," against Spanish trade. In the last uneasy years of peace between the two nations, piracy was regarded by the Crown in much the same way as state-sponsored terrorism is viewed today: an ideal way to strike one's enemy and hide the blade.[29]

The colorful career of Sir Francis Drake is a fine example of this policy. With a commission from the Crown and the encouragement of Elizabeth, Drake set off on a round-the-world voyage in which he sacked and burned Spanish ports in the Americas and seized Spanish ships with impunity. He returned to England with a fortune in captured gold. England and Spain were still at peace throughout the voyage, and an enraged King Alfonso III sent repeated entreaties to England begging Elizabeth to capture and execute the pirate. When the Queen appeared at Deptford to be presented to Drake, the captain was understandably nervous. Senor Mendoza, the Spanish ambassador, had extracted Elizabeth's promise that if she ever saw Francis Drake again she would "strike his head from his body." Reminding the assembled company of that pledge, the Queen handed a sword to a French emissary standing nearby. Thus it was the Frenchman who, with Elizabeth's sword, knighted Sir Francis Drake.

As Drake's history reveals, sponsored piracy aided the state in numerous ways. First, it trained future captains by testing their skills against the Spanish before the navies could meet in force. Second, it bled Spanish resources and frustrated their governance of empire, most particularly in the New World. Third, it vastly enriched the English government, providing for the construction of the new fleet. Fourth, it provided a huge resource of trained and experienced seamen to man the fleet once it was ready. Finally, and most important, it provoked the Spanish into waging war before they were fully prepared, on the necessity of countering a pirate menace that struck at the very heart of its empire. It is interesting to note that only one of these motivations was exclusively monetary. Drake, Raleigh, and others brought an enormous haul of Spanish gold into England, setting the bar for generations of future pirates, yet pecuniary aims were secondary to political ones. The sacking of Cartagena and other Spanish ports terrorized not only Spain's government but also its people, distracting the navy and reinforcing the impression of England as a nation of ruthless conquerors. As a political weapon this was without par, for it conditioned Spain to anticipate defeat even before its Armada sailed.[30]

While historical connections should not be overly stretched, this "private war" has considerable resonance. The case for correlating piracy and terrorism relies on an understanding of piracy as more than theft for private gain. In its Elizabethan form, privateering—like modern state-sponsored terrorism—was a means of employing force and terror to achieve political ends. States could strike at one another through their privateers, yet still retain the pretense of diplomatic relations. Today we call this concept "deniability." Elizabeth and her ministers regularly commissioned privateers on the one hand, and stoutly denied it on the other. In our own era, hostile governments continue to finance terrorist organizations while maintaining diplomatic relations with the United States. In both cases, the benefit for the sponsors is the same: a cheap and easy way to harass one's enemy without committing the full resources of the state to all-out war.

The English privateers also provide a precedent for distinguishing between different kinds of state-sponsored terrorism. If the terrorist group merely accepts money or other forms of aid from a state, it still remains an independent entity. Ideally, under a model definition of terrorism, the state itself would be liable under the law of conspiracy as an accomplice. Yet the terrorist group would not lose its status. This is akin to the situation in the late seventeenth and early eighteenth centuries, where English pirates regularly found safe haven in the Atlantic colonies, yet were ruthlessly pursued and often hanged by England herself. Evidence of colonial aid and succor did not rebut the charge of piracy, although it certainly did embarrass certain colonial governors.[31]

If, however, the terrorist organization not only accepts aid but also acts on the direct orders of the state, it is impossible to maintain that it is anything other than an agent of that state. This is akin to the status of the privateers, whose actions were indistinguishable from those of ordinary pirates, yet who acted at the behest of the Crown. After the confusion of the sixteenth century, when England and other states deliberately hid their relations with their privateers, a system was developed whereby states regularly granted privateering commissions during time of war. These commissions clearly stipulated the terms under which the privateer operated, and made it explicit that if he exceeded or violated those terms, he was liable for the charge of piracy. In England such commissions were granted under the Great Seal of the Admiralty, and thus bore not only the imprimatur of the state but its navy as well. Consequently, until the nineteenth century, privateers were defined under law as combatants, not pirates. They could be captured and imprisoned as prisoners of war, but not hanged. In short: soldiers, not criminals. For an alleged terrorist to rebut that status, he or she must likewise be proved to be acting under the direct orders of a state. In that context, if the suspect has launched an attack against another state, that attack is construed not as an act of terrorism, but an act of war.

CONFLICT AND COMPROMISE: *HOSTIS HUMANI GENERI* VERSUS SEA ROBBERS

For well over two thousand years, the common understanding of piracy was of a private war waged between bands of criminals and states. Theft was only one of many offenses, which included hijacking, ransoming, and outright murder. The idea of piracy as robbery at sea, and all the limitations that term implies, is in contrast a relatively recent one. It was formulated at a time of diplomatic crisis, and was intended to patch over the gaping holes of English piracy law. Yet it is this image that survives intact, while the other has been largely forgotten.

While this chapter is devoted to reviving the notion of private war, especially as it applies to contemporary terrorism, it is worth noting how piracy as sea robbery came into being. This is particularly important because the principle objection to conflating piracy with terrorism centers on motive: terrorists—so the objection states—want political/social/religious change, whereas pirates just want money.[32] This distinction is even codified in the UN Convention on the Law of the Sea, which defines piracy as depredations committed "for private ends," as distinguished from political ones.

Yet piracy has never been free from politics, and the two

were never more entwined than the era in which sea robbery came into being. For centuries, beginning not long after the Norman conquest, English courts squabbled over jurisdiction for piracy cases. The problem came down to the dual structures of common and civil law. If pirates were ordinary criminals, in the same class as highway robbers, then they should be tried by jury under the common law as felons. But if they were *hostis humani generi*, their acts became of form of petit treason,[33] removing them from common to civil law, under the jurisdiction of the Admiralty.

The English Crown favored the latter definition. The recognition that acts of piracy transcended the common law devolved principally from the transnational aspects of the crime. When English pirates attacked foreign vessels, it threatened the peace between those countries. Consequently, as early as 1289, Edward I established a commission to inquire into "trespasses" committed by English vessels against the King of France. The commission found that an equal number of English vessels had been plundered by the French, among others.[34] This led to the first letters of marque granted by the Crown to English sailors to reclaim stolen property at sea from foreign pirates, as mentioned above. These commissions also recognized the newly created post of the Lord Admiral as the proper venue for declaring and disposing of captured goods.[35]

The intention here was most likely to limit legal remedies and prevent wars breaking out over petty mercantile squabbles: by granting Commissions, the Crown established the reverse prerogative that any English sailor engaging in piracy without such commission transgressed against the Admiralty.[36] Thereafter piracy would not be construed as an act of war, but a crime against the Crown. And since that crime was directed against the King's person (through his subordinate, the Lord Admiral) it was properly understood as petit treason. The actual elements of the crime —specifically, theft and murder at sea—were secondary to the outrage of violating the King's trust by sailing without commission.

Obscurity in the law left the Admiralty and the common-law

courts fighting over jurisdiction. Both had a viable claim. Common-law juries were notoriously reluctant to convict pirates. Ordinary folk, particularly in seaside communities, often identified with the accused, either through social or commercial ties. Edward III became so incensed at the rate of acquittal that in 1352 he attempted to wrest jurisdiction of piracy from the common law courts by declaring piracy a petit treason triable by civil law under the Statute of Treasons, 25 Edward III, Statute 5, Chapter 2.[37] An earlier case, decided in 1350, gave legal precedent for this: three English sailors and a Norman captain were tried before the assizes on several counts of piracy. The Norman was convicted only of robbery, but the Englishmen were found guilty of treason by reason of having taken up arms with a nonsubject against the trade of the Crown.[38] Edward turned this decision into an extension of the Crown's legal prerogative by employing its rationale to incorporate piracy within the commission granted to the admiralty courts. The coast of England and Wales was divided into nineteen districts, each granted a vice-admiral to oversee all coastal and foreign trade and a judge empowered to decide cases involving the breach or detriment of that trade.[39]

Edward III's efforts led to a revitalization of the claim for Admiralty prerogative and ultimately to the dissolution of all common-law piracy jurisdiction. In 1361, for example, a prior order to try a piracy case in a common-law court was revoked and replaced by an order from the Crown for "our Admirals" to try the pirates "according to maritime law."[40] As Alfred Rubin writes, piracy law was "distinguished from the common law of England by the very fact of royal promulgation of a Code; the power of interpretation was given to Admirals as beneficiaries of royal patronage rather than common law judges with their own traditions of independence."[41]

Yet until the sixteenth century there were no permanent tribunals under Admiralty jurisdiction, but rather ad hoc affairs convened by commission from the king. Meanwhile the problem of piracy was becoming increasingly acute. It was not that the Crown lacked the will or inclination to try pirates, but rather that the civil law lacked the mechanisms of common law for dealing with "ordinary" crime. Predicated on the presumption that pirates were traitors, it required that "they must plainly confess their offenses (which they will never do without torture or pains) or else their offenses be so plainly and directly proved by witnesses indifferent, such as saw their offenses committed, which cannot be gotten but by chance at a few times."[42]

This quote, taken from the preamble to the statute of 27 Henry VIII, Chapter 4 (1535), provided the justification for wresting piracy jurisdiction from the Admiralty and giving it back to the common-law courts. Henceforth, piracy at sea would be treated the same as a felony committed upon land. This was accomplished by devaluing the term *piracy* and replacing it with a list of offenses committed at sea. A second statute passed one year later, 28 Henry VIII, Chapter 15 (1536), made a telling alteration. The preamble to the first statute referred to "pirates, thieves, robbers, and murderers." The second dropped the term "pirate" altogether, replacing it with "traitors" and "confederators" (an early term for mutineers).[43] Piracy was a loaded word, carrying with it the concept of *hostis humani generi* and the weight of customary international law. Parliament clearly wanted to avoid the complexities of multinational transgressions at sea, which were more easily understood as an Admiralty prerogative, and focus instead on the elements of the crime—the *actus reus*—that were synonymous with the common-law felonies of robbery and homicide.

Yet Parliament's attempt to obscure piracy by its own elements found spirited resistance from the Crown, which reacted by using the term as often as possible. Distinguishing between privateers under Admiralty commission and those who had none, Elizabeth I declared the latter "pyrats and rovers upon the seas" who were "out of her protection, and lawfully to be by any person taken, punished, and suppressed with extremity."[44] This was a conscious echo of the Roman precept that pirates, as *hostis humani generi*, were subject to universal jurisdiction, meaning they could be captured anywhere on earth, by anyone

that found them. In practical terms, "piracy" as such declared
was still within the connaissance of the Admiralty, as an act of
petit treason (Sir Edward Coke wrote in 1628 that "if a subject
had committed piracy upon another this was holden to be petit
treason, for which he was to be drawn and hanged, because
pirata est hostis humani generi").[45] Yet the crime existed in
name only, for in nearly all instances the Admirals were
required to turn captured pirates over to common-law courts
for trial on the grounds that they had committed one of the enumerated felonies of the 1536 statute.

By the end of the sixteenth century, a fissure had developed
between Crown and Parliament on the proper jurisdiction for
piracy. As it would throughout the following century, the
Crown saw piracy as a means of extending its bureaucracy: by
1600, the Admiralty handled all matters of prize, commission,
letters of marque, and reprisal.[46] It also held commission to
capture and prosecute "pirates," although the 1535 and 1536
statutes had gutted that term of all practical meaning. All
"felonies" at sea committed by Englishmen were remitted to the
common-law courts, and even those who breached Admiralty
commissions, or sailed without them, were beyond its purview.

Writing in 1628, jurist Sir Edward Coke defended and outlined common law jurisdiction for piracy in his *Institutes of the
Laws of England*. Acts of piracy, he wrote, are acts occurring at
sea "which by an act of Parliament (8 H. 6, 42) are to be
enquired of, heard and determined according to the course of
the common law, as if they had been done upon the land." This
included "all treasons (28 H. 8, 15), felonies, robberies, mur-
ders and confederacies committed upon the sea."[47] Coke reiterated the need for common-law jurisdiction, referring to the
"mischief of the statute" whereby piracy cases had previously
been tried by the Admiralty under civil law, wherein:

> traitors, pirates, thiefs, robbers, murderers, and confederators
> on the sea many times escaped unpunished, because the
> common law of this realm extended not to these offences, but
> were judged and determined before the lord admiral after the

course of civil laws, the nature whereof is, that before any judgment of death they . . . either must plainly confess their offenses (which they never would do without torture or pain) or by witness indifferent.[48]

While upholding the prerogative of the common law courts, Coke recognized that piracy was not, by definition, a common-law crime. It did not emerge from English case law, but rather from the civil law regarding international commerce and relations. Its precepts, likewise, were transnational in character, most especially pirates' status under law as *hostis humani generi*. While piracy shared criminal elements with domestic felonies, it would be regarded under law not *as* a felony but *as if it were* one. "Before this statute," Coke wrote, referring to 28 Henry VIII, "piracy was no felony, for that it could not be tried, being out of all towns and countries, but was only punishable by the civil law. This statute did not alter the offence . . . but giveth it a means of trial in the common law, and inflicteth such pains of death as if they had been attainted of any felony done upon the land."[49] Coke reinforced this distinction by referring to Butler's Case, where it was held that since piracy was not a felony under common law, there could be no felonious accessories to the crime.[50]

The question of jurisdiction was never successfully resolved until long after the threat of piracy had receded. The compromise, whereby civil-law piracy cases were tried in common-law courts, existed in theory but the mechanics of actual prosecution were left obscure. The few piracy cases of the seventeenth century, until the Every trials of 1696, appear indistinguishable from other common-law prosecutions. This can be seen in the trial of Capt. John Cusack and his crew, held at the Old Bailey in January 1674.[51] Cusack's piracies had been committed against French vessels off Martinique, yet the preface to the printed account of the trial stressed its connections to more mundane felonies:

> The world hath long been entertained with accounts of
> Highwaymen and Land-robbers, but Piracies and Sea-
> Robbers being for the most part perceived either under the
> protection of some states . . . or on the pretense of some
> commission from some Prince engaged in a War with his
> neighbors; therefore it is hoped that the following Account
> shall be received and read generally.[52]

The relative scarcity of such cases may explain why the rules of
procedure were not clarified. In the following century, another
jurist was content to restate Coke without any addition, writing
that "formerly [piracy] was only cognizable by the admiralty
courts, which proceeded by the rules of civil law. But it being inconsistent with the liberties of the nation that any man's life should
be taken away, unless by the judgment of his peers, or the common
law of the land, the statute 28 Henry VIII, Chapter 15 established
a new jurisdiction for this purpose, which proceeds according to
the common law."[53] Similarly, Sir Matthew Hale in his *Pleas to the
Crown* echoed Coke in declaring that "the statute alters not the
offence, but it removes only an offense by civil law . . . and
gives trial per course of common law"[54] for crimes of piracy.

Yet the traditional definition of pirates as *hostis humani
generi* did not disappear, despite Parliament's attempts to bury
it. Even as he defended the common-law courts' right to prosecute pirates, Sir Edward Coke offered the Ciceronian definition
for pirates themselves—the first English jurist to do so.[55] In a
piracy trial occurring in 1668, the presiding judge not only reiterated the idea of pirates as enemies of all but also articulated
(for the first time in English jurisprudence) the doctrine of universal jurisdiction as applied to them. Pirates were "enemies not
of one nation only, but of all mankind," Sir Leoline Jenkins
declared, concluding that consequently "everybody is commissioned, and is to be armed against them, *as against rebels or
traitors*, to subdue and to root them out."[56]

Over one hundred years later William Blackstone, in his
Commentaries on the Laws of England, credits Coke for being
among the first to rearticulate the Roman precept and goes on

to offer a concise definition in the English context: "As, therefore, he [the pirate] has renounced all the benefits of society and government, and has reduced himself afresh to the savage state of nature by declaring war against all mankind, all mankind must declare war against him."[57]

It remained to be seen how the compromise between common and civil courts would work in practice. The opportunity arose in 1696, during the trial of the crew of the pirate ship *Fancy*, captained by Henry Every. Every, the first mate of an English trading ship, had seized the vessel in a bloodless mutiny in 1694, and convinced the majority of its crew to join him. Cruising around the Indian Ocean in search of prey, the *Fancy* came upon the *Ganj-i-Sawai*, a ship belonging to the Great Mughal of India and carrying on board his own daughter and one of his wives. It also carried several million English pounds' worth of gold coin, which Every promptly transferred into the *Fancy*.

The scandal following Every's piracy was doubled by the fact that the Great Mughal and England were trading partners, and consequently Indian trade was effectively closed in protest. East India Company agents were beaten and imprisoned in Bombay, and the Mughal demanded that Every be caught and hanged before any commerce resumed. The English Crown began a worldwide manhunt but succeeded in capturing only six of Every's crew. It was these six who appeared on trial at London's Old Bailey in October 1696.

To understand the importance of the trial, it is necessary also to note the unique role of public opinion in early modern England. While Henry Every and his crew were enemies of both the English Crown and the Great Mughal, their exploits on the high seas found favorable reception among the English public. Every's stunning success placed him among the pantheon of other notable English sea rovers: Walter Raleigh, Sir Francis Drake, Sir Henry Morgan. Even as early as the seventeenth century, piracy was already beginning to assume mythical, romantic dimensions. By the time of the trial, for example, ballads had already been composed in Every's honor—one, at least, by

Every himself. Consequently the burden on the Crown was twofold: satisfy the vengeance of the Great Mughal and provide a narrative of piracy to counter the surging groundswell of popular support for the practice.

The Every trial was also a working example of the fusion between civil and common law outlined by Sir Edward Coke almost seventy years before: a piracy trial with a common-law jury, convened at the Old Bailey, yet under the rules of admiralty law. How well that compromise would function—particularly as there were a dearth of contemporary precedents to draw from—was not clear.

Opening for the prosecution, Sir Robert Newton framed the crime of piracy in nationalist terms. An offense to trade, he told the jury, was an offense to England herself—and, consequently, an act of war. By provoking the Great Mughal, the Every pirates invited the retribution of that monarch on England; Newton vividly cast the image of ravaging Moslem hordes sweeping through the streets of London. In framing the issue of piracy as an act of war, Newton's opening address could have been copied almost verbatim from Cicero's before the Roman Senate. Not only war, but treason: the pirates, by inviting the Mughal's wrath, had betrayed their nation. Few statements have ever so clearly articulated the relationship of piracy to international relations. In closing, Newton went yet further. Dismissing the common-law idea of pirates as mere robbers, he stressed instead how their crimes were unique: "piracy *by so much exceeds Theft or Robbery at Land*; as the Interest and Concerns of Kingdoms and Nations, are above those of private Families, or particular Persons: For suffer Pirates, and the Commerce of the World must cease."[58]

Besides presenting the Crown's case against the defendants, Newton was also articulating a particular view of piracy: pirates were *hostis humani generi*, and when their depredations embarrassed their mother country or hampered its relations, that action was treason. This, as will be recalled, was the view espoused by the English Crown and the Admiralty, which conflicted with Parliament's attempts to make piracy a crime under common law. By reiterating it at trial, Newton hoped to impress upon the jury the great importance of their decision for the Kingdom, and the world at large. Whatever his intentions, however, popular opinion won out: all six pirates were acquitted of all charges.

It would be hard to overstate the crisis this posed for the English government. Indian commerce was the cornerstone of its foreign relations, and a central part of its trade. A conference was hurriedly convened at Whitehall, while the pirates themselves still languished in prison, and the following day— October 31, 1696—the bewildered defendants found themselves again in the dock, answering "other charges." These charges related not to the piracy, but the act of mutiny whereby the *Fancy* was seized. Yet the court left no doubt as to the true nature of the complaint. The head justice, Sir Charles Hedges, chose to frame the crime in a different light. Dismissing the unique and transnational character of piracy, which might otherwise lend it spurious legitimacy as an act of war, Hedges attempted to recast it in analogous terms to ordinary felony. In doing so, he left behind an expression that would become famous: "Now Piracy is only a Sea term for Robbery," he began, "Piracy being a Robbery committed within the Jurisdiction of the Admiralty; if any man be assaulted within that Jurisdiction, and his Ship or Goods violently taken away without a Legal Authority, this is Robbery and Piracy."[59]

Piracy as sea robbery was not entirely original: Coke had once compared the taking of a vessel at sea to stealing a horse, and maintained in his third Institute that a pirate was "a robber on the sea." These comments had been made to bring piracy more closely in line with common-law felonies, and a similar attempt was being made here. By adopting an almost homey, popular understanding of pirates' activities, no different from highwaymen ashore, pirates lost both the majesty and the menace traditionally accorded them under the law. Yet the contrast between Hedges's definition and the weight of precedent was glaringly apparent even when compared with the first Every trial.

Whether Hedges's words shifted the balance or not, the second trial did result in convictions. It also introduced the term *sea robbery* into both legal and social lexicons, creating an alternate definition of piracy that ignores the salient international aspects of the crime—which jurists since the Roman Republic have identified—and focuses instead on one element: theft. The irony of this definition is that it was not even appropriate when it appeared: the Every scandal struck at the very heart of England's international relations, as Sir Robert Newton made clear. In retrospect, Justice Hedges was likely not attempting to dismiss the gravity of piracy, but rather make it more understandable to a jury composed of solid London bourgeois whose limited imaginations boggled at anything more tenuous than simple felony. The tension between his definition and Newton's reflects the tension within English law itself, a long struggle between Crown and Parliament over which courts should have jurisdiction for piracy trials. As such, sea robbery emerged out of a unique set of political circumstances and merely reflects the conflicting aims of early modern England, not a profound shift in perceptions of piracy overall.

Nevertheless, it has survived. Even as recently as 2008, commentators balked at ascribing the word *terrorist* to the Somali pirates, claiming that since their primary motive was monetary, the term could not apply. Yet what the Somali pirates were guilty of was not sea robbery at all, but hijacking and ransom—two crimes that the United Nations has long defined as synonymous with terrorism. Moreover, these commentators also ignored the fact that much of the ransom money was being paid over to insurgency groups within Somalia itself, many with alleged links to international terrorist organizations. In spite of all this evidence, the popular myth of piracy prevailed.

The crowning irony of the sea robbery argument is not that it was merely inappropriate when formulated, but that it was abandoned almost immediately afterward. The brief combination of circumstances that led Coke and Hedges to attempt to limit piracy to its felonious elements were arcane even by the beginning of the eighteenth century. Thenceforth, and throughout the so-called pirate wars that saw the most successful extermination of piracy in recorded history, pirates were repeatedly and almost universally defined as *hostis humani generi*. The threat of piracy to the sovereignty of states was recognized, and states themselves employed the full weight of their military power to stamping it out. Sea robbery largely faded away, rarely appearing in trial records or government policy until the twentieth century, when a second set of political circumstances again led to its revival.

WAR AGAINST ALL THE WORLD

In the first three decades of the eighteenth century, the nations of Europe declared war against a global scourge, piracy, and won. Of all the precedents mentioned thus far, for our own war on terror this is the most salient because of both how states framed and waged that war and how the pirates defined it themselves.

These men were a new breed. After the Peace of Utrecht in 1718, the absence of war meant no more privateering commissions, and states that had formerly sponsored and protected pirates now turned their navies against them. This meant that mariners choosing piracy no longer came from the same patriotic mold as Francis Drake, Henry Morgan, or even Henry Every. They did not regard their profession as a war against England's enemies, but war against England herself—England, and every other civilized nation. Much like the Cilicians of Republic Rome, pirates of this new era forged relationships and communities based on the principle of the eternal outcast: having forcibly divested themselves of the restraining bonds of their societies, they remade a world of their own. These pirate bands existed not only apart from states but also in defiance of them. Historian Marcus Rediker writes: "Pirates constructed that world in defiant contradistinction to the ways of the world they left behind, in particular to its salient figures of power . . .

and to the system of authority those figures represented and enforced. . . . They erected their own ideal of justice, insisted upon an egalitarian, if unstable, form of social organization, and defined themselves against other groups and types."[60]

It was the presence of these alternate pirate communities, as much as the depredations of the pirates themselves, that motivated England and other nations to exterminate them. Piracy was no longer confined to sea robbery, but a profound challenge to the very idea of statehood itself. Daniel Defoe tells of one pirate who "reduced himself afresh to the savage state of nature by declaring war against all mankind." Capt. Charles Bellamy employed almost exactly the same language as he lambasted a recalcitrant merchant captain:

> Damn ye, you are a sneaking puppy, and so are all those who submit to be governed by laws which rich men have made for their own security. . . . I am a free prince and have as much authority to make *war on the whole world* as he who has a hundred sail of ships and an army of a hundred thousand men in the field.[61]

The pirate captains of the eighteenth century came, unlike their corsair predecessors, from universally low beginnings. Most had served in England's merchant marine as ordinary seamen, toiling years before the mast with no prospects for advancement. Officer ranks were reserved for gentlemen until well into the nineteenth century. Thus it was not uncommon for a boy of seventeen years to command a vessel crewed by men who had spent up to forty years at sea.

Piracy was both a way to escape this penury and revenge oneself against those who enforced it. Pirate captain Bartholomew Roberts summed up the choice facing him and his men: "In honest service there is thin commons, low wages and hard labor. In this [piracy] there is plenty and satiety, pleasure and ease, liberty and power. And who would not balance creditor on this side when all the hazard that is run for, at worse, is only a forelock or two at choking?"[62]

The idea of piracy as personal war against civilization is recurrent throughout the literature of the time. The most common shared sentiment among the pirates was vengeance. It surfaced even in the names they chose for their ships. Blackbeard commanded the *Queen Anne's Revenge*, while Capt. Richard Worley sailed in *New York's Revenge* and later, after the loss of that ship in battle, *New York Revenge's Revenge*. Pirates had a healthy sense of irony, and the idea of a silly name striking terror into the hearts of merchant captains seemed a rich joke. Thus we find pirate ships with names like *Childhood*, *Amity*, *Blessings*, *Most Holy Trinity*, *Happy Delivery*, and *Peace*. Perhaps the best joke of all belonged to pirate Edward Low, who named his ship the *Merry Christmas*.[63]

It was Low, in fact, whose example gave the era its name. His career began, according to Defoe, when he "took a small Vessel . . . hoisted a Black Flag, and declared *War against all the World*." Low's war was one of personal vengeance waged against a society he felt had wronged him from birth, and he waged that war avidly and with breathtaking brutality. Describing the capture of a Portuguese ship, one chronicler related how the ship's captain jettisoned its cargo (eleven bags of gold) to avoid it being captured. In retaliation, Low "cut off the said Master's lips and broiled them before his face, and afterward murdered the whole crew of thirty-two persons."

Many pirates seemed to take an almost erotic thrill in inflicting punishment on their captives. Keel-hauling, branding, slashing with broken bottles, scalping, tarring, and even boiling victims alive were not uncommon. Some pirates were even more inventive. One account described victims that "had slender cords or matches [fuses] twisted about their heads, till their eyes burst out of their skull." Such sadism suggests a motive more complex than mere avarice, even vengeance. On the one hand, there is the pleasure derived from inflicting humiliation on those who once held power over one: the same motivation that drove the Cilician pirates to make Roman citizens "walk the plank." On the other, there is the knowledge of how such acts of cruelty will reverberate when reported back to the states themselves. The pirates of the eighteenth century were acutely aware of their notoriety at home, and they reveled in it. It served two purposes: first, as with the Vikings, to spread fear and panic ahead of themselves, making captures all the easier; second, to trumpet their defiance to the nations they had declared war against. One modern commentator described it thus: "Pirates of old were terrorists. Not only did they seize ships and all persons and property aboard, not only did they murder, rob, and rape, but they also did so by creating fear and panic among their intended victims and seafarers everywhere." This concept of piracy is echoed in the definition of terrorism proposed by the 1999 Terrorist Finance Convention:

> Any other act intended to cause death or serious bodily injury to a civilian . . . when the purpose of such an act, by its nature or context, is to *intimidate* a population or to compel a government or an international organization to do or to abstain from doing any act.[64]

If pirates were terrorists, then by far the most successful of these was Edward Teach, alias Blackbeard. More than any other pirate before or since, Teach understood the symbiotic relationship of terror and piracy. While some pirate captains gave quarter to their captured prizes and were often deposed as weaklings by their own crews in response, Blackbeard was a terrorist par excellence. He rarely took prisoners, and ill-treated those he did. Although pirates usually melted away if they encountered serious resistance, Teach never refused a fight. He invented his own primitive form of weapon—Defoe described them as "grenadoes"—consisting of a rum bottle filled with gunpowder and shrapnel, and delighted in hurling them at his adversaries. When one of his victims asked him fearfully, "Who are you and whence come you?" Teach answered, "I come from hell and I will carry you there presently." Even his own crew believed him invincible, an agent of the devil, a superstition that Teach encouraged. One evening he challenged his shipmates to create a "hell" in the tween-decks, lighting brimstone and sulfur until the heat and smoke drove out all but he. When boarding a prize in battle, he wove long-burning fuses into his enormous beard, wreathing his face in green smoke and giving himself a truly satanic appearance.

Teach's antics illuminate another central link between the crimes of piracy and terrorism; the deliberate use of terror to achieve a desired result. Nor was he the only pirate to engage in such psychological manipulation. Pirates were often far outmatched in guns and men by the ships they preyed upon, and had to rely heavily on a reputation for ferocity. In the eighteenth century, pirates fashioned Jolly Rogers with distinctive symbols (Teach's displayed a pirate—possibly himself—stabbing his blade through a human heart) that acted as advance warning of the horrors awaiting crews foolish enough to resist. While brutality and barbarism have been hallmarks of all human conflict, this was something different: the *threat* of barbarism, instilled to achieve a desired result.

Still, if pirates like Teach were merely isolated individuals, their threat to the sovereignty of states would have been negligible. The danger came from cohesion and community. In the so-called pirate colonies of Madagascar, New Providence, and elsewhere in the Caribbean, as well as on their ships, pirates self-consciously fashioned an alternate, egalitarian universe. Law and social order were upended, in what one historian describes as "a world turned upside down." Captains were often democratically elected,[65] and shares in each voyage were portioned out fairly, with the captain receiving only slightly more than the lowest mate. Democracy, comradeship, and a desire for order are all reflected in the rules of conduct that pirates fashioned for themselves. These "pirate articles" were often as specific and meticulous as acts of Parliament. An excerpt from those of Capt. John Phillips in 1723 provides an example of their scope and breadth:

1. Every man shall obey civil Command; the Captain shall have one full Share and a half in all prizes; the Master, Carpenter, Boatswain, and Gunner shall have one Share and a quarter.

2. If any Man shall offer to run away, or keep any Secret from the Company, he shall be maroond [*sic*] with one Bottle of Powder, one Bottle of Water, one small Arm, and Shot. . . .

9. If at any time you meet with a prudent Woman, that Man that offers to meddle with her, without her Consent, shall suffer present Death.[66]

These articles suggest that the pirates did not exist in the state of Hobbesian anarchy so often attributed to them, but were instead often as organized and disciplined a crew as any in the Royal Navy. Pirate captains sometimes furthered this image by mimicking the Royal Navy's practice of reading the Articles of War aloud each Sunday after prayers. While the crew stood at attention, the pirate captain recited each article and punishment with due solemnity.

The pirate articles are of particular relevance when considering the nature of piracy and its relation to organized terrorism, for they provide an early example of an organization with its own administrators, codes of conduct, and punishments, functioning for the sole purpose of wreaking havoc. A pirate ship was a quasi state unto itself, a legal anomaly that customary international law recognized by granting universal jurisdiction on its capture.

Ironically, the more organized (and arguably "civilized") the pirate world became, the more it worried nation-states. When pirates were lone individuals tracking merchant ships and raising havoc, that was problem enough. But by coalescing, forming communities, and developing into a distinct society, the pirates created an antistate, a direct challenge to their mother countries.

Whereas English society thrived on structured hierarchies, with an idle aristocratic class maintained by the labors of the poor, pirates offered a tempting alternative: a world that enshrined personal liberty, egalitarianism, and easy life, with the added chance of achieving great wealth. Little wonder so many mariners abandoned their hard life for this one; little wonder, too, that states began to fear it. Just as Cicero had predicted, piracy posed a grave challenge to the very foundation of the nation: not merely its trade and foreign relations, but the laws and institutions, mores, and social structures upon which it relied.

The pirate wars began in the first decade of the eighteenth century, when, as one historian writes, "the English government moved on a broad front to bring order to the empire."[67] Nor did it act alone. With the resumption of peace in 1718, the nations of Europe were primarily concerned with reestablishing trade relations with one another and the rest of the world, and making their colonies turn a profit. Both enterprises were threatened by the pirates. Historian Robert Ritchie offers his own interpretation of their new policy: "The roistering buccaneer did not suit the hard-headed merchants and imperial bureaucrats, whose musty world of balance sheets and reports came into violent conflict with that of the pirates."[68]

The war against piracy was more than a business decision. For centuries, the line between pirates as agents of the state (privateers), enemies of the state, and robbers at sea had been drawn and redrawn. But now, with states seeking to consolidate their empires, any threat to those empires was tantamount to an act of war. Thus the pirate wars were correctly identified as such by both sides. For the pirates, it was a war against all the world; for governments, it was a private war to stamp out a global menace. Contained within this zeal was the germination of international law: a recognition that as empires expanded and began to interact with one another, state policy no longer could be contained within its own borders, but rather had to respond to international pressure both from other states and from an emerging international order. This, historian Elizabeth Mancke argues, led states with overseas interests "to control or suppress privatized violence," including (and especially) piracy.[69] Piracy, as a threat to trade and an infraction of international customary law, posed a grave challenge to the maintenance of amicable relations between empires. Consequently, "international pressure, as well as complaints from the East India Company, contributed to a crackdown on piracy spearheaded by the Board of Trade after the Treaty of Ryswick in 1697."[70]

The legal counterpart to the navy's worldwide war was the return of *hostis humani generi* with a vengeance. Noticeably absent in the case law of the eighteenth century was the careful parsing of sea robbery and ordinary felony that appeared in the seventeenth. In the 1701 trial of Capt. William Kidd, the presiding judge echoed Cicero in declaring, "I need not tell you the heinousness of this offence which they [Kidd and his shipmates] are charged, and what ill consequence it is to all trading nations. Pirates are called *hostis humani generi*, the enemies of all mankind, but they are especially so to those [who] depend on trade."[71]

At the 1704 trial of pirate John Quelch in Massachusetts, the presiding judge looked past the preceding centuries and reiterated Cicero's definition verbatim, even its contentious corollary: "A pirate was therefore justly called by the Romans *hostis humani generi*: And the civil law saith of them, that neither faith nor oath is to be kept with them. . . . for pirates are not entitled to law, not so much as the law of arms." The judge even went on to comment that the trial itself was unnecessary since, under the law of universal jurisdiction:

> Captors are not obliged to bring them into any port, but may expose them immediately to punishment by hanging them on the mainyard: a sign of its [piracy] being of a very different and worse nature than any crime committed on the land; for robbers and murderers, and even traitors themselves, may not be put to death without passing a formal trial.

This was stunning, for it not only negated the entire debate over sea robbery but also effectively turned the clock back past the entire history of privateering, past Edward I and the Cinque Ports, past even the Vikings, and found as the only workable model the ruthless antipiracy policies of Rome. Pirates were neither robbers nor even felons, but "beasts" who had renounced their citizenship and therefore were owed nothing by their former countries. In 1718, at the trial of Major Stede Bonnet in South Carolina, another judge made this explicit:

> As to the heinousness or wickedness of the offense, it needs no aggravation, it being evident to the reason of all men. Therefore a pirate is called *hostis humani generi*, with whom neither faith nor oath is kept. And in our law they are termed "*brutes*" and "*beasts of prey*" and that it is lawful for anyone [who] takes them, if they cannot with safety to themselves bring them under some government to be tried, to put them to death.[72]

A fundamental shift was occurring in the law, driven by the perceived threat of pirate colonies and their challenge to the order and structure of states. These trials are crucial in developing our understanding of the unique nature of piracy in the law, for not since the Roman Republic had the *crime* of piracy been so expressly articulated. When confronted with a seemingly new problem, lawyers inevitably look back to find a precedent to help them understand, define, and deal with it. The jurists of the eighteenth century chose to look past the intervening centuries of pirate sponsorship and embrace a concept of piracy as a threat to the nation-state. This accorded precisely with how the pirates regarded themselves, as we saw earlier.

The corollaries between the golden-age pirates' war against the world and modern organized terrorism are striking. In both we find a group of men who band together in extraterritorial conclaves, remove themselves from the protection and jurisdiction of the nation-state, and declare a personal war against civilization itself. One might argue that the comparison fails on the grounds of motivation. While the pirates sought nothing more politically than to strike back at their states, most international terrorists seek by their acts to effect a political transformation. Yet once again, the means outweigh the motivations. Both parties have effectively declared war against the state, a form of state versus nonstate conflict that is otherwise unique. Moreover, both use the same tools—homicide, terror, wanton destruction, and disruption of trade—to achieve a common aim: gaining notice to themselves.

This parallel cannot be stressed enough, for it represents the most significant nexus between terrorism and piracy yet mentioned, and in itself forms the basis for a new understanding of terrorism based on piratical antecedents. The idea of attracting attention to one's self and one's cause is the modus vivendi of all terrorism, whether government sponsored, organized, or anarchic. Compare, for example, the pirates war against all the world with this definition of terrorism promulgated by the academic community:

> Terrorism is an anxiety-inspiring method of repeated violent action, employed by (semi-) clandestine individual, group or state actors, for idiosyncratic, criminal or political reasons. . . . [Its] main targets are used to manipulate the main target audiences, turning it into a target of terror, a target of demands, or a target of attention, depending on whether intimidation, coercion, or propaganda is primarily sought.[73]

Terrorism is a means of projecting individual, extragovernmental aims through the commission of acts so horrific as to captivate the world's attention. Hence the pivotal issue is not whether the terrorists seek by their acts to achieve a change of governmental policy, a revolution, or even (as with the nineteenth-century anarchists) a collapse of all governments—it is only whether they employ terror to achieve this notice. If they do, then theirs is also a war against all the world.

Second, we can also look to the pirate wars of the eighteenth century as a valuable precedent for our own war on terror. The link between the two has even been noted by historians: Peter Earle, who penned the definitive work *The Pirate Wars*, writes that the extermination of pirates was "an epic story, since pirates, like terrorists, their modern counterparts as enemies of mankind, were hard to eliminate." Why so? For the same reasons as terrorist groups are today: by forming secret, cellular enclaves, they required militaries to strike everywhere at once. "Like weeds or Hydras," one contemporary noted, "they spring up as fast as we can cut them down." The states' solution was to go after the safe havens, the colonies that still harbored pirates, and the myriad islands where they congregated. In 1701 a successful raid by the English Navy destroyed the pirate colony at St. Mary's, in Madagascar; in 1718, following the Treaty of Ryswick, ex-pirate Woodes Rogers arrived at another pirate bastion, the Bahamas, and proceeded to clean house. Coupled with constant patrols and frequent raids by the combined navies of England, France, Holland, and Spain, these efforts ultimately paid off. Just as Pompey had done, "the expanding tentacles of European empires gradually eliminated more of the bases and havens on which pirates depended until, by the nineteenth century, there was hardly anywhere left on the globe which was safe from imperialist attention."

This gives us a clue for how to wage our own, twenty-first-century fight against terrorism. If terrorists thrive, as pirates did, from the existence of safe havens and sympathetic states, the logical first step in eliminating the groups altogether is to remove those havens. This makes it more difficult for the groups to communicate, to train, to plan. A later chapter will be devoted to the mechanics of how piracy law can be used to help gain the cooperation of states for such an action, as well as providing legal defense for those times when it is necessary to raid and destroy a terrorist camp within a hostile state. For now, however, the critical point is not that it *can* be done, but that is has *already* been done. The precedent is there.

THE PIRATE PRECEDENT

It is dangerous to extrapolate too greatly from the past. The pirate wars are not perfect cognates to our war on terror, as many who read this book will doubtless point out. Rarely, if ever, does history provide a perfect example of repeated circumstance that does not require a little artful retouching. The purpose of this chapter is not to attempt to pack and stuff the notion of a war on terror into eras where it did not exist, any more than to suggest that our own problems are no different from those of the Roman Republic. Yet the history of piracy is crucial, for it provides the foundation for establishing a precedent.

Precedents do not have to be perfect. In fact, they never are. Lawyers searching through volumes of case law hardly ever come upon one with exactly the same facts. They look instead for similarities, points of connection. The magic of the law, as well as history, is that these connections almost always can be found. Even something as seemingly unique as twenty-first-century international terrorism can be linked, in acts and motivations and circumstances, to events that seem at first glance both remote and arcane. Once that connection is made, the groundwork is in place to define, understand, and resolve our current conflict.

This chapter has raised four points in establishing the historical linkages between piracy and terrorism. First, since its earliest manifestation, the directed use of terror has been an integral part of piracy. One finds it throughout history, from the Vikings to Sir Francis Drake and Edward Teach. Each understood the political, as well as personal, benefits of terror. Terror inspired fear in the breast of the victim before the first shot was fired, an invaluable reputation that facilitated many bloodless captures. Each also understood that piracy, unlike other forms of conflict, did not obey gentlemen's rules. Ferocity and barbarism were essential components to the trade. Thus, piracy represents the first use of terror as a means of coercion by a non-state actor against the flag and trade of a nation-state.

Second, the history of piracy as a political tool of governments negates its popular image as mere sea robbery, a definition that bears little similarity to terrorism. Piracy must properly be understood as being as much a political as a commercial enterprise. From the time of the Punic Wars until the eighteenth century (and, as we shall see in later chapters, well into the nineteenth), governments employed pirates as privateers to hinder an enemy's trade, distract its navy, frustrate its relations with its empire, deplete its coffers, and sometimes drive it toward open warfare. The extralegal aspect of government-sponsored piracy provided a means of wounding a hostile state while continuing to maintain diplomatic relations. As such, it bears remarkable similarity in both execution and purpose to modern government-sponsored terrorism. In both instances, the pirate/terrorist is a private individual (or organization) acting beyond the nominal purview of the sponsor state, yet whose actions are directed toward a coercive political aim of that state.

Third, when employed not as an agent of governments but as a weapon against them, as in the so-called pirate golden age, the motivations of piracy have strong resonance with contemporary terrorism. The pirates' war against the world provides a crucial historical example of nonstate versus state conflict, the same sort of war that al Qaeda wages today. This form of conflict must be distinguished from revolutions and civil wars in that here the aggressors detach themselves both politically and (more important) physically from the nation-state—leading the revolt from without rather than from within. The argument that international terrorists are revolutionaries falls apart on these grounds, for revolutions are defined as uprisings within a state to change its government. A terrorist organization, by becoming international and therefore extralegal in character, divorces itself from such terminology.

Likewise, the methods of the contemporary terrorists have much in common with their piratical forbears; the terrorist, like the pirate, appears suddenly, attacks his target, and disappears. The amorphous, extraterritorial composition of modern terrorist organizations provides much the same function as the Atlantic did for their predecessors. Al Qaeda terrorists move covertly through the world like ships across a vast ocean, surfacing without warning, wreaking havoc, and retreating into an obscure mist of anonymity.

The last and most important connection is pirates' status since the Roman Republic as *hostis humani generi*. Coupled with this definition is the legal and political conception of piracy as a private war between states and nonstates. The threat that piracy posed to the nation-state was unprecedented: a band of private individuals divorced from the state, existing in enclaves outside its jurisdiction, whose actions threaten the safety and the sovereignty of the community as a whole. All these elements are present in the current composition of international terrorist organizations. They lack only the legal recognition that should long have been awarded them: enemies of the human race. This would involve recognizing, first, that terrorism, like piracy, is not a legitimate political tool; second, that states may not use it as a means of political coercion; third, that all instances of terrorism—as defined by international covenant—are equally unlawful, whether state sponsored or not; fourth, that terrorism, like piracy, is therefore an international crime, not to be confused with the recognized right of peoples to change their forms of government; and fifth, that terrorists, as *hostis humani generi*, are likewise subject to universal jurisdiction.

While the historical precedent is critical, it must not be extended too far. Historical parallels, at best, are merely indicators that the problems currently posed by the war on terror are not wholly unique. They do not prove that piracy and terrorism are the same crime, nor that the same means used against the pirates would be equally effective against the terrorists. For that, we must turn from the European context to our own, and from the past to the present.

NOTES

1. For a complete history of piracy in ancient Rome, see Henry Omerod, *Piracy in the Ancient World: An Essay in Mediterranean History* (Baltimore: Johns Hopkins University Press, 1997).

2. Quoted in Alfred S. Bradford, *Flying the Black Flag: A Brief History of Piracy* (Westport: Praeger, 1999), pp. 49–50.

3. A complete account of this incident can be found in Ormerod, *Piracy in the Ancient World*, pp. 13–42.

4. *Trials of Joseph Dawson, et al. at the Old Bailey, Oct. 31, 1696* (London: John Everingham, 1697), p. 6.

5. Omerod, *Piracy in the Ancient World*, p. 80.

6. Alan Villiers, *Men, Ships and the Sea* (Washington, DC: National Geographic Survey, 1973), p. 29.

7. Ormerod, *Piracy in the Ancient World*, p. 157.

8. Alfred Rubin, *The Law of Piracy* (Irvington-on-Hudson, NY: Transnational Publishers, 1985), p. 11.

9. Ormerod, *Piracy in the Ancient World*, p. 221.

10. Bradford, *Flying the Black Flag*, p. 44.

11. Rubin, *Law of Piracy*, p. 10.

12. Quoted in ibid., pp. 10–11.

13. Bradford, *Flying the Black Flag*, p. 50.

14. Marcus Tullius Cicero, *De Officiis*, bk. 3, chap. 29, p. 107.

15. Ormerod, *Piracy in the Ancient World*, p. 8.

16. Pomponius, *Ad Quintum Mucium*, bk. 2, n. 118.

17. Ulpanius, *Corpus Juris Civilis* XLIX.15.24.

18. Hugh Rankin, *The Golden Age of Piracy* (New York: Holt Rinehart, 1969), p. 4.

19. Bradford, *Flying the Black Flag*, p. 63.

20. Ibid., p. 62.

21. Robert Ritchie, *Captain Kidd and the War against the Pirates* (Cambridge, MA: Harvard University Press, 1986), pp. 5–6.

22. Takeo Tanaka, "Japan's Relations with Overseas Countries," in *Japan in the Muromachi Age*, ed. John Whitney Hall and Toyoda Takeshi (Berkeley: University of California Press, 1977), pp. 173–74.

23. Piero Belli, *De Militari et Bello Tractatus*, pt. 2, quoted in Rubin, *Law of Piracy*, p. 26.

24. Cesare Beccaria, *An Essay on Crimes and Punishment* (Brookline, MA: Branden, 1992 [1819]).

25. M. Cherif Bassiouni, "The History of Universal Jurisdiction and Its Place in International Law," in *Universal Jurisdiction: National Courts and the Prosecution of Serious Crimes under International Law*, ed. Stephen Marcedo (Philadelphia: University of Pennsylvania Press, 2004), p. 43.

26. Quoted in Burdock Britten, "The Law of Piracy," in *Piracy at Sea*, ed. Eric Ellen (Paris: ICC Publishing, 1989), p. 159.

27. Rubin, *Law of Piracy*, p. 30.

28. Consider the example of recent events in Iran, wherein protesters following the 2009 election were labeled "terrorists" by the government in power and punished ruthlessly.

29. Hugh Rankin, *The Golden Age of Piracy* (New York: Rinehart, 1969), p. 4.

30. Barry Hart Dubner, *The Law of International Sea Piracy* (New York: Holt Rinehart, 1969), pp. 40–45.

31. See Douglas R. Burgess, *The Pirates' Pact: The Secret Alliances between History's Most Notorious Buccaneers and Colonial America* (New York: McGraw-Hill, 2008).

32. The second most common objection, that piracy can only occur at sea, is likewise fallacious and will be addressed later.

33. Sir Matthew Hale, *Pleas of the Crown* (London: Richard Tonson, 1678), p. 77. Hale writes that piracy was a species of "petit treason, if done by an English subject." A similar argument was made by Coke, which is discussed later.

34. R. G. Marsden, ed., *Documents Relating to the Law and Custom of the Sea* (London: Naval Records Society, 1915), pp. 10–11.

35. Rubin, *Law of Piracy*, p. 47.

36. Ibid.

37. Hale, *Pleas of the Crown*, p. 77.

38. John William Bund, *A Selection of Cases from the State Trials* (London: Cambridge Warehouse, 1879), pp. 8–9.

39. Sir Edward Coke, *Institutes of the Laws of England; Concerning High Treason, and Other Pleas of the Crown and Criminal Causes* (London: E & R Brooke, 1794 [1628]), pt. 4, "Articuli Admiralitatis," p. 136.

40. Marsden, *Documents*, p. 88.

41. Rubin, *Law of Piracy*, p. 48.

42. 27 Hen. VIII c.4 (1535) in Danby Pickering, *The Statutes at Large* (Cambridge: John Burgess, 1795), p. 348.

43. 28 Hen. VIII c.15 (1536) in ibid., pp. 441–43.

44. Marsden, *Documents*, p. 224.

45. Coke, *Institutes*, p. 113.

46. Rubin, *Piracy Law*, p. 61.

47. Coke, *Institutes*, p. 111.

48. Ibid., p. 112.

49. Ibid., p. 113.

50. While it is dangerous to impute outside circumstances to Coke's legal writings, Stephen White has noted that Coke wrote his *Institutes* while in severe political disfavor with Charles I, whose administration he criticized openly. This might have influenced Coke's defense of common-law jurisdiction for piracy, especially as it could be regarded as a check on the Crown. Stephen White, *Sir Edward Coke and the Grievances of the Commonwealth* (Chapel Hill: University of North Carolina Press, 1979), pp. 9–10.

51. *An Exact Narrative of the Tryals of the Pyrats George Cusack, Henry Lovewell, et al. . . . held at the Old Bailey on Thursday and Saturday the 7th and 9th of January, 1674* (London: 1675).

52. *The Grand Pirate, or the Life and Death of Captain George Cusack* (London: 1675), p. 3.

53. William Blackstone, *Commentaries on the Laws of England* (Chicago: University of Chicago Press, 1978), p. 67.

54. Hale, *Pleas of the Crown*, p. 84.

55. Coke, *Institutes*, p. 113.

56. Rubin, *Piracy Law*, p. 97.

57. Blackstone, *Commentaries*, p. 66.

58. *Trials of Joseph Dawson et al.*, p. 4.

59. Ibid., p. 6.

60. Marcus Rediker, "'Under the Banner of King Death': The Social World of Anglo-American Pirates, 1716–1726," *William & Mary Quarterly* 3, vol. 38 (April 1981): 203–27.

61. Charles Johnson, *History of the Pyrates* (New York: Creation Books, 1999), p. 78.

62. Rankin, *Golden Age of Piracy*, p. 23.

63. Ibid., p. 28.

64. Ben Saul, *Defining Terrorism in International Law* (Oxford: Oxford University Press, 2008), p. 59.

65. A process hinted at in R. L. Stevenson's *Treasure Island*, when Long John Silver's crew elects to "depose" him.

66. Rankin, *Golden Age of Piracy*, p. 31.

67. Ritchie, *Captain Kidd*, p. 149.

68. Ibid., p. 2.

69. Elizabeth Mancke, "Empire and State," in *The British Atlantic World, 1500–1800*, ed. David Armitage and Michael J. Braddock (New York: Palgrave, 2002), pp. 175–95.

70. Ibid., p. 185.

71. Graham Brooks, ed., *The Trial of Captain Kidd* (London: William Hodge, 1930), pp. 30–47.

72. *Trial of Major Stede Bonnet at the Court of Vice Admiralty, 5 George I. 1718*, pp. 1234–37.

73. Brian Jenkins, *Future Trends in International Terrorism* (New York: Parrit, 1986), pp. 41–42.

Chapter 2

PIRACY AND THE AMERICAN EXPERIENCE

The most crucial test for defining terrorism as piracy in American law lies is whether the case law for piracy will sustain such a claim. It is not enough to raise historical parallels, for such parallels have ultimately little weight on legislators' minds when they look for sources of law, nor for jurists when they define the parameters of that law in our courts.

The recent surge of piracy off the coast of Somalia, the capture and rescue of Capt. Richard Phillips, and most of all the extradition of a Somali pirate for trial in New York have sent admiralty lawyers and State Department officials scurrying through dusty libraries, hunting up American law of piracy. They will have a meager reward for their efforts. The Piracy Act of May 15, 1820, remains in force, only slightly modified, today. The Supreme Court case construing that act, *US v. Smith*, was decided that same year and Justice Story's opinion is still the most commonly quoted source for understanding piracy in the American context. The actual incidents of out-and-out piracy against American vessels are almost nonexistent after the second decade of the nineteenth century. Consequently, the majority of case law is devoted to determining whether other acts—mutiny, hijacking, confederate privateering, accidental ramming, even slavery—can be construed as piratical. The answer to most of these queries has been no.

This would appear to be inhospitable ground for building a workable precedent for extending piracy law to terrorism. But the law is not as limiting as it seems. On the contrary, just as the last chapter revealed obscure but critical links between the private wars of terrorism and piracy, so too does the American example, if properly understood. That will be the purpose of this chapter. We will begin by looking at the foundations of American piracy law from the Constitution to the first statutes, America's struggle with the Barbary pirates, and the attempts—formulated in response to that struggle—to extend American law to pirates in foreign waters under the right of universal jurisdiction. From there we will turn to consider the role of piracy in the Civil War and the concurrent threads in European history and law that ultimately led to the understanding of pirates that exists today.

What we find is that American law embraces a concept of pirates as *hostis humani generi*, reinforced by its own experiences with the Barbary corsairs and Confederate privateers. While attempts to apply the law to nonpiratical acts have rarely met with success, the overall trajectory of that law is one of expansion, not limitation. It is, in fact, the law's uniquely broad conception of piracy that allows and encourages these attempts. In the relative absence of actual piracy (either of the sea robbery or private war variety), American law and policy have gradually moved toward a more nuanced understanding of the term: pirates as "maritime terrorists."

THE ORIGINS OF AMERICAN PIRACY LAW

The history of piracy in the American colonies was closely bound to that of their mother country, England. Throughout the pirate golden age of the seventeenth and eighteenth centuries, the seaports of Newport, New York, Charlestown, Philadelphia, and Boston actively protected and financed the pirates, often in direct opposition to English policy. Nearly every colony profited from illegal pirate voyages, which not only enriched its denizens but also offered them a choice of stolen merchandise outside the strictures of the Navigation Acts. Bound up as it was with notions of free trade and independence, charter colonies like Rhode Island and Massachusetts also regarded piracy as an essential element of their liberty, and zealously guarded it from imperial interference. English administrators railed against the "private colonies," accusing them of being places where "privateers and Red Sea pirates [are] entertained . . . while the King's own colonies dwindle to nothing."[1] Yet at the same time, colonial governors like Samuel Cranston warned their assemblies not to accede to the Crown's demands on piracy, lest they allow their children to "fall into bondage . . . a word to the wise is sufficient."[2]

This was the muddied legacy that the framers of the Constitution inherited. Adding to the general confusion over defining piracy was the Continental Army's extensive use of privateers during the Revolutionary War, which acted in place of a conventional navy. The framers were anxious to distinguish the actions of their own privateers (and, by extension, the Red Sea piracies of their fathers and grandfathers) from legal "piracy," and correspondingly deferred the definition to Congress while obliquely offering a suggestion on what form the law should take. Article I, Section 8, Clause 10 of the US Constitution states that "Congress shall have the Power . . . to define and punish Piracies and Felonies committed on the high seas, and Offenses against the Law of Nations."

By binding piracy, felony, and crimes against the "law of nations," the framers clearly envisioned a definition of piracy considerably broader than sea robbery. This was reflected in the first substantive law of piracy, which appeared in the Act of April 30, 1790. Statute 112 extends the definition to include murder, robbery, running away with a ship, voluntarily aiding a pirate, violence against a ship's master by a seaman, and mutiny; in short, nearly every act of depredation or violence "upon the high seas, or in any river, haven, basin or bay, out of the jurisdiction of any particular state."

Congress's blanket definition was much in keeping with its predecessor the English Crown's ongoing attempts (discussed previously) to broaden piracy for political ends. Here the political ends were more subtle, but no less present. The United States, as a new nation, wished to establish its legal prerogatives around the world. The first and easiest means for doing so was to assert jurisdiction as frequently as possible. In 1798 the attorney general advised John Adams's cantankerous secretary of state, Timothy Pickering, that the United States could deny Great Britain's extradition request for three pirates of dubious citizenship on the grounds that "the criminal tribunals of the United States are fully competent to try and punish persons who commit murder or piracy on the high seas . . . [even] supposing them [the defendants] to be foreigners, . . . I deem it more becoming the justice, honor, and dignity of the United States that the trial should be in our courts."[3]

This early assertion of universal jurisdiction was echoed soon after by Justice Story of the US Supreme Court, who in 1812 broadened the definition of "high seas" to include foreign harbors: "Any waters on the sea coast which are within the boundaries of low watermark, although such waters may be in a roadstead or bay within the jurisdictional limits of a foreign government." This was stunning, for it extended the United States' jurisdictional reach not only across oceans but within the territorial bounds of other states as well. Theoretically, the United States now had the power under law to capture pirates anywhere on earth, even within states. After 1818, and the Supreme Court decision rendered in *US v. Palmer*, this included not only pirates who had committed offenses against the United States but all pirates everywhere. Justice John Marshall wrote, "The Constitution having conferred on Congress the power of defining and punishing piracy, there can be no doubt of the right of the legislature to enact laws punishing pirates, although they may be foreigners, and may have committed no particular offense against the United States."[4]

The jurisdictional reach of the United States was lengthening, even as its own definition of piracy appeared to encompass almost any defendant whose crimes were "offenses to the Law of Nations." This universalist language began to creep into both judicial opinions and acts of Congress. In the pivotal 1818 case *US v. Klintock*, Justice Marshall definitively stated the operating definition for universal jurisdiction that would mark all such cases up to the present day: "Persons of this description [pirates] are proper objects for the penal code of all nations, and we think that the general words of the Act of Congress applying to all persons whatsoever [including foreigners] . . . ought to be so construed as to comprehend those who acknowledge the authority of no state."[5]

Here Marshall not only lays out the United States' claim for universal jurisdiction but also echoes the Roman definition of pirates who have renounced statehood altogether. The Act of September 30, 1790, Marshall writes, "does extend to all persons on board all vessels which throw off their national character by cruising piratically and committing piracy on other vessels." Such criminals can be captured and adjudicated by the United States regardless of whether their offenses touched that nation, since they are "persons who by common consent are equally amenable to the laws of all nations." One year later, Congress reinforced Marshall's broad reach (and his implied criticism of the lack of an explicit piracy law for foreign subjects) by combining both universal jurisdiction and the understanding of piracy as an offense to the law of nations in the Act of March 3, 1819, which states, "That if *any person or persons whatsoever*, shall, on the high seas, commit the crime of piracy, *as defined by the law of nations*, and such offender or offenders shall afterwards be brought into or found in the United States, every such offender or offenders shall suffer upon conviction thereof . . . be punishable with death."[6] This statute was supplanted by a second passed one year later, which repeated its wording verbatim. That statute, the Act of May 15, 1820, remains in force today.

From its inception, then, the United States had a vested interest in defining piracy in the broadest terms and extending its own jurisdiction over the greatest possible area. With a mandate from the Constitution, both Congress and the Supreme Court embraced the concept of pirates as *hostis humani generi*, enemies that could be captured anywhere in the world, by anyone who found them. Much of this appears to have been aimed at distinguishing pirates from privateers, especially in the context of both the Revolutionary War and the War of 1812. But there is also evidence that the United States wished to extend its purview as widely as possible, particularly after the confrontation with the Barbary corsairs in 1804. Consequently, American law is furnished with both a definition of piracy and jurisdictional bounds that are—if not unique—certainly among the broadest among the community of nations. Both make it exceptionally amenable to incorporating the crime of terrorism within the definition of piracy and justifying the application of universal jurisdiction against terrorists around the world. In fact there is already a precedent for so doing, in the tumultuous case law of the mid-nineteenth century.

PUSHING THE DEFINITION: PIRACY, SLAVERY, AND THE *MALEK ADHEL*

By the end of the War of 1812, traditional piracy (that is, piracy not in some way connected to the state, as with privateering) was declining. Much of the case law emanating from this era, therefore, deals with the extension of the term *piracy* to crimes that might not otherwise be considered piratical. These cases, anachronistic for almost two centuries, now have renewed relevance as we attempt to expand the definition of piracy to include terrorism.

The substantive law, as noted above, left open the possibility to apply the definition and legal mechanics of piracy almost at will. Congress included all manner of depredations at sea (including mutiny and conspiracy) in its definition, then compounded that broad mandate by deferring to "the law of nations," wherein pirates were defined as stateless international criminals. This left open an exciting possibility: that if the law of nations were to declare a certain species of criminal as pirates, regardless of whether their actions were expressly piratical, the United States would be obliged to follow suit.

This logical inference was tested in the case of *The Antelope*, 23 US (10 Wheaton) 66 (1825). It began in England, where momentum had been building for some time to abolish the slave trade throughout the world. At the Congress of Aix-la-Chappelle in 1818, British foreign secretary Lord Castlereagh laid out the case for extending piracy law to the slave trade on the grounds that both shared a status as crimes against the law of nations:

> If the moment should have arrived when the traffic in slaves shall be universally prohibited, and if, under these circumstances, the mode shall have been devised by which this offense shall be raised to the Criminal Code of all civilized Nations to the standard of piracy; they conceive that this species of piracy . . . will, by the Law of Nations, be amenable to the ordinary Tribunals of any or every particular state. . . . The verification of the fact of piracy, by sufficient evidence, brings them at once within the reach of the first Criminal Tribunal of competent authority.[7]

Lord Castlereagh was not arguing that piracy and slavery were the same crime per se, nor even that they shared compelling elements. Instead, his argument was based on the understanding that any behavior that is both universally abhorred and transnational in scope is construed as an offense against the law of nations, and must therefore be prosecuted *as if* it were the original international crime—piracy. Crucially, this included the central element of piracy law: universal jurisdiction. What

Castleraugh advocated was thus an extension of *hostis humani generi* to include other criminals besides pirates whose actions were equally iniquitous to the international legal order.

Castlereagh's argument became the basis for a trial that appeared before the Supreme Court in 1825. The facts of the case were labyrinthine, involving a Venezuelan slaver captured by an American privateer (which, for reasons left undefined, was flying the flag of an unnamed "Oriental republic"), and the subsequent attempts of the privateer's crew to sell the captured slaves in Florida. The crew was charged with piracy under the 1820 Act, stemming not from their status as privateers but having participated in "an offense against the Law of Nations," the slave trade. Justice John Marshall, speaking for the court, declined to uphold the charge of piracy. Interestingly, his legal basis was not that the slave trade could *never* be defined as piracy, but rather that it could not *at present*. The distinction lay in what constituted an offense to the law of nations. The African slave trade was contrary to the law of nature, he wrote, but was not prohibited by the positive law of nations: "Although the slave trade is now prohibited by the laws of most civilized nations, it may still be lawfully carried on by the subjects of those nations who have not prohibited it by municipal acts or treaties. The slave trade is not piracy unless made so by the treaties or statutes of the nation to whom the party belongs."[8]

Just as he had once chided Congress for not providing a coherent definition of piracy allowing for universal jurisdiction, Marshall now laid the blame for the lack of consensus on slavery as a universal crime with the intransigence of an unlikely participant:

> The parties to the modern law of nations do not propagate their principles by force, and Africa has not yet adopted them. Throughout the whole extent of that immense continent, so far as we know its history, it is still the law of nations that prisoners are slaves. Can those who have themselves renounced this law be permitted to participate in its effects by purchasing the beings who are its victims?

Until all the nations of the world agreed on a legal norm, it could not be properly considered universal. As Marshall pointed out, "both Europe and America" had practiced the slave trade until the last decade, "and for nearly two centuries it was carried on without opposition and without censure." One could not fault the African states for failing to proceed apace. Nor, Marshall lectured, could England or the United States maintain that Africa's vote was irrelevant. His conclusion was a powerful statement on the difficulty of achieving international consensus:

> No principle of general law is more universally acknowledged than the perfect equality of nations. Russia and Geneva have equal rights. A right, then, which is vested in all by the consent of all can be divested only by consent, and this trade, in which all have participated, must remain lawful to those who cannot be induced to relinquish it. As no nation can prescribe a rule for others, none can make a law of nations, and this traffic remains lawful to those whose governments have not forbidden it.
>
> If it [the slave trade] is consistent with the law of nations, it cannot in itself be piracy. It can be made so only by statute, and the obligation of the statute cannot transcend the legislative power of the state which may enact it.

While Marshall's decision had a quashing effect on attempts to bring slavers to trial under piracy law, its language boldly validates the principle behind the attempt: if a crime is universally adjudged to be an offense to the law of nations, it can be prosecuted *as if it were* an act of piracy. Moreover, the law would not merely bind one state, but all states equally. In other words, if the United States were to announce the principle that slavers were *hostis humani generi*, and this statement were not contradicted by the laws of any other state, it would become perforce a *jus cogens* norm under the law of nations. This was illustrated by a second slavery case decided in 1855, where the presiding judge likewise ruled that there was no international consensus against the slave trade to warrant its definition as a crime against the law of nations. Yet once again the judge upheld the concept of extending the law under the proper circumstances: "If the nations of the so-called civilized world . . . could for once unite in defining that some one act should be regarded as a crime by all, it may be that after such an agreement by all the world, the courts of any one nation might without reference to the nationality of the individual undertake to punish the offense he had committed."[9]

The slave trade failed that test in 1825 and 1855, but what of international terrorism in 2010? Are there any states that would willingly declare terrorism as anything other than an offense to the law of nations? It seems doubtful. The weight of international treaty and convention stands against such a proposition, and even those states that might finance or harbor terrorists *sub rosa* are not likely to defend the practice openly (indeed, given their clandestine involvement, they are perhaps the least likely to do so). The central question of the nineteenth-century jurists was not whether the slave trade was reprehensible, nor even whether it was criminal, but whether it was *universally recognized* as such. Unfortunately for Castlereagh and the abolition societies, no such consensus existed. But if it could be said to exist today for terrorism—if, in other words, the United States can maintain that the practice of terrorism is a crime against the law of nations, and no nation's laws contradict it—then the precedent set by the *Antelope* case and those following it appears to provide Congress with the ability to define terrorism as a species of piracy, subject to universal jurisdiction.

It is worth noting that none of the arguments advanced above relate to the similarities between terrorism and piracy, which was the focus of the first chapter. My purpose in raising the slavery example is to show how even the most seemingly disparate crime can, under certain circumstances, be defined as piracy. This argument does not rely on any similarity between the two crimes, save one: the recognition that both are offenses to the law of nations. In the nineteenth century, before the establishment of such institutions as the United Nations and the International Court of Justice, the definition of such an offense had to be inferred. It was only after the Nuremburg tribunals of the twentieth century that international crimes were delineated and defined: crimes of aggressive war, crimes of genocide, crimes against humanity. All rely on a shared understanding that such actions are a violation of natural law, law that is shared by every people and every state, regardless of individual circumstances. The legal principle is thus one of defining a certain class of persons as *hostis humani generi*, and springs from the same origin: the laws of piracy. Piracy, as the first international crime, provided the foundation for all subsequent law. Thus it is not surprising to find nineteenth-century jurists attempting to place the most predominant evil of their day—the slave trade—within its definition. The guiding impulse is the same as that which motivates this book: the recognition of a scourge that transcends national barriers, and the urgent need to place it within the parameters of existing law so that it can be confronted and eradicated.

In fact, the correlation of piracy and terrorism is a much easier sell than piracy and slavery, whose only kindred component lay in the fact that both occurred on the high seas. Interestingly, a case that reached the Supreme Court during the mid-nineteenth century provides the legal foundation for making that connection. At roughly the same time that the court rejected repeated attempts to extend the definition of piracy in other venues, it easily jettisoned one of the oldest and most persistent shibboleths of the crime: that it must have some element of robbery either as its motive or in its acts. In *US v. the Brig Malek Adhel*, 43 US 2 How. 210 (1844), an American cargo ship bound from New York to California inexplicably turned renegade off the coast of Mexico and fired upon numerous vessels, including two British and one Portuguese. Evidence given by the first mate indicated that the vessel's master, Captain Nunez, was insane. A snippet of dialogue preserved in the record indicates the bizarre nature of the voyage: "[The English] captain asked me why Nunez had fired at him; I said I did not know; the captain had ordered it. He asked me where we were bound. I said, 'God only knows.'"

Intercepted and captured by the navy brig *Enterprise*, the captain and crew of the *Malek Adhel* were charged with piracy. The defendants answered that there was no piracy, as their intent had merely been to harass and/or sink the vessels, not plunder them. Justice Story rejected this argument, and articulated a view of piracy that was at the same time markedly different from sea robbery and yet entirely consistent with the broad definition adopted by Congress. Contrary to the claimant's defense that piracy under law "must unequivocally demonstrate that the aggression is with a view to plunder, and not for any other purpose, however hostile or atrocious or indispensable such purpose may be," Story declared instead, "We cannot adopt any such narrow and limited interpretation of the words of the act [of May 15, 1820], and in our judgment it would manifestly defeat the objects and policy of the act, which seems designed to carry into effect the general law of nations on the same subject in a just and appropriate manner." Arguing that piracy also included acts of "hatred, revenge, or wanton abuse of power," Story proceeded to record the most articulate and compelling definitions of piracy ever given, and one with powerful resonance for our own understanding of contemporary terrorism:

> A pirate is deemed, and properly deemed, *hostis humani generi*. But why is he so deemed? Because he commits hostilities upon the subjects and property of any or all nations, without any regard to right or duty, or any pretense of public authority. If he willfully sinks or destroys an innocent merchant ship, *without any other object than to gratify his lawless appetite for mischief*, it is just as much a piratical aggression, in the sense of the law of nations, and of the act of Congress, as if he did it solely and exclusively for the sake of plunder, *lucri causa*.[10]

Story's definition of piracy is thus akin to the private war much discussed in the last chapter. In an earlier case (*Marianna Flores,*

24 US [11 Wheaton] 1 [1826]) the justice made this connection explicit. A Portuguese captain had mistaken a US warship for, of all things, a pirate vessel, and he opened fire. Brought up on the ironic charge of piracy himself, the captain was rescued by Justice Story, who wrote for the court that piracy could not exist without a *mens rea* (mental state) of intention to commit such acts. In other words, there could be no piracy by mistake. In distinguishing the actual crime from the actions of the unfortunate, befuddled Portuguese, Story restricted piracy to vessels engaging in "a private unauthorized war." Tellingly, this war need not be restricted to depredations against merchant vessels; by deciding the case on the base of the *mens rea*, the logical conclusion must be that if the captain *had* piratical intentions in mind, the fact that he attacked a naval vessel and not a merchantman would not have mattered in determining the crime as one of piracy.

In returning to the traditional definition of pirates as *hostis humani generi* engaged in a war against all the world, the United States was following (and in some ways leading) a trend in international law that began early in the century and culminated with the Treaty of Paris in 1856. It is appropriate to briefly turn our attention from the American example and consider how events beyond its shores ultimately had a critical impact on its laws, and ultimately on the eradication of piracy throughout the world.

FROM THE SHORES OF TRIPOLI TO THE TREATY OF PARIS: THE LAST PIRATE WAR

Frequently when I am called upon to speak on the links between piracy and terrorism, someone in the audience will raise the inevitable precedent of the US Marines' first engagement against the Barbary corsairs in 1805. Inasmuch as it represents the earliest known example of the US military's engagement in a state versus nonstate conflict, this precedent has merit. I suspect, however, that the most tempting reason for its frequent reference is the chilling concept of a "war against Islam."

This is a dangerous precedent and one that must be examined with great care. It is not my intention to fall into the same brambles that have beset many legislators and commentators by conflating the eradication of a band of international criminals with bombastic, xenophobic notions of a twenty-first-century crusade. It is critical, when considering the definition of international terrorism, to isolate it from the socioreligious penumbra that surrounds it. This is harder than it seems, for many terrorist organizations identify themselves as religious warriors, leading some members of the US leadership to abandon the term *terrorism* altogether in favor of *Islamic extremism*.

The problem, however, is that such terminology incorrectly incorporates motive into the definition of the criminal. On the contrary, criminal law rarely inquires *why* someone breaks the law, unless the reason would justify that person's actions or otherwise mitigate culpability. No one would seriously suggest that identification with a religious cause can, *per ipsum*, rebut the charge of engaging in terrorist acts. The critical element in the law is not motive but the acts themselves. A cognate example would be of a pirate who, at trial, declares he is not really a pirate but (as one described himself) "a free prince" with "as much authority to make war on the whole world as he who has a hundred sail of ships." Such a declaration would not transform a pirate into a state; nor does the existence of a political/religious motive rebut the charge of terrorism.

The Barbary corsairs are nevertheless critical for understanding the Western world's ultimate rejection of privateers and the resurgence of pirates as *hostis humani generi*. We have already seen how American law moved gradually toward a broad definition of piracy that acknowledged its status as an offense to the law of nations and included virtually any act of depredation at sea—even if it occurred in the territorial waters of another state, and even if it involved neither theft nor intent to steal. While this legislation partly emerged from the desire to extend America's presence around the world, it also came from a unique set of geopolitical circumstances predating the American Revolution by several centuries.

As Western piracy waned and waxed and waned again, Mediterranean piracy achieved something close to stasis. It will be recalled from the first chapter that even as far back as the Roman Republic, the Mediterranean was an ideal hunting ground for pirates. In the sixteenth century, at the same time as Elizabeth I of England was busily commissioning corsairs like Francis Drake, another form of state-sponsored piracy emerged. From the regencies of Algiers, Tunis, and Tripoli came the *corso*, tightly-knit pirate bands whom the English dubbed the "Barbary corsairs." These corsairs came from a different culture than those developing to the north: steeped in the long history of crusades and counter-crusades, they looked upon English vessels in the Mediterranean as interlopers in "their" territory. Barbary piracy was thus fueled by a potent strain of patriotism inextricably linked with the persistent Muslim regard for Christians as "infidels," and vice versa. Piracy against European vessels was thus not only profitable but part of a greater war against Christianity itself. Pirate voyages were often as much about capturing slaves as cargo; going "Christian stealing," as the English consul in Tripoli described it.[11]

Just as the English corsairs obtained commissions from Elizabeth, so too did the Barbary corsairs claim fealty to the regencies that harbored and financed them. Thus their quasi-religious war was as much state policy as was English privateering. As historian Peter Earle describes it, "The men who sailed and fought these vessels carried commissions from their rulers and saw themselves as legitimate warriors of Islam . . . whose only function was to capture Christian shipping and cargoes and enslave Christian men and women."[12] By 1642, forty years after the death of Elizabeth, the problem had only worsened: in a twenty-year period some three hundred English ships alone had been seized, along with seven thousand Englishmen who had, almost universally, been sold into slavery.

More than any effect on its shipping, the knowledge that

thousands of its subjects lived in bondage under the Muslim warlords fueled an unprecedented rage in England. Some historians, most notably Linda Colley, even credit the depredations of the Barbary corsairs for the corresponding emergence of British nationalism, best embodied by the famous 1740 verse by Thomas Augustine Arne:

> Rule, Britannia! Britannia rules the waves,
> Britons never, never, never shall be slaves!

But from the sixteenth century through the nineteenth Britons *were* slaves, and so to a lesser extent were French, Spanish, Portuguese, Dutch, and even American sailors captured by the corsairs. It might be expected, therefore, that these states would have banded together. Despite the corsairs' resiliency, it cannot be doubted that such an alliance would have dispatched them quickly—best evidenced by the brief and bloody struggle that wiped piracy off the Atlantic in the mid-eighteenth century. Yet the alliance refused to materialize. Instead, throughout the eighteenth century, Britain and other European powers chose to bargain with the corsairs, pay tributes to their warlords, and employ them as mercenaries in their own wars against one another. Suspicion, greed, and realpolitik were the primary motives. Constantly distrustful of one another, any attempt to deal with the Barbary pirates by one state was invariably assumed by others as a guise for some other form of adventuring. Moreover, the century between the Treaty of Utrecht in 1713 and the Battle of Waterloo in 1815 was marked by near-constant wars between the European powers; even if the consensus existed to combat the pirate menace, states could not pause long enough in their own wars to do so. Subsumed by the much larger conflagration on the European continent, the Muslim war against Christendom appeared almost quaint.

So began a crucial shift in relations between Europe and the Barbary corsairs. Britain, for one, chose to overlook the past century of mutual enmity and formed a close alliance with Algiers. France soon followed suit with Tunis. The "warriors of

Islam," for their part, chose to suspend their ongoing battle with Christianity in favor of a negotiated (and profitable) truce. Correspondingly, for the remainder of the eighteenth century until the first decade of the nineteenth, the Barbary corsairs became paid mercenaries for both sides, routinely waging their own personal wars against one or the other's shipping, with commissions granted by regencies now allied either with France or Britain. Such alliances were ephemeral at best, and the corsairs' benefit as privateers was offset by the mutually deleterious effects for both European powers. Indeed, the only true beneficiaries during this tumultuous time were the corsairs themselves (and, by extension, their Muslim protectors), who now enjoyed not only the benefits of their plunder but also the patronage of their European allies.

Yet relations forged by the exigencies of war rarely survive peace, and so it was for the corsairs. A decade before the ultimate defeat of Napoleon at Waterloo, they had already proved to be more trouble than they were worth. In 1805, the same year that Nelson achieved decisive naval victory over Villeneuve's fleet at Trafalgar, only a few hundred miles further along the coast another battle was being waged between the Barbary corsairs and the US Navy. Weary of paying the exorbitant tributes demanded by the Barbary states of Algiers, Tunis, and Tripoli, the US government under President Thomas Jefferson dispatched a fleet of fifteen naval vessels to attack Tripoli in 1801. A campaign of four years ensued, ending with a treaty negotiated between the two powers in 1805. The corsairs were far from destroyed, but for the first time they had been successfully checked.

The American precedent would not be followed by the European powers until the end of the Napoleonic Wars a decade later. At that time, however, England and her erstwhile enemies soon rediscovered the same truism that bedeviled their trade and international relations two centuries before: the cessation of war does not mean an end to privateering, but its continuance as outright piracy. The corsairs, freed from the enforced strictures of alliance, preyed on both French and English ships alike.

A century of European sponsorship had achieved the inverse of what its proponents intended: the Western powers and their navies emerged weakened, and the corsairs were wealthier and more formidable than ever before.

The problem of the corsairs was compounded by the continued inability of the Western states to act cohesively against them, even after the Congress of Vienna in 1815. Mutual distrust persisted, fueling and fueled by ongoing attempts to create separate peaces with individual warlords and employ the corsairs—as much as they could now be employed—in private wars against the trade of former enemies. A new imperial mentality could now be discerned, whereby Western powers willingly employed so-called barbarian mercenaries to engage in acts that they themselves eschewed and would, if accused of promoting, vehemently deny.

This sort of government sponsorship seems, at first glance, like the old Elizabethan policy writ large, but there was a crucial difference. The combined influences of English law, burgeoning empires, and the Enlightenment affected a profound shift in the Western conception of piracy. It became, in effect, an act of savagery. When committed by an Englishman, Frenchman, or anyone belonging to the fraternity of states that comprised "Western civilization," piracy was treason, tantamount to declaring oneself at war with the nation-state. But if committed by "savages" it was not only permissible but also politically useful. By terming piracy an act of barbarity, the law was thus able to meld the competing doctrines of political utility and *hostis humani generi*. A pirate, in this latest incarnation, was a ruthless savage whose existence was in conflict not only with the nation's laws but also with civilization itself.[13]

This led to a paradoxical situation, for the more the imperial powers employed pirates against each other, the more their laws responded by driving the definition of piracy further toward *hostis humani generi*, until it finally achieved its modern definition as a crime so heinous and barbaric that all who committed it were not just criminals but enemies of the human race.

The nineteenth century's bizarre double standard for piracy came back upon itself when the European governments in the 1850s realized they had created a beast they could no longer control. The corsairs continued their attacks on trade long after peace was concluded, a source of prolonged embarrassment and a serious economic threat to the Great Powers. It was a pattern repeated throughout the history of government-sponsored piracy, from the Hanseatic League to the Enlightenment. Now, however, the perceived barbarity of the pirates gave Western nations an added impetus for declaring it an act of *hostis humani generi* once and for all. As early as 1775, Edward Rutledge of South Carolina, speaking to his colleagues in the Continental Congress, expressed the hope that it would not authorize privateering, lest it "ruin the character and corrupt the morals of all seamen." He was ignored, but the precedent was set.

By the time of the Crimean War (1853–1856) England and France had become allies, and the usefulness of the corsairs as mercenaries was nil. There was a shared recognition, too, that the European states had erred in financing the privateers, whose activities were now regarded as counterproductive to the general trend of centralizing force and promoting imperial trade. "War," as one statesman declared, "is now an affair of Governments."[14] Pirates, under any guise, no longer fit with the general trend of history. Or, as Queen Victoria put it, "Privateering is a kind of piracy which disagrees with our Civilization, [and] its abolition throughout the world would be a great step in its advance."

Proposals for abolition had been circulating as early as 1820, but not until 1856, at the end of the Crimean War, would consensus among the European powers finally be reached. At peace negotiations in Paris, Count Walewski of the French delegation recommended the adoption of a statement on the principles of maritime law, to which the British agreed. The Declaration of Paris, as it came to be known, banned piracy, privateering, and pirate sponsorship in all its forms: the legal distinction between pirates and privateers was voided in favor of a general (and much simpler) definition as *hostis humani generi.* The seven European states that were parties to the conference were the first to sign. Over the next several years, the original peace treaty expanded into a multinational pact, drawing from the example of the Congress of Vienna and presaging international organizations like the League of Nations and the United Nations. By 1860, nearly every developed nation had signed on.

The significance of the Declaration of Paris cannot be overstated, for it brought to an abrupt conclusion several thousand years' worth of tension between states' desire to stamp out piracy and their equal willingness to employ the pirates in war. It was this duality that allowed piracy to survive, much as terrorism today benefits from both the lack of an international definition and the continued willingness of some states to capitalize on that fact by promoting it. What the declaration represented was, in effect, a statement that there were some forms of behavior that were simply beyond the pale, and no state could be party to them. This recognition was a critical advance in state relations, a precedent for the laws of war eventually adopted at the Hague in 1899 and the much broader Geneva Conventions of 1949. As for piracy, the adoption of a shared definition accomplished what centuries of naval battles never could: pirates, as a threat to nation-states, disappeared. While individuals might still harass shipping lanes, they would never again bear the imprimatur of sponsor states nor find any safe havens ashore. Thus the declaration transformed the war against piracy by presenting the pirates with a united front of condemnation and coordinated response. I would argue that much of the reason piracy seems anachronistic today (or did, until the events off Somalia's coast) was the rapid and stunning success of international policy after 1856.

The chain of events leading to the adoption of the declaration bears a chilling similarity to the crisis facing us today. Just as England and France created the renewed menace of piracy through their sponsorship of the corsairs, so too is the United States credited for manufacturing its own enemy by training, funding, and outfitting terrorist groups in the Middle East during the Cold War. Indeed, criticism that the United States is responsible for the very threat it now seeks to eliminate has been a formidable stumbling block against the creation of any new international law on terrorism.

But the lesson to be drawn here is not merely one of history repeating itself, nor even a reaffirmation of the close historical linkages between the problems of piracy and terrorism. Here, the history of piracy law provides not only a precedent to our current dilemma but also the solution. The 1856 Declaration of Paris is, on one level, recognition of shared guilt and a promise that the behavior of states that produced the problem will not be repeated. On another level, it represents the first recognition since the Roman Republic of piracy as a crime in and of itself, separate from state sponsorship. The central premise of *hostis humani generi* is that a pirate is not an enemy of the state but of humankind itself. He exists like a malevolent satellite to the law of nations, waging war upon them not only through his acts but also through his identity. Until 1856, international law recognized only two legal entities: persons and states. Persons were subject to the laws of their own governments; states were subject to the laws made between them. The Declaration of Paris and subsequent legislation created a third entity: persons who lacked both the individual liberties and protections of law to be citizens, and the legitimacy and sovereignty of states.

The creation of this third legal entity—pirates—was recognition by the states that piracy as a political tool was beyond the pale of legitimate state behavior and that pirates themselves forfeited the right to the protections of citizenship. In order to create a just and lasting body of law on organized terrorism, states must apply a similar understanding of their own behavior and of the crime itself.

A TRANSFORMATION OF IDENTITY:
PIRACY, INSURGENCY, AND THE CIVIL WAR

Aside from Mexico and Spain, only one nation of any promi-
nence declined to sign the Declaration of Paris: the United States.
While the declaration would eventually come to have a crucial
effect on US policy, the tumult of civil war precluded immediate
adoption. The circumstances were much like those surrounding
the creation of the International Criminal Court in 1998,
wherein the United States began by leading the charge, only to
suddenly reverse itself and retire from the field. President James
Buchanan fully supported the aims of the declaration at the time
of its adoption, stating that "the genuine dictates of Christianity
and civilization would be to abolish war against private property
on the ocean altogether."[15] Later, however, as the threat of seces-
sion became apparent, he reversed himself: the US Navy was not
at full strength, and the administration wished to keep its
options open. By 1861 this decision was moot: the Confederacy
embraced privateering and relied on the quiet but crucial aid of
Great Britain (much to the dismay and furor of the Union) to
replenish and repair its commercial raiders in seaports throughout the Caribbean and Bermuda.

In the context of melding the definitions of piracy and terrorism, one aspect of Civil War piracy is especially significant.
While the Confederacy's commercial raiders have long been recognized as the last privateers employed by a recognized power
(though not, technically, a state), the secessionists also adopted
what might today be termed guerilla tactics on the high seas,
aimed not only at seizing Union vessels but also at spreading
panic and discord in the fleet. These were the so-called insurgent
passengers, defined thus by legal scholar Samuel Menefee in the
early 1990s.[16] Insurgent passengers were not mutineers, but
civilians posing as ordinary supercargo who seized control of
their vessels through violent means.

The first precedent was not, perhaps, an auspicious one. In 1861
a heavily veiled lady boarded the Union packet *St. Nicholas*. She

never spoke, was commonly understood to be French, and traveled with a considerable cargo of steamer trunks. Halfway through the voyage, the veils were lifted and the trunks opened, revealing a Confederate officer named Richard Thomas Zarvona and a vast store of munitions. Zarvona and several fellow "passengers" successfully captured the ship and sailed it to a Southern port as a prize.[17]

While sometimes comical in the details, the effect of such captures was anything but. Not only did it hamper Union trade, it accomplished the same result as a conventional privateer with considerably less manpower. This was precisely the argument made by the United States in a later case involving the seizure of a schooner named the *Joseph L. Gerrity*, in maintaining that the captors were pirates *jure gentium*. The "pirates" in question were now in British custody, and hence the case came before the Queen's Bench in the spring of 1864.

The case raised several critical issues. First, could insurgency be considered piracy? The majority of the court ruled that it was. "Looking at the evidence," Justice Crompton wrote, "what was done by the prisoners is either the taking of a ship for plunder, which would be piracy *jure gentium* . . . or an act of war."[18] This raised a second issue, of whether the defendants were military combatants and thus immune from extradition. Confederate secretary of state Judah Benjamin advanced this claim, arguing that an insurgent government like the Confederacy must often engage in "irregular" warfare. The British court agreed in principle, but Chief Justice Cockburn narrowed the definition and, in so doing, left a critical precedent for understanding so-called political piracy. The case for defining pirates versus military combatants rested on whether the defendants were acting on orders from a recognized power, not whether they professed themselves to be: "If the act is not done with piratical intention, but the bona fide intent to aid one of the belligerent parties, they [the defendants] cannot according to any recognized law be treated as pirates. *But it is not because persons assume the character of belligerents that they can protect themselves from the consequences of an act really piratical.*"[19]

What this means is that the distinction between legal warfare and illegal piracy is not what the pirates' motives are, but whether they are acting as agents of a state. A pirate might truly believe that his or her actions are in furtherance of a political objective, but absent a military commission, such beliefs are irrelevant to the presumption of piracy. This is a critical point that we will return to again when considering the dimensions of political piracy in the twentieth and twenty-first centuries.

Similar to our own contemporary struggles to distinguish between states, insurgent governments, and terrorist organizations, the legality of piracy in the 1860s hinged on whether the pirates' sponsor, the Confederate States of America, could be regarded as a state. The British court ruled that it could, and accordingly denied extradition of the *Gerrity* pirates. Not surprisingly, the position of the United States was different. In 1864, Confederates John Beall and Bennett Burley, posing as passengers, seized control of the steamer *Philo Parsons* on Lake Erie and employed the vessel as a makeshift raider, taking a second ship, the *Island Queen*. Captured in Canada, Beall and Burley were held in a Toronto prison while the United States and the Confederacy both claimed jurisdiction. Acutely aware of the earlier failure with the *Gerrity* defendants (and of Canada's status as a British Dominion), President Lincoln warily requested an opinion from Attorney General Bates "whether their extradition *as pirates* may be demanded under the Ashburton treaty," which obligated Britain and the Commonwealth to extradite criminals acting against the United States. Bates replied that it could, and consequently the case came before a Toronto court in early 1865. The defendants produced both a privateering commission and an endorsement by Jefferson Davis himself, yet the court demurred. Citing Justice Cockburn's famous opinion that pirates could not protect themselves from the charge by calling themselves belligerents, the court granted extradition of both defendants to the United States.[20]

Though neither of these cases occurred in America, both had profound consequences for American understandings of piracy.

They demonstrate that even as early as the mid-nineteenth century, piracy was transforming. As it did so, many of the shibboleths that marked its earlier history and definition became irrelevant or arcane.

First, the emergence of an insurgent government, the Confederacy, tested the traditional distinctions between legitimate privateering and illegal piracy. It is worth noting that, as stated earlier, this dispute had already been resolved in Europe, after the Declaration of Paris in 1856. But for the United States it remained critical: how to classify acts against civilian vessels committed for allegedly political aims, yet not necessarily on the direct orders of a recognized government? Were they acts of war or piracy? Thus we find an early example of the conundrum that faces the United States and other nations today: distinguishing legal and illegal combatants, soldiers from civilians, and states from insurgent groups.

Second, and following from this debate, was the question of the pirates' motives. If one professed to act for a political cause, did that rebut the presumption of piracy? The obvious answer would be that it did not, yet debate rages even today between scholars of maritime law on the so-called political exclusion in the UN definition of piracy, which states that piracy must occur for private ends as opposed to political ones. This restriction has been argued by some to discount virtually all acts of maritime terrorism on the grounds that the captors did not seek treasure but rather notoriety or some other nonmaterial aim. Here Chief Justice Cockburn's opinion provides the codex for resolving this dispute: it does not matter what the pirates consider themselves to be, nor what their motives are; the only question at issue is whether they act on the direct orders of a recognized political body. A similar recognition, if applied to crimes of international terrorism, would revolutionize both the definition and the parameters of a states' ability to seize and prosecute—as we shall see later.

Finally, and most important, the inclusion of insurgents as pirates *jure gentium* by American, British, and Canadian courts revolutionized the definition and stood in stark contrast with the customary two-ship model that can still be found in some legal codes today. Pirates could attack not only from without but also from within, seizing hostages and vessels in choreographed raids that are indistinguishable from modern-day hijackings. Thus the Civil War insurgency cases are the earliest precedents in American law of the link between piratical and terrorist acts, a melding that would persist through the combined histories of aerial piracy (otherwise known as airplane hijacking) and maritime terrorism throughout the twentieth century.

FROM INSURGENCY TO HIJACKING TO TERRORISM

After the end of the Civil War, the number of piracy cases appearing before American courts dwindled to almost zero. This was scarcely surprising: traditional piracy itself had virtually disappeared from the Atlantic and was in severe decline around the world. Consequently, the few instances of "piracy" in the late nineteenth and twentieth centuries must always include scare quotes, as they do not fit the traditional model. Two such incidents are of critical importance, however, as they represent a development from the insurgent passenger cases arising during the Civil War. Both involved passenger vessels seized by an onboard coup; both were labeled, correctly, acts of terrorism.

In 1961, a band of Portuguese and Spanish insurgents led by Enrique Galvão seized control of a Portuguese liner, the *Santa Maria*, en route from Miami to Curaçao. Their objective was political: raising awareness and instigating a revolt against Spanish dictator Francisco Franco in the African and Iberian colonies. As the attack occurred near American waters, the Portuguese government requested assistance from the United States. Initially it complied, dispatching navy vessels to monitor the *Santa Maria* and, if possible, recover the ship by force.

Meanwhile, the American government joined Portugal and Spain in decrying the incident as an act of piracy, despite the fact that it was an insurrection from within.

As the situation dragged on, however, the United States eventually chose a diplomatic route, engaging in dialogue with the hijackers and arranging for asylum for Galvão and his followers in Brazil. Galvão was convicted of piracy *in absentia* in Portugal and became something of a media celebrity in the United States. Many of the passengers sold narratives of their captivity to newspapers, and Galvão himself wrote a book on the entire incident. Overlooking the fact that the *Santa Maria*'s third officer had been murdered in the attack, public perception of the hijackers adopted the spurious trappings of benign rascality—in other words, conforming with the popular myth of pirates as ruffians with a heart of gold.

Seen from a twenty-first-century perspective, the actions of the American government and the attitude of its citizens seem almost incomprehensible. This reflects how much our attitude toward acts of terror has changed. In 1961, with insurgent groups rising up and challenging imperial authority throughout the world, there was still something romantic about a band of men seizing a ship for no other reason than to bring awareness to their cause. Galvão was not unlike Ahmed ben Mohammed el Raisuli, the famous Moroccan outlaw whose 1904 capture of an American diplomat, as a challenge to the corrupt sultan, had led Theodore Roosevelt to issue "the wire that ran around the world." Such underdog antics resonated with Americans, who themselves had overthrown imperial rule in 1776. The seeming appeasement of the Kennedy administration was also very much in keeping with the spirit of the age, where the predominant attitude was not to crush acts of individual terror but to prevent them from escalating into wider conflicts between states. The fact that Francisco Franco was universally despised by Americans made the eventual diplomatic solution all the more likely.

Nevertheless, American passivity when confronted with piracy and terrorism left a devastating precedent. Less than fifteen years later, it was no longer Portuguese and Spanish victims, but Americans. The seizure of the *Achille Lauro*, outlined at the opening of this book, was a transformative event in the combined histories of piracy and terrorism. Here was the concept of the insurgent passenger in its fullest expression: a band of terrorists gaining control not merely over an airplane or small passenger vessel (the *Santa Maria* was only 5,000 tons) but over a major ocean liner capable of carrying thousands of persons at a time. The *Achille Lauro* did not itself alter American attitudes toward hijacking and terrorism in general; the recurrence of aerial hijackings in the 1970s had already accomplished that, as we shall see in the next chapter. What it did, however, was to finally divorce hijacking at sea from the romantic vestiges of Hollywood piracy, which were apparent in responses to the *Santa Maria* incident, and introduce a new term to the lexicon of international crime: maritime terrorism.

Although never explicitly articulated, the link between conventional piracy and maritime terrorism resurfaced in the United States' most recent efforts at formulating a working law on piracy. In June 2007, the Bush administration released a reworked version of the National Strategy for Maritime Security that dealt specifically with piracy "and other criminal acts of violence against US persons."[21] Several aims were identified in the document, among them the prevention of future pirate attacks, the fortification and security of American vessels, and—more broadly—the preservation of the freedom of the seas and continuing "to lead and support international efforts to suppress piracy."

Yet the timing of this document renders these limited (though laudable) aims somewhat suspect. While jurists recognized that the United States "lacked a single, coordinated document that contained all of our national objectives and policy guidance on the issue,"[22] incidents of piracy had actually *declined* over the last several years. None were against American-registered vessels. What had increased, alarmingly so, were high-profile acts of terror launched against ships. Al

Qaeda was credited with two such attacks in the last six years: the bombing of the USS *Cole* in 2000, and the similar raid launched against the MV *Limburg*, a tanker carrying 297,000 barrels of crude oil, in 2002. More recently, Iraqi al Qaeda leader Farik al-Zarqawi claimed responsibility for a third strike on the same model—a Zodiac craft loaded with explosives detonated alongside a larger vessel—in the 2004 bombings of oil terminals at Khawr Al-Amaya and Al-Basrah in Iraq. In that same year, terrorists belonging to the Abu Sayyaf Group (ASG) and Rajah Soliaman Revolutionary Movement (RSRM) targeted a civilian craft, the Philippine *Superferry 14*. Twenty sticks of dynamite were hidden in a television set, then detonated at sea. The ensuing fire claimed 116 lives.

The US government was not prepared to label these acts "piratical" without further definition of the term. Its most recent laws consciously eschewed such terminology, creating a blanket category of "violence against maritime navigation," which included "seizing control of a ship by force or intimidation, placing any device on the ship that is likely to cause damage or endanger the vessel, destroying a ship or causing damage to its cargo . . . or destroying logistical facilities in the maritime sector, such as ports and harbors."[23]

Some of these offenses were indistinguishable from traditional piracy, others less so. The United States, however, was persuaded that the time had come to meld the definitions into a single, workable whole. This, as it turns out, was much in keeping with the general trend. In its annual report, the International Maritime Bureau in 2006 combined the terms *piracy* and *armed robbery at sea* in a single definition: "An act of boarding or attempting to board any ship with the apparent intent to commit theft *or any other crime* and with the apparent intent or culpability to use force in the furtherance of that act."[24] Earlier, the Baltic and International Maritime Council (BIMCO), the largest shipowners' association in the world, advocated an even more radical step: combining piracy, cargo theft, human trafficking, drug smuggling, and maritime terrorism under the umbrella definition of "maritime crime." The linkage of piracy and terrorism was explicit, and much commented on at the time.[25]

The recommendations of the Bush administration were more cautious, yet nevertheless reflected a conscious effort to apply the existing law of piracy over a broader sphere of criminal conduct. While largely a restatement and encapsulation of existing law, the new policy contained a revealing instruction: for the first time, the responsibility of combating piracy was shifted from the US Navy to a shared prerogative between the assistant to the president for National Security Affairs and the assistant to the president for Homeland Security and Counterterrorism. While historical parallels do not always jibe, it is hard not to see the similarities between this decision and that of the English Crown in 1696, when it recognized the menace posed by piracy to international security and responded by transferring responsibility to a new bureaucratic agency, the Board of Trade. In both instances, the state recognized that the crime of piracy had taken on new dimensions—evolved, in fact, from a peripheral problem to a critical threat.

This recognition likewise paves the way for an even broader extension: that of piracy law to *all* acts of international terrorism. Much of the groundwork has already been done. Consider, for example, the US Code's inclusion of attacks on ports and harbors in its definition of maritime violence. While primarily concerned with attacks similar to those launched against the Iraqi oil ports in 2004, this provision extends the idea of maritime terrorism to attacks committed on land—a crucial step that moves us yet further from traditional piracy and closer to a more inclusive concept of interstate violence.

CONCLUSION

The history of piracy and the United States furnishes a strong case for a joint definition of piracy and terrorism under American law. This chapter has attempted to prove that the linkages between the two crimes already exist in both our history and our legal code. In concluding, let us briefly highlight them again.

Since its foundation as an independent nation, the United States has sought to extend its jurisdiction for piracy cases over the widest parameters possible. This reflects the desire of the founding fathers to bolster America's presence around the world and legitimize its claim as a viable state. Ultimately, this ambition also left present-day jurists with one of the broadest mandates in any legal system for pursuing and capturing pirates under the doctrine of universal jurisdiction. The United States can, by its own law, seize and prosecute pirates who have injured not only its own citizens but also citizens of other states. Applied to crimes of terrorism, this precedent would allow American courts to prosecute international terrorists whose crimes might or might not have included American targets—indeed, under the law of conspiracy, it might also cover those whose only crime is belonging to a terrorist organization that has plotted or engaged in these acts.

Yet universal jurisdiction cannot be successfully argued unless it can be shown that the crimes of piracy and terrorism are comparable. Here we find three traditional objections: that piracy must involve some act of theft, that it must occur between two vessels, and that it must occur for private and not political ends, thereby seemingly excluding political terrorism.

The first objection can be easily dispensed with. Justice Story's opinion in the *Malek Adhel* case explicitly stated that no actual taking was required for piracy, only a "lawless appetite for mischief." This is reflected in many subsequent cases in which the piratical objective often lay in either capturing the vessel for military or even political ends, as we saw during the Civil War.

Indeed, the definition of piracy has evolved dramatically over the last two centuries, embracing both activities and actors radically different from the traditional model. Perhaps the most telling example is that of the attempted extension of piracy to the slave trade. Here the argument for extension lay not in the acts (which were obviously incompatible) but in the shared notion of a crime against the law of nations. Likewise, the attempt failed not because piracy and the slave trade were fundamentally different, but rather that—as Justice John Marshall argued—slavery had not yet attained the status of an offense to international law. The inference is that any crime that *has* attained such status can be conflated with piracy.

It must be noted that these opinions were written a century before the creation of the United Nations and the codification of international crimes under UN law: genocide, war crimes, and crimes against humanity. We cannot, therefore, take Marshall's words to mean that all these crimes are akin to piracy. What we can conclude, however, is that American law allows for the extension of piracy's unique legal status (specifically, a crime of universal jurisdiction) for international criminals whose acts constitute an offense to the law of nations. If terrorists fit that definition—if, in other words, a consensus exists among states that crimes of terrorism are abhorrent and not to be tolerated—then the United States has the right to pursue and prosecute known terrorists wherever they may be found.

The second and third objections are less concerned with the acts constituting piracy than with the nature of the pirates themselves. The two-ship rule of piracy comes from attempts to distinguish piracy from mutiny and other forms of internal conflict on board ship. Yet during the Civil War, insurgent passengers posed as great a threat to Union vessels as conventional privateers. This was reflected in the response of both the British and American governments, which recognized that such acts constituted piracy, even if they differed on the appropriate response. In both instances, the finding of piracy was based on a shared understanding of the nature of the offender. Whether boarding the ship or taking it from within, the pirate was an outsider. He was not a member of the ship's crew, but rather one who had boarded the vessel under false pretenses. In legal terms, the act of boarding for piratical purposes could be accomplished either during actual battle or much earlier, at port. If the miscreant had piratical intentions in both instances, that was sufficient for a finding that piracy had occurred.

This concept of the insurgent passenger transformed conventional understandings of piracy, bringing it much closer to modern-day examples of aerial hijacking. It also suggests a vital recognition in the law of where the crime of piracy begins—not on a ship, nor even on the high seas, but in the mind of the miscreant. By this logic, piracy is defined by the intention to commit the act, not when or under what circumstances the act occurs. This may seem like a trivial point, but it assumes critical importance when applied to crimes of terror. If we can argue that terrorism begins not with the act but the intent to commit, then the logical inference is that the location of the crime is of secondary importance. Thus the determination of piracy or terrorism would not turn on whether the crime occurred on land or sea (or *descent* by sea, as we shall consider later) but on the acts themselves and the intent behind them. If the acts and the intent of piracy and terrorism are the same, then they must be the same crime, wherever the crime takes place.

The final step to meld piracy and terrorism is the introduction of political motivation, as found in the more recent cases of the *Santa Maria* and the *Achille Lauro*. As we shall see in the next chapter, the UN Convention on the Law of the Sea defines piracy as a crime committed for private ends, as opposed to political ones. Since its adoption in 1958, this limitation has been cited by conservative legal scholars to prevent extension of the crime of piracy to acts of maritime terrorism—and would, naturally, also prevent an even more radical application of piracy to all international terrorist crimes. The parameters of this debate will be considered later, but it is worth noting that the most cogent response was given in 1864, when Justice Cockburn argued that "it is not because persons assume the character of belligerents that they can protect themselves from the consequences of an act really piratical." Only if it can be shown that the defendant is acting on the orders of a state, as a military combatant, can the charge of piracy be rebutted. That is the correct interpretation of the political clause: it does not refer to defendants with a political motive, but rather to defendants who act as agents of their country. A terrorist organization is not a state and cannot declare itself one. Its motives may be political, social, religious, pecuniary, or some combination of the above, but this cannot transform terrorist acts into legitimate warfare.

One might argue that the politicization of piracy goes as far back as Elizabeth's corsairs (indeed it is my own belief—articulated in the first chapter—that piracy and politics have always been intertwined); nevertheless, it is significant that the two most publicized acts of aggression in the twentieth century against a commercial vessel were both committed for a political cause. The *Santa Maria* and *Achille Lauro* incidents suggest that, whatever the status of the law, the reality of piracy in recent decades has evolved. The response of the American government in both instances is indicative of this evolution. In the former example it prevaricated, first labeling the act as piracy and later shying away from that term, ultimately choosing to regard the incident as a sort of sophomoric prank.

This deference to the traditional image of pirates as goodhearted swashbucklers, closely allied to the image of terrorists as romantic freedom fighters, was absent in 1985. After two decades of aerial hijackings, bombings, hostage takings, and the horrors of the 1972 Olympics, the United States had begun to reckon with a new reality: international terrorism. Consequently, in the aftermath of the *Achille Lauro*, President Reagan termed the hijackers as "pirates" and the United States urged the passage of a declaration against acts of "maritime terrorism" at the United Nations. This concept of maritime terrorism has developed a trajectory of its own, resulting in the articulation of a new law of piracy that includes such acts by the Bush administration in 2007.

In sum, the evolution of American law and the American experience of piracy have moved toward a recognition of pirates as maritime terrorists, engaging in the same acts of violence at sea that their confreres do on land. Meanwhile, despite the relative dearth of piracy cases, our courts have given us several crucial precedents for defining piracy in broad terms, applying the definition to crimes that do not fit the traditional mold, and extending jurisdiction over cases and criminals throughout the entire world. Since Justice Marshall first articulated the concept in 1825, it remains the policy of the United States to extend its jurisdiction to all persons whose crimes constitute an offense to the law of nations. These persons can, under American law, be prosecuted *as if they were* pirates.

It must be concluded, therefore, that there is nothing in our laws of piracy that prevents their application to terrorist crimes. But that is only half the problem. For the United States to articulate and pursue this policy successfully, it must have the cooperation—or at least the consent—of a majority of states. Unilateralism has isolated the United States and hampered its war on terror. If we were to simply announce that terrorists are pirates under our law and use this definition as a blanket justification for renditions and other forms of illegal capture, little would be gained except a renewed hostility to the United States.

The final task of this section, then, is to consider the amenability of international law to a joint definition of piracy and terrorism.

NOTES

1. William Beeston to the Lords of Trade, July 22, 1696, CSP 1696–1697, p. 14n101.

2. Stevens Collection, John Carter Brown Library, vol. 8, n. 510.

3. Alfred Rubin, *The Law of Piracy* (Irvington-on-Hudson, NY: Transnational Publishers, 1985), p. 141.

4. Quoted in ibid., p. 155.

5. *US v. Klintock*, 18 US (5 Wheaton) 144 (1820).

6. 3 Stat. 510, 15th Cong., 2d sess., chap. 77.

7. Quoted in Rubin, *Law of Piracy*, p. 161.

8. The Antelope, 23 US (10 Wheaton) 66 (1825).

9. *US v. Darnaud*, 3 Wallace 143, 3rd circ. (1855).

10. *US v. the Brig Malek Adhel*, 43 US (2 Howard) 209 (1844).

11. Peter Earle, *The Pirate Wars* (New York: Methuen, 2005), p. 40.

12. Ibid., pp. 41–42.

13. Peter Earle, *Corsairs of Malta and Barbary* (London: Sidgwick & Jackson, 1970), p. 266.

14. Robert Ritchie, "Government Measures against Piracy and Privateering in the Atlantic Area, 1750–1850," in *Pirates and Privateers*, by David Starkey (Exeter, UK: University of Exeter Press, 1989), p. 23.

15. Ibid.

16. See Samuel Menefee, "Piracy, Terrorism and the Insurgent Passenger: A Historical and Legal Perspective," in *Maritime Terrorism and International Law*, ed. Natalino Ronzitti (Boston: Martinus Nijhoff, 1990).

17. Ibid., p. 47.

18. Quoted in ibid., p. 49.

19. Quoted in ibid., p. 48.

20. Ibid., p. 53.

21. George W. Bush, "Maritime Security Policy," June 14, 2007.

22. James Kraska, "Developing Piracy Policy for the National Strategy for Maritime Security," in *Legal Challenges to Maritime Security*, ed. Myron Nordquist et al. (Boston: Martinus Nijhoff, 2008), p. 334.

23. 18 USC 2280, September 13, 1994, 108 Stat. 1975.

24. International Maritime Bureau, Piracy and Armed Robbery against Ships Annual Report, 1 January–31 December 2006.

25. See John Parker, "Pirates or Terrorists? BIMCO Links the Two Together in an Effort to Increase Ocean Shipping Security," *Traffic World* 31 (December 3, 2001).

Chapter 3
A NEW HYBRID
Political Piracy and Maritime Terrorism

Piracy has returned.

Properly speaking, it never left. For decades the Malacca Straits in the South China Sea, the Gulf of Aden, and to some extent the Caribbean have been pirate hunting grounds. Before 2005, however, incidents in such locales garnered little media attention and were primarily of interest only to maritime insurers. Nor can Somali piracy be described as a new phenomenon: vessels of numerous flags have been raided off its shores since civil war broke out in the country in the mid-1990s. Yet even as the number of captured vessels ticked steadily upward, few outside the maritime community noticed or cared. Pirates in the late twentieth century were an anachronism, as remote to the public imagination as highwaymen or riverboat cardsharps. The few articles that described attacks by the Somalis and other pirates invariably began with a cautionary preamble: pirates are not what you think they are.

What changed? In short, the scope and frequency of the attacks, and the boldness of the pirates themselves. In 2005 the cruise liner *Seabourn Spirit* was harassed by Somali pirates firing machine-gun rounds and rocket-propelled grenades into the ship; it repelled the invaders with a combination of sound cannons and high-pressure fire hoses. The incident was the first to make major headlines, primarily as it involved a passenger vessel (the diminutive *Spirit*, a vessel of less than 10,000 tons displacement that resembles a large yacht, was inevitably morphed by media accounts into a "major ocean liner"). Interestingly, the attack was not regarded as a warning that pirates were becoming more ambitious but was dismissed with a self-congratulatory smirk that they could be so easily deterred. I am reminded of the ocean liner *Arizona*, which in 1879 rammed full-speed into an iceberg and survived with a crumpled bow. The lesson drawn was that ships had overmastered the elements, and captains continued to plow full-speed through ice fields until one particular night in April 1912.

No singular incident of the *Titanic* scale served to demonstrate the growing danger of piracy in the twenty-first century, and so the response of the international community was sluggish. This in turn emboldened the Somali pirates, who capitalized on their early successes to equip themselves with more sophisticated tools and technology, and began venturing farther from shore. The list of captures from 2005 to 2009 reveals a slow but steady accrual of tonnage, from the Chinese fishing trawler *Ching Fong* in May 2007 to the 163,257 GRT super-tanker *Sirius Star*, carrying two million barrels of crude oil, in November 2008. By the time of the latter's seizure, the news media had not only seized upon the story but was raising familiar questions: How could a small band of criminals capture such a gigantic prize? Why were ransoms being paid? Why did it seem as though states' navies were powerless? Most of all, how could this scourge have developed apparently unnoticed by the rest of the world?

One dubious but salutary effect of these recent events is that the preamble quoted above is no longer necessary. We know that pirates are more than eye-patched, peg-legged, rum-swilling figures of fantasy. Even as popular culture reinforces this myth, images from around the world belie it: none more so than the bedraggled but smiling figure of Captain Phillips rescued from his ordeal aboard a lifeboat of the *Maersk Alabama* in April 2009. In contrast to the buccaneers of old, piracy today conjures up different and more compelling icons: flak jackets and khaki, assault rifles and Zodiac boats.

I call this change salutary because it provides the visual reinforcement for the argument of this book: the link between piracy and terrorism. We no longer need to dispense with hoary and inaccurate stereotypes to see this relationship; it is revealed not only by the Somali pirates' methods but also by the political motivation behind them.

So-called political piracy has been the subject of a pitched debate between legal scholars for over half a century. In the second half of the twentieth century, as the previous chapter alludes, piracy was distinguished from other forms of violence at sea (mutiny and acts of war) on the grounds that it was private versus political warfare; that is, committed by individuals for personal ends, not acting on behalf of a state or revolutionary organization. This distinction was necessary, as we shall soon consider, since the preceding history of piracy from the late nineteenth century to the mid-twentieth reflects a move in precisely the opposite direction: imputing "piracy" on acts of war ranging from submarine aggression to the bombing of coastal cities from offshore. The reasoning, as we shall see, was purely political. Piracy in its conventional form had all but disappeared, yet the word *pirate* still held the powerful connotation of "enemy of the human race." Much as Castlereagh had attempted in the 1820s, the Western powers from 1856 onward deemed as piracy such behavior that was anathema to them under the logic that it offended natural law.

An inevitable backlash followed in the wake of the Second World War, when under the aegis of the United Nations, jurists began delineating international crimes. The crime of piracy had become overextended past all coherence, applied to almost any behavior a state wished to brand as especially harmful. Consequently, the thrust of the 1958 UN Convention on the Law of the Sea (UNCLOS) was a ruthless return to basics. Piracy was specifically distinguished from any behavior that could be construed as an act of war, and pirates themselves could not, by definition, be acting on the behest of a state or under its flag.

While the need for clarification was undeniable, this chapter will argue that it has gone too far in the opposite direction: narrowing the definition so greatly that almost no one—not even the Somali pirates—falls within it. UNCLOS notwithstanding, the general trend of the last century has been toward a recognition that politics lie at the very heart of piracy, and piracy itself encompasses a great deal more than sea robbery. This recognition has also motivated recent attempts of scholars, maritime consortiums, shipowners, insurers, and even individual states to rework the definition to reflect existing realities. Their efforts have been directed toward the melding of piracy (in all its traditional and modern forms) and maritime terrorism. The logic of incorporation is clear: in today's world, in virtually every incident recorded in the last thirty years, the two crimes are intertwined.

Hence, the final step in arguing for the congruity of piracy and terrorism is to consider how they have moved closer together, not only in definition but in actual events around the world. We will begin by considering attempts by the British government in the late nineteenth century to expand piracy to acts committed against its vessels and colonies, then look at how these attempts served as the foundation for much more radical extensions in the early twentieth century. Then we will turn to examine how, in spite of a narrowed definition, political and social conceptions of piracy broadened in the late twentieth century to include a new—or at least newly identified—menace: aerial and maritime terrorism. This became the basis for a recent body of law devoted to identifying such crimes and distinguishing them from ordinary homicide: in effect, the first glimmering of an international law on terrorism. The potential was there, but not the realization, as such laws lacked the legal precedent afforded by piracy—specifically, universal jurisdiction and pirates' status as *hostis humani generi*. It took the events of the last few years to finally bring the two crimes together in fact, if not in law. Consequently, we will conclude by examining how the explosion of Somali piracy ironically furnishes both the United States and the international community with an invaluable opportunity to recognize the linkages between piracy and terrorism, to jettison stale and arcane debates over political versus private piracy, and to prepare the ground for an even more momentous step: the application of piracy law to all crimes of international organized terrorism.

PIRACY AND EMPIRE: THE BRITISH EXPERIENCE

The Washington and Nyon agreements, which extended piracy to overt acts of warfare, represent the culmination of a trend extending back for almost a century. It was motivated, as legal scholar Alfred Rubin writes, by the desire of the British government in the early nineteenth century "to find a rationale for naval activity against those who, for whatever reason, interfered with British merchant shipping in the Mediterranean Sea."[1] At first glance this does not seem all that remarkable, as piracy was traditionally defined as "interference" with trade. Yet the British carried this argument further, hinging recognition of statehood on whether that state had amicable trade relations with Great Britain. Thus sheiks, beys, and sultans who were in obeisance to the British Crown were "legal," and all others were "pirates."

Cynical it might have been, but it was nevertheless a neat inversion of the law. Pirates had long been defined as stateless persons—stateless not by chance, but by choice. It was this very quality that led jurists from Cicero onward to consider them a separate species: neither ordinary criminals nor warring states, but a hybrid of both. The British, in their zeal to subjugate the Mediterranean princes and consolidate their trade, claimed a logical corollary: if pirates were defined as stateless, then states that engaged in piracy were presumed to have renounced their legitimacy. Such states were therefore not at war with Britain but rather mere pirate bands.

It was not a bad argument, and indeed might serve as an early precedent for the principle set down at Nuremberg over a century later: even princes can engage in acts that delegitimize both themselves and their states. The problem was not in the logic of the concept, but its application. Who was to define what constituted piracy against British trade? Britain herself. Consequently, the British government termed any act of aggression against its trade as piracy, even when it involved nothing more than the refusal to enter into commercial treaties.

In its unilateral qualities and ruthless implementation, this nineteenth-century British "war against piracy" shared much in common with an earlier precedent: Imperial Rome. Rubin notes dryly that the language emanating from Whitehall at this time "is reminiscent of the Roman conception of a permanent war with '*pirata*' who opposed the establishment of Roman hegemony in the Eastern Mediterranean."[2] Viewed from a legal perspective, this policy is appalling, as it disregards centuries of carefully constructed barriers between piracy and warfare; moreover, it gives Britain the prerogative to declare anything inimical to its interests as piratical and thus sets up the dangerous precedent that the dominant nation is the definer and arbiter of all international law.

In other words, the mistake of the British government in the nineteenth century was precisely that of the American government in the twenty-first: employing a bogeyman expression—"pirates" or "terrorists"—to recast its international policy in Manichean terms. There is no better example than President George W. Bush's famous declaration to states: "You are either with us or with the terrorists." But who exactly were these terrorists? Aside from members of al Qaeda, the term remained nebulous. Certainly there were terrorists, but as time went on a howl of criticism rose up against the Bush administration both from within and from without the United States that it was applying the expression at will ("terrorist" states, "terrorist" regimes, "terrorist" sympathies) and—in so doing—devalued the term entirely.

Today, the British precedent is most commonly remembered as an example of legal overreach prompted by imperial greed.[3] It was. Moreover, even if Britain's motives had not been centered on the bottom line, its actions still provided the blueprint for later attempts to politicize piracy, and stretch the definition of the crime beyond all recognition.

Nevertheless, it is wrong to dismiss the British argument entirely. To claim that all states that resisted its overtures were piratical was clearly false, but the question remained: can states ever be guilty of piracy? For most scholars, the answer is no.[4] If a state engages in piratical acts—seizure or destruction of another vessel, capture of its goods, homicide at sea—these are not piracy but *causus belli*, acts leading to war. Yet what of a state whose entire livelihood is based on such acts? Or one that cannot or refuses to contain its pirates?

The question turns not so much on the definition of piracy but on that of statehood. In our own time we might take the case of Somalia, which has existed in a state of civil war since the mid-1990s. It is clearly a state in that it has an established territory, a flag, and a provisional (albeit ineffective) government. Yet by almost every other measure it falls short: no police, no standing army, no adjudicative structures. Consequently its pirates operate with near-total freedom. Recently the question arose of whether the United States or other nations were justified in launching attacks on the pirate bases along Somalia's coast. Were these legal under the law of universal jurisdiction for pirates, or were they a violation of Somalia's sovereignty?

One answer is found in a British case, *In Re the Magellan Pirates*, decided in 1853.[5] Writing for the court, Dr. Stephen Lushington summed up the issue of pirates acting under a foreign flag. His words could easily have been written today:

> Even an independent state may, in my opinion, be guilty of piratical acts. What were the Barbary pirates of olden times?

What many of the African tribes at this moment? It is, I believe, notorious, that tribes now inhabiting the African coast of the Mediterranean will send out their boats and capture any ships becalmed upon their coasts. Are they not pirates, because, perhaps, their whole livelihood may not depend on piratical acts? I am well aware that it has been said that a state cannot be piratical; but I am not disposed to assent to such a dictum as a universal proposition.[6]

Implicit in Dr. Lushington's opinion are certain key assumptions about states. States may engage in acts of illegal war, but they also do other things: build roads, make treaties, investigate crimes. In short, their raison d'etre is diffused, not directed upon one solitary object. But what of states that wholeheartedly embrace piracy, put it at the center of their "whole livelihood," or lack the means (or will) to suppress it? Can these properly be called states at all?

Considerations of this kind, raised in 1853, found their fullest expression just three years later in the Declaration of Paris. By declaring piracy separate from and beyond the pale of state behavior, the European nations also left open a possible corollary. States were not only abjured from granting piratical commissions themselves but also obligated to take their share of responsibility in hunting down pirates offshore. Consequently, if a state *did* engage in piratical acts, granted commissions, or failed through weakness or indifference to curtail pirates sailing from their shores, it could be perceived as relinquishing its legitimacy.

This was the essence of the argument advanced by the British government, without the cynicism. The declaration indicated a willingness to return to the fundamentals of piracy law, distinguishing it from warfare on the one hand and entwining it with the law of nations on the other. This precluded unilateralism: piracy could not be declared so by one nation, but must be agreed upon by all (or at least a preponderance of) states. By the time of its passage, even Britain had come around to this mentality, abandoning its attempts to define piracy as an affront to British mercantile policy and accepting (coolly, but with good grace) the primacy of international law. In 1854, possibly in response to the decision in the *Magellan Pirates*, a legal report promulgated by the Law Officers of the Crown adopted a more nuanced definition:

> That all persons (whatsoever their origin, or under whatsoever Flag or Papers they may Sail, or to whomsoever their ship may legally belong) will be pirates by the Law of Nations who are guilty of forcible robberies, or captures of Ships or Goods upon the High Seas without any lawful Commission or authority. They . . . may be captured by Officers and Men in the public service of any Nation, and may be tried in the Courts of any Nations. . . . It is of no consequence where, or upon whom, they have committed their Crimes, for piracy under the Law of Nations is an offence against all Nations, and punishable by all Nations.[7]

Such language is both broadening and limiting. It reinforces Britain's claim to universal jurisdiction, offering perhaps the broadest mandate yet codified. Likewise it extends this prerogative to all nations, reaffirms the right of all nations to adjudicate captured pirates, and asserts that the capturing state need not be the principle victim. Yet, for all the apparent power it vests in states (Britain certainly among them), it also limits the definition of pirates as those "without Commission or authority" and defers that determination to the "law of nations." Clearly, the message conveyed is that Britain is willing to work in conjunction with other states to stamp out piracy and will relinquish her claim as the sole arbiter of the law to further that end. The success of this policy was manifest: among the signatories to the Declaration of Paris was Britain's longtime nemesis, Turkey.

British attempts to expand piracy law in the nineteenth century were shamelessly self-serving, but they raised critical issues that shaped legal discourse and policy throughout the next century. By conflating piracy with a "war on trade," Britain forced the international community to consider anew what such a war entailed. Could states be guilty of piracy or held accountable for the piracy of their citizens? Could one state declare an act piratical, or must it seek consensus among its peers? Could a state even lose its legitimacy by engaging, promoting, or condoning acts of piracy?

On the most obvious level, such questions demonstrate that the distinction between political and private piracy is a line drawn by wind upon water. Piracy *was* political; the two were inseparable. The charge of piracy, invoked by one state against another, sent a distinct message: you are acting illegally and in danger of relinquishing your status. Piracy, as an offense to the law of nations, extended the category of *hostis humani generi* to include those states that harbored or aided such criminals. This was the first articulation of a concept imminently familiar to us today: the rogue state. It therefore raises a fascinating parallel: if states in the nineteenth century could lose their legitimacy by engaging in acts of piracy, could a state that sponsors terrorists be so treated today? It is an open question, but one worthy of some consideration.

Nevertheless, attempts to conflate piracy and warfare in the nineteenth century are also cautionary, reminding us of the necessity for distinguishing between piracy and ordinary acts of warfare. By extending piracy to states, Britain devalued one of the most crucial aspects of the definition: the concept of piracy as a war against the world. Pirates renounced their citizenship when they took up the trade, and piracy itself since Roman times was defined *in opposition* to states, not in conjunction with them. The logic for such a distinction was clear, and never more so than in the nineteenth century: if acts constituting piracy could be committed by states, then these were not piracy but acts of war, and thus piracy and sea warfare would be indistinguishable and the crime of piracy would lose its meaning altogether. This is precisely what happened in the early twentieth century, which ultimately led to a draconian attempt to distinguish piracy from any vestiges of state behavior.

SEARCHING FOR BALANCE IN THE
EARLY TWENTIETH CENTURY:
THE WASHINGTON AND NYON AGREEMENTS
AND THE HARVARD DRAFT CONVENTION OF 1933

Just as nineteenth-century attempts to broaden piracy rested on the uniquely horrendous status of the crime, so too did those of the twentieth century. Piracy was not merely a crime but one invested with anarchic overtones. Like terrorism today, it was invoked in cases where ordinary criminality seemed insufficient—in short, for behavior that was beyond the pale.

The horrific effects of unrestricted submarine warfare in the First World War produced, as with poison gas, a strong sentiment for abolition in the early postwar period. In 1922, the nations of France, Italy, Japan, Britain, and the United States (but not, interestingly, Germany) signed the Washington Agreement, pledging to punish "as if for an act of piracy" any submarine commander violating its stringent codes of conduct. "Unrestricted" submarine warfare, a German policy after 1915, eschewed the traditional requirements for a submarine to surface and warn its target before firing the first torpedo, giving the ship's crew time to escape. The German Admiralty found this needlessly time consuming and dangerous, and instead ordered its commanders to fire on sight. The effects were horrifying, most famously in the case of the sunken British ocean liner *Lusitania*. Consequently, the 1922 declaration did not rest on any shared historical linkages between piracy and submarine warfare, but rather on a perception of such tactics as beneath the dignity of states. It may seem quaint to us today, but sentiments of this kind were common in the aftermath of the First World War, a conflict that tested and ultimately decimated every concept of a "gentleman's war." The Washington Agreement was undertaken in the same spirit as the Kellogg-Briand Pact, concluded in 1928, that proposed to outlaw warfare altogether.[8]

If nothing else, the Washington Agreement demonstrated that private/political distinctions for piracy were obsolete, and the term itself had become so malleable as to be effectively without a definition. This was further underscored a decade later. The Spanish Civil War, which quickly devolved into a proxy war between the Axis and Communists, produced a second treaty, even more explicit than the first. The Nyon Agreement of 1937, concluded between Egypt, Greece, Turkey, Romania, France, Belgium, Britain, and the USSR, purported to extend universal jurisdiction against unidentified vessels and aircraft attacking merchant shipping on behalf of the Spanish insurgents. In doing so, the agreement specifically referred to "piratical acts" by submarines and all other like attacks "which should justly be treated as acts of piracy."[9]

Neither the Washington nor Nyon agreements had the slightest impact on actual policy and must be regarded more as aspirational declarations than binding agreements. For this reason, they have not fared well in retrospect. Postwar legal scholars were appalled, and the Washington and Nyon Acts were widely criticized for stretching the meaning of piracy beyond all recognition by outlawing numerous forms of legitimate state versus state warfare. Certainly the Nyon Act blurred the distinction between the two: by punishing revolutionaries as pirates, the concept of pirates as *hostis humani generi* was substantially diminished. Two years later, in the wake of the Nazi's U-boat strikes, these agreements went from being irksome to absurd; appropriate adjuncts to the Kellogg-Briand Pact outlawing war. Nevertheless, they demonstrated a willingness on the part of states to extend the definition of piracy when it suits their purposes, even to acts that are patently not piratical.

As such, these precedents cannot be discounted, for they are a potent rebuttal to critics who would oppose the extension of piracy law to acts of terrorism on the grounds that it has never been done before. Moreover, the Washington and Nyon agreements evidence a recognition of the interconnection between piracy, terrorism, and politics. This is especially true of the Nyon Agreement. By equating acts by nonstate aggressors with piracy, it effectively achieved exactly what this book intends.

The inclusion of attacks by aircraft underscores this fact, demonstrating that the drafters were not hidebound to traditional notions of piracy occurring on the high seas. The Washington and Nyon agreements, taken together, may represent a model approach for contemporary attempts to draw a new international law for organized terrorism from the existing law of piracy.

*   *   *

Even as world leaders began applying piracy to expressly political acts and blurring the distinction between private actors and states, a small cadre of legal scholars moved in the opposite direction. The purpose of this book is not to provide an exhaustive overview of conflicting legal opinions regarding piracy; in this case, however, the debates surrounding the promulgation of the Harvard Draft Convention of 1933 are critical, for they represent the most coherent and conscious attempt to formulate a working definition of piracy for the modern world. In part this came in response to the blurring of definition by states, but it was not exclusively retrogressive. The drafters were not attempting to save piracy from obscurity, but they were trying to predict its course for the rest of the century. Piracy, they reckoned, would not disappear, and the law needed to be prepared for its resurgence. When it came, it did so in such a form as they could barely have envisioned: maritime terrorism. And yet ultimately it would be they, and not the states, that best anticipated and shaped the definition of piracy in the postwar world.

It would only be a slight exaggeration to claim that modern piracy law owes its existence to the obstinacy of a small group of Romanian academics. Alone among the member states in the League of Nations in the early 1930s, Romania pressed for a codified series of international crimes, the basis of an international criminal code. Piracy was meant to be the forerunner, and model, for all international criminal law. This proposal was met with mixed response by the other nations. Yet persistency finally prevailed, and the league agreed to assemble a research group to codify the law of piracy internationally as a precursor to future, more pertinent crimes. For this task, the league turned to Harvard University Law School. The result was the 1932 Harvard Draft Convention, or, more fully, Harvard Research in International Law, *Draft Convention on Piracy with Comments*, 26 *American Journal of International Law* 749 (1932). The draft, a ponderous document replete with notes, corrections, and explications, purported to classify the crime of piracy in concise legal terms, including its attendant *actus reus* and *mens rea*.

Regardless of whether it accomplished this task, the most notable aspect of the draft lies not in its conclusions but its motivations. The draft was a seminal document, for it created a species of criminal jurisdiction distinct from both municipal law and international treaty, springing instead from a declaration by an international covenant of sovereign states. While previous treaties and municipal laws had recognized pirates as *hostis humani generi*, some even acceding the principle of universal jurisdiction, the discourse was based hitherto on a state's *right* to suppress piracy. The draft, in contrast, transformed this right into an obligation. As pirates were enemies of the human race, it was the duty of all states to pursue, capture, and adjudicate pirates, wherever they were found, whosoever should find them. The group made this expanded jurisdiction explicit: "[The] draft convention should include the recognition of a special authority—or jurisdiction—to prosecute foreigners for piratical offences beyond the state's ordinary jurisdiction. . . . Piracy, however it is defined, is a special basis of jurisdiction; judicial, legislative, executive, and administrative."[10]

The practical result of making piracy the basis of a new "special basis of jurisdiction" was to create the first true international crime. The drafters wholly espoused the concept of pirates as a special case, *hostis humani generi*. They even quoted from the judgment in *US v. Smith*, stating that "a pirate, under the law of nations, is an enemy of the human race; being an enemy of all, he is liable to be punished by all."[11] The crime of piracy, under this definition, outweighs the specific acts comprising it, becoming a distinct crime that identifies more with the odiousness of its perpetrator than the elements of his crime. It is the pirate who must be suppressed, not solely by virtue of his deeds but by what he represents: an enemy of the human race, waging private war against civilization itself.

This theme surfaced repeatedly as the drafters attempted to define the crime of piracy and the limits of universal jurisdiction. It cannot be overemphasized, for it is tantamount to a recognition that the threat posed by certain crimes, such as piracy, far exceeds the individual harm inflicted by their occurrence. It is an argument that could well be made for acts of terrorism. The task, then, is to inquire whether terrorism can be defined as a species of piracy, within the limitations of the Harvard Draft Convention.

Ultimately this inquiry comes down to three critical questions: first, is piracy confined to sea robbery; second, is it limited to private ends, excluding political ones; third, is it limited to the high seas? If the answer to all three questions is no, then terrorism is perforce synonymous with piracy.

Let us first consider the offenses listed as constituting piracy in the Harvard Draft Convention. They are as follows (italics provided for emphasis):

1) Robbery committed by using a private ship (a pirate ship) to attack another ship.
2) Intentional, unjustifiable *homicide*, similarly committed for private ends.
3) Unjustifiable *violent attack on persons* similarly accomplished for private ends.
4) Any unjustifiable *depredation or malicious destruction of property* similarly committed for private ends.
5) *Attempts* to commit the foregoing offenses.
6) Cruising (in a pirate ship) with the purpose of committing any of the foregoing offenses.
7) Cruising as professional robbers in a ship devoted to the commission of such offenses as the foregoing.

8) Participation in sailing a ship (on the high sea) devoted to the purpose of making similar attacks in territorial waters *or on land, by descent from the sea*.[12]

The first question as to the limitations of the crime is quickly answered. The drafter's definition was a far cry from sea robbery; as indicated above, actual theft represents only one of eight separate offenses. The definition notably includes destruction of property without an act of taking, as well as homicide. Numbers 6, 7, and 8 comprise the conspiratorial element of the crime, extending jurisdiction to those who assist in planning acts of piracy before they occur. In sum, there is no requirement at all that an actual taking occur; the enumerated acts comprising piracy herein could have been more succinctly expressed by referring to *In Re Piracy Jure Gentium*, defining piracy as "any act of armed violence at sea which is not an act of war."[13]

An earlier report, brainchild of the ponderously named Subcommittee of the League of Nations Committee of Experts for the Progressive Codification of International Law, similarly concluded that "piracy consists in sailing the seas for private ends without authorization from the Government of any State with the object of committing depredations upon property or acts of violence against persons." Robbery is defined as theft with violence. Yet in all these definitions, the emphasis is on the *violence*, not the theft. It is the violent aspect of piracy that distinguishes it from mere theft at sea and warrants "special jurisdiction" under international law.

As to the question of political versus private ends, the draft is more limiting, perhaps reflecting an early reaction to the all-encompassing qualities of the Washington Agreement. The most damning language occurs on p. 786, where it states:

While the scope of the draft convention is controlled by the international law of piracy, it is expedient to modify in part the traditional jurisdiction because of modern conditions. The modification may work in both directions. It may be thought advisable to exclude from the common jurisdiction certain doubtful phrases of traditional piracy which can now be left satisfactorily to the ordinary jurisdiction of the state . . . and it may be expedient to concede common jurisdiction over certain sorts of events which are not beyond dispute piracy by tradition, but bear enough analogy to cases of undoubted piracy to justify assimilation under the caption. *Therefore the draft convention excludes from its definition of piracy all cases of wrongful attack on persons or property for political ends, whether they are made on behalf of states, or of unrecognized belligerent organizations, or of unrecognized revolutionary bandits.*[14]

A definition of piracy that expressly excludes political acts cannot accommodate terrorism. But that is not necessarily what the draft provides. Comparing the earlier section with the italicized, there is an apparent dichotomy. If certain acts of 'piracy by analogy' *should* be conceded, why does the draft conclude that "therefore" political ends are not piracy? The question hinges on the drafters' definition of "political." A cursory glance seems to provide the answer: acts on behalf of "states, unrecognized belligerent organizations, or unrecognized revolutionary bands" are deemed political, suggesting that terrorists—as "unrecognized revolutionary bands"—would likewise be precluded from jurisdiction. But reliance on the words of the draft alone is misleading. Consideration must also be given to its context, the political climate in 1932. At that time, the European empires were still much in force, and the advent of terrorist organizations—as we know them today—was decades away. In 1932, "political" referred solely to states, and those persons or organizations wishing to change the government of their states. Hence the political aim of the "unrecognized belligerents" could only be national, not international, in scope. This leads to quite a different interpretation of the distinction between private and political acts: private acts are those that are neither state sponsored nor undertaken to effect a change of state government.

In the draft's exclusion of acts "on behalf of states," we find a modern reworking of the old distinction between pirate and privateer. The drafters equated "political purpose" with actions taken under color of the state, removing piracy from the private realm to that of diplomatic interplay between nations. As a result, the relevant question for determining political purpose was whether the pirate was, de facto, an agent of the state.

The draft's reference to "belligerent organizations" and "revolutionary bands" is, likewise, far more limited and context-specific than it appears. This is indicated by the quotation within the *Draft of Halleck on International Law* (3rd ed.) volume 11, page 120 footnote: "It is an open question whether privateers, commissioned by a deposed sovereign, are pirates or not."[15] The problem facing the drafters lay in the quasi-legitimate status of revolutionary governments. The right to self-determination was already a recognized principle of international law. Understandably, the drafters did not wish to create a definition that would allow besieged governments to cry "piracy" against their revolutionary opponents. The effect would be to reduce all insurgents to international criminals. Instead, the drafters elected to confer a faux-state status on such organizations, distinguishing them from common pirates.

But this recognition was clearly limited to rebels against an established government. Were it otherwise, pirates could declare (as they had in the 1690s) that they were at war with the world, and thus be spared from piracy jurisdiction as "unrecognized belligerent organizations." Such a possibility was precluded by the draft's reliance on the concept of *hostis humani generi*, as well as its quotation of Wheaton on international law: "If a foreigner knowingly cruises against the commerce of a State under a rebel commission, he takes the chance of being treated as a pirate *jure gentium*, or a belligerent. In law, his foreign allegiance or citizenship is immaterial."[16]

In this respect, it is also immaterial whether or not the sovereign whose subject he is has recognized the rebel authorities as belligerent. It is not the custom for foreign nations to interfere to protect their citizens voluntarily aiding a rebellion against a friendly state if that state makes no discriminations against them. The distinction between private and political in the Harvard Draft Convention recalls our earlier discussion of the three recognized actors in international relations: states, individuals, and international criminals (pirates). While the first and second are self-evident, the third is a term of art: an artificial classification created by customary and conventional international law to define those persons whose activities excommunicate them from their states. It is not surprising, therefore, that the draft members should wish to distinguish these persons from legitimate state actors. It is also logical that the drafters should extend the political category beyond its customary state parameters to include insurgents and revolutionaries. The private ends requirement reflects an understanding that the desire for a change of one's government is not criminal, nor is it a crime to revolt against that government.

This must be distinguished, however, from organized terrorism. Even if their aim is one of regime change, international terrorist organizations waging war against nations other than their own forfeit—by this definition—the right to call themselves revolutionaries if their attacks are against outside citizens, they shift from legal status as insurgents to *hostis humani generi*, pirates. Also notable is the lack in the Harvard Draft Convention of any equation between private ends and pecuniary ones. Recall Hedges et al. and the earlier limitations of piracy to acts of monetary gain. Such a limitation in the Harvard Draft would not only run contrary to the obvious intent of the drafters but also be in direct conflict with its specified elements of piracy. How, for example, could there be a private (pecuniary) end in "intentional, unjustifiable homicide" or the "malicious destruction of property"? The drafters merely wished to distinguish acts of piracy from legitimate acts of maritime warfare, and there was need for such a distinction. Absent a private-ends requirement, navies could be condemned for acts of piracy whenever they fired on an enemy vessel. What the drafters most certainly did *not* intend was to limit piracy jurisdiction to old-fashioned ideas of loot and plunder. Dispelling the popular identification of piracy with this Hollywood cliché was the chief purpose of the Harvard Draft Convention.

The third and final question concerns whether acts of piracy must be committed on the high seas. The drafters concluded decidedly in the negative, for several reasons. First, there was the issue of new technology. In 1932, air routes were still in their infancy, but the potential was there. The Reply of Rumania, conjuring up images of pirate airplanes swooping hawk-like upon their prey, nevertheless ends by suggesting a presentience of aerial hijacking fifty years before its advent: "[T]he word 'aircraft' might be added, especially as it is quite possible that piracy may be practiced in the future by means of hydroplanes. . . . [The] notion of piracy by aircraft may find a new application in the future if certain regions of the air above State territory are ultimately regarded as free."[17]

The drafters themselves considered the possibility of aerial piracy a viable challenge to traditional concepts and explained its inclusion within the draft thus:

> The pirate of tradition attacked on or from the sea. Certainly today, however, one should not deem the possibility of similar attacks in or from the air as too slight or too remote for consideration in drafting a convention on jurisdiction over piratical acts. With rapid advance in the arts of flying and air-sailing, it may not be long before bands of malefactors, who now confine their efforts to land, will find it profitable to engage in depredations in or from the air beyond territorial jurisdiction. Indeed there may even occur thus a recrudescence of large-scale piracy. *A codification of the jurisdiction of states under the law of nations should not be drafted to fit only cases raised by present conditions of business, the arts, and criminal operations.*[18]

Second, the draft members deferred to "traditional wisdom" on the permissible locus of piracy. The fanciful possibility of aerial piracy was joined by a much more concrete example:

piracy in unowned territories. Although a century of Western imperialism had taken its toll, there were still unclaimed corners of the world in 1932. They were, like the high seas, outside the jurisdiction of any state. Why, the drafters argued, should the same acts that would be piracy at sea be unpunishable on terra incognita ashore? Pressing their case by the hypothetical, the drafters displayed a surprisingly fertile imagination:

> It is quite untrue that the special legal notion of piracy is due to its maritime character. . . . Besides the high seas, there are also *unowned territories*, and though, of course, they are always becoming rarer, they still exist; and until some State acquires exclusive sovereignty over them, every State, in virtue of the principles described above, will naturally have a theoretical right of punitive jurisdiction over them. Supposing, for example, that a band of brigands in some unowned territory attacks and plunders a convoy or caravan and escapes capture by its victims, what is the difference from the legal point of view between piracy on the high seas and pillage in unowned territory? If the act was committed in unowned territory, it is universally punishable *in virtue of the same principles* as those which make piracy on the high seas universally punishable. It would therefore be most desirable to substitute for the term "high seas" the words "places not subject to the sovereignty of any State."[19]

Yet whimsical depictions of rogue hydroplanes and roving brigands could only go so far. Even allowing these special circumstances, nonmaritime piracy was still seemingly confined to areas outside state jurisdiction. The drafters noted that the "central idea in recent times of the traditional concept of a common jurisdiction to all states over piracy has been that the offence occurs out of the territory of every state—generally on the high sea." The backhanded use of "traditional" suggests that the drafters did not concur. This was further proven by their recognition of acts of piracy occurring "by descent from the sea," as quoted above. In support of this extension, the drafters referred to Hall on *International Law*: "Piracy no doubt can take place independently of the sea, under the conditions at least of modern civilization; but the pirate does not so lose his piratical character by landing within state territory that piratical acts done on shore cease to be piratical."[20]

The door was thus opened for a third possibility alongside aerial and unappropriated lands: acts of piracy on established state territory. The only limitation seemed to be that the pirates come upon the territory by sea, as evidenced by the inclusion of a second passage from Hall stating: "If the foregoing remarks are well founded, piracy may be said to consist in acts of violence done upon the ocean or unappropriated lands, *or within the territory of the state through descent from the sea, by a body of men acting independently of any politically organized society.*"[21]

What this descent from the sea actually entailed could be loosely defined. Did it mean sailing brazenly into a port city, dropping anchor, and sending the jolly boats ashore? Clearly not. The inclusion of aerial piracy suggests that the menace could come from above the horizon as well. In fact, the definition of "descent" is so vague as to allow virtually any person arriving from overseas and committing a piratical act to be deemed a pirate—even if that act occurred, not in the coastal cities of Boston or New York, but in Butte, Montana.

In sum, the Harvard Draft Convention provides a definition of piracy that is *generally* applicable to contemporary organized terrorism. Clearly, it is stronger on some points than others: piracy is not limited to the high seas, nor to acts of robbery, but the question remains over political piracy. While the drafters could not have envisioned the rise of terrorism in the late twentieth century, its express language excluding "belligerent organizations" is a thorny problem. It is ameliorated somewhat, however, by the provision of Article XVI, which reads: "The provisions of this convention do not diminish a state's right under international law to take measures for the protection of its nationals, its ships, and its commerce against interference on or over the high sea, when such measures are not based upon jurisdiction for piracy."[22]

Legal scholar P. W. Birnie argues that this provision, apparently at odds with the rest of the draft, may have been the genesis of a modern legal recognition of acts of maritime terrorism.[23] But if the Harvard Draft Convention predated maritime terrorism, to what does Article XVI refer? The answer must be the aforementioned belligerent organizations and revolutionaries. Article XVI sheds further light on the "political" dilemma, providing more evidence that the drafters intended only to distinguish between the internal problems of insurgency and revolution (affecting only an individual state) and the external problem of international piracy.

The political question, never fully answered by the Harvard Draft Convention of 1932, would return to haunt the UN Conventions of 1958 and 1982. It remains open to this day.

PIRACY AND THE COLD WAR: THE 1958 AND 1982 UN CONVENTIONS ON THE LAW OF THE SEA

The collapse of the League of Nations in the wake of the Second World War meant, among other things, a postponement sine die for the creation of an international criminal court. It would take sixty years and a new century for the ICC to finally emerge. International criminal law, however, received a powerful boost in the Nuremberg trials of 1945. Faced with the unimaginable horror of the Holocaust, the trials of the Nazi war criminals established the precedent that there were certain crimes so heinous as to shock the conscience of the world. As offenses not against the state but against all states, such crimes merited universal jurisdiction.

The Nuremberg trials enumerated these crimes as aggressive war, crimes against humanity, and war crimes. The International Criminal Court awarded jurisdiction for these and added a fourth: genocide. Customary international law supplied the fifth and final: piracy. Of the four, piracy seems anachronistic. The others are "new" crimes, emerging from the technological and political history of the twentieth century. While acts of barbarity and genocide were hardly unique to that era, Nuremberg marked a turning point in international perception from regarding them as the private prerogative of states to the international responsibility of the United Nations. Piracy, in contrast, owed its place on the list to historical precedent. It was the first crime of universal jurisdiction, the most debated, the most articulated. The idea of *hostis humani generi*, previously specific to piracy, became the legal norm to describe all international criminals.

Yet it was not until 1958 that the issue of piracy specifically found expression in international law. When it did, in the Geneva Convention on the High Seas of 1958, it was retrogressive. The convention purported to adopt nearly verbatim the Harvard Draft Convention, which was its principle source. In fact, it did nothing of the kind. In the twenty-six years between the two documents, the international political climate had changed radically. The murky definition of "political" acts offered by the draft in 1932 was soundly repudiated in 1937, with the passage of the Nyon Agreement. The agreement, discussed *supra*, branded acts of unrestricted submarine warfare piratical and in so doing turned the draft's fine distinctions between state and individual on their heads. The Nyon Agreement recognized the folly in attempting to distinguish political and private ends in piracy. Piracy consisted of the act itself and accompanying *mens rea* of— as the US Supreme Court would have said—"hatred or criminal mischief." Beyond that, inquiry into the pirates' motivations was both unnecessary and counterproductive.

Both the Nyon Agreement and the 1958 Geneva Convention were products of their time: the Nyon Agreement of rising fears of Nazi aggression, the Geneva Convention of the Cold War. In the late 1950s, as the Maoists assumed command of the People's Republic of China, the disenfranchised nationalists began intercepting vessels on the high seas bound for China. The USSR, citing the Nyon Agreement, proposed before the United Nations that such actions be declared piratical. The Czech government further proposed that the issue of piracy be reexamined, with a view toward expanding the definition to include the nationalists' activities.[24]

Over the course of three years, beginning with the seventh session of the International Law Commission in 1955 and ending with the Geneva Convention on the High Seas of 1958, the political dimensions of piracy were heatedly debated. Among the commission's first acts was to disavow all competency to discuss political piracy altogether. After receiving numerous reports from various countries concerning free navigation in Chinese waters, as well as a memorandum from the Polish government stressing the relevancy of the Nyon Agreement, the commission declined to address the "political considerations" of piracy. A flurry of memoranda followed, as the democratic nations congratulated the commission on their sagacity and the communist nations protested stridently. The debate was obviously not over. The distinction between private and political ends, in fact, became the chief bone of contention. Sir Gerald Fitzmaurice summed up the problem: "The real antithesis which needed to be brought out was between authorized and unauthorized acts and acts committed in a public or in a private capacity. An act committed in a private capacity could have a political purpose but be unauthorized—as, for example, the seizure of a vessel by the member of an opposition party."[25]

The same problem facing the Harvard drafters now bedeviled the commission: where to distinguish between private and political acts of piracy in a miasma of rebels, insurgents, and civil war? Some argued that this was simply beyond the competency of the commission, claiming that questions of "whether parties to a civil war constituted belligerents or not, as well as that of governments which were not universally recognized" were far too "complex and controversial" to address.[26] Despite these reservations, the commission eventually broke down along ideological lines. The communist representatives, led by Zourek and Krylov, argued strongly for inclusion of political acts within the definition of piracy.[27] Zourek commented that he "considered, in particular, that the acts of violence and depredation referred to in Article XIV [of the 1956 draft] constituted acts of piracy even when committed (a) for political ends; (b) by warships or

military aircraft; or (c) by aircraft or seaplanes against foreign
aircraft or seaplanes."[28] The opposition of democratic nations,
led by Sir Gerald Fitzmaurice, argued for a traditional definition
of piracy. Yet even Sir Gerald harbored some misgivings, for
while he saw his stance as necessary to counter the Russian
threat, he regretted that such a limitation would be a step back-
ward, rendering the crime of piracy obsolete and incapable of
dealing with new realities. He commented wistfully, "It would be
a pity to delete the reference to private aircraft, because the
Commission should not disregard an aspect of piracy that was
both novel and potentially real."[29]

Ultimately, the democratic nations won out. Piracy was narrowly construed in Article XXXIX of the 1958 Geneva Convention on the High Seas to refer to:

1. Any illegal act of violence, detention or any act of depredation, committed for private ends by the crew and passengers of a private ship and directed:
   a) On the high seas, against another ship or against per-
      sons or property on board such a ship.
2. Any act of voluntary participation in the operation of a
   ship or of an aircraft with knowledge of facts making it
   a pirate ship or aircraft.

So anxious was the commission to thwart possible communist
piracy claims that they effectively brought the definition of piracy
back two centuries. Whereas the evolution of both municipal law
and international law had been toward a broader, more inclusive
definition of piracy encompassing both political objectives and
political actions occurring other than on the high seas, the Geneva
Convention introduced a slightly expanded version of Justice
Hedges's definition: sea robbery with violence. Piracy was confined to "the high seas or in any other place outside the jurisdiction of any State," and limited to private vessels.[30] The comment
to Article XXXIX now read: "Save in the case provided for in
Article XL, piracy can be committed only by private ships and

not by warships or other government ships." The exception of Article XL referred to ships that had been seized by mutineers.

The commission also specifically repudiated the Nyon Agreement, in its comment to Article XIV. This comment also serves to highlight the tensions between two ideological poles and offers and insight on exactly what the commission considered political:

> With regard to point (iii), the Commission is aware that there are treaties, such as the Nyon Agreement of 14 September 1937, which brand the sinking of merchant ships by submarines, against the dictates of humanity, as piratical acts. But it is of the opinion that such treaties do not invalidate the principle that piracy can only be committed by private ships. In view of the immunity from interference by other ships which warships are entitled to claim, the seizure of such ships on suspicion of piracy might involve the gravest consequences. Hence the Commission feels that to assimilate unlawful acts committed by warships to acts of piracy would be prejudicial to the interests of the international community. *The Commission is unable to share the view held by some of its members that the principle laid down in the Nyon Arrangement confirmed a new law in process of development.*[31]

The stridency of this comment seems to represent a sharp break from the Harvard Draft Convention. In fact, however, it is entirely consistent with the draft's definition of "political"—even reaffirming it. Both the draft and the commission perceived the menace of political piracy to lie in the gray area of state sponsorship and rebellion. Both define "political" as state oriented, meaning either actual state actions (such as piracy by warship), state-sponsored piracy (privateering), or piracy by revolutionary quasi governments. None could have anticipated the creation of a third category, distinct from internal state conflict: terrorists. The law, therefore, does not reflect this potentiality.

It does, however, provide some guidance on how it *would* approach the problem of organized terrorism. By centering the concept of political piracy within the framework of inter- and intrastate conflict, the law suggests that other forms of politically motivated piracy committed outside this framework would still be termed piracy under the law. This reading is reinforced by the comment quoted above, saying that the "questions arising in connection with acts committed by warships in the service of rival governments engaged in civil war are too complex." The purpose of the antipolitical commentary is to distinguish the crime of piracy from legitimate acts of war. But war, as I stated in my introduction, can only be conducted between states or between rival factions within a state. Terrorism is not a war by any definition, as it occurs outside the geographic scope of conflict, is cellular and international in character, and pursues its political objectives solely through the illegitimate means of terror and coercion.

Despite its retrogressive elements, the 1958 Geneva Convention unwittingly facilitated the interpretation of terrorism as an act of piracy by defining what piracy was *not*. It is not to be found in naval war between states, nor between revolutionaries and the state. The inference, however, is that it *is* to be found in all other allegedly political circumstances.

*   *   *

The 1982 UN Convention is remarkable only in that it completely ignored twenty-four years of evolution in piracy law and deferred, almost word for word, to the terms of the 1958 Geneva Convention.[32] Among the most notable documents emerging in the interim was the International Law Association Report of 1970, defining piracy as the unlawful seizure of a vessel by violence, threats of violence, surprise, fraud, or other means.[33] This definition, which would have included maritime hijacks (in fact was specifically intended to do so) was not even addressed in the commentary of the 1982 UNCLOS. Instead, it offered a warmed-over definition of piracy nearly identical to its 1958 precedent, with the added element of new, more stringent concepts of jurisdictional zones. As one commentator lamented, "the old weaknesses and ambiguities not only remain, but are exacerbated by the zonal provisions." Piracy was thus defined as:

a) any illegal acts of violence or detention, or any act of depredation, committed for private ends by the crew or the passengers of a private ship or private aircraft, and directed:
    i) on the high seas, against another ship or aircraft, or against persons or property on board such ship or aircraft;
    ii) against a ship, aircraft, persons or property in a place outside the jurisdiction of any State.
b) any act of voluntary participation in the operation of a ship or of an aircraft with knowledge of facts making it a pirate ship or aircraft;
c) any act of inciting or intentionally facilitating an act described in sub-paragraphs (a) or (b).[34]

As the 1982 UNCLOS was the last published statement of piracy law, it remains in force to this day. On the one hand, it offers a depressingly limited and quite arcane concept of piracy; a fact that has led commentators for the last twenty years to suggest revision. But, on the other hand, it is very amenable to expansion. There is no limitation to acts of sea robbery, and the acts against "persons or property" outside of state jurisdiction is a short step from the "descent from the sea" concept discussed earlier. Moreover, the familiar phrase of "private ends" is offered without comment and thus is open to liberal interpretation. Desire to inflict terror for political reasons could certainly be considered "private ends"; I can scarcely imagine many other reasons for an attack on innocent civilians without any intention to steal. In short, the 1958 and 1982 conventions leave open the possibility for expansion of piracy law to include all forms of organized terrorism.

PIRATES, TERRORISTS, AND POLITICS:
RECENT ATTEMPTS AT DEFINITION

In the summer of 1999, the Joint International Working Group on Uniformity of the Law of Piracy met in London to draft a model definition of piracy. The impetus for this gathering came from the efforts of numerous scholars to extend the UN definition of piracy beyond its traditional parameters (as articulated in the 1982 UN Convention), particularly in regard to acts of so-called political piracy. The working group drew from numerous sources, both international and municipal. As a starting point, it circulated a questionnaire among the member states requesting summaries of their laws on piracy.[35]

This elicited a number of interesting responses, most especially that of the United States. The US Maritime Law Association delivered a report stating that US piracy law was based upon Sections 1651–55 of Title 18 of the US Code. Section 1651, discussed earlier, defers the question of definition to the law of nations. Sections 1652 and 1653 define jurisdiction for acts of piracy as against anyone who attacks in a piratical fashion a US citizen or is property "on board a vessel, ship, or maritime structure and is afterward brought into or found in the United States." Section 1654 concerns American citizens committing acts of piracy. Section 1655, by far the most controversial, defines as piracy acts of privateering—including acts for political purposes—provided that the act is against a US citizen or within US jurisdiction. Taken together, US law provided a model example of jurisdiction against political pirates.

The extension of piracy to political acts was further reinforced by the definition suggested by the marine insurance industry. The proposed insurers' definition included acts against vessels from shore, a significant departure from the "high seas." Similarly, the International Maritime Bureau (IMB) offered its own definition of piracy as "an act of boarding any vessel with the intent to commit theft or any other crime and with the intent or capability to use force in the furtherance of that act."[36]

Much of this language traces itself back to a single source: the 1988 Rome Convention. The convention, which came about largely in response to the *Achille Lauro* incident, altered the traditional jurisdiction for maritime crimes in areas outside all state jurisdiction to include attacks against vessels moored in roadsteads, harbors, even tethered to wharves. Moreover the list of prohibited offenses was greatly broadened to almost any act of violence against a ship, its cargo, or its crew. Under Article III, paragraph 1(c) of the convention, it is illegal to intentionally destroy a vessel or use it as a weapon against harbor facilities. This is a critical provision, as author Rudiger Wolfrum points out, for it provides the maritime corollary to the attacks against the World Trade Center on September 11, 2001.[37]

It was precisely that occurrence which prompted a 2005 Protocol to the Rome Convention, dealing specifically with terrorist offenses. Among the acts proscribed are:

> using a ship in a manner that causes death or serious injury or damage; transporting on board ship any explosive or radioactive material, knowing that it is intended to be used to cause . . . death or serious injury or damage for the purpose of intimidating a population, or compelling a government or an international organization to do or abstain from doing any act.[38]

Scholars distinguish the Rome statute and subsequent legislation from piracy by terming the former maritime terrorism. This is a relatively new concept, and it represents in part an attempt to separate avowedly political crimes at sea from conventional piracy. Among the more recent definitions of maritime terrorism as a discrete crime is that offered by the Council for Security Cooperation in the Asia Pacific (CSCAP):

> The undertaking of terrorist acts and activities (1) within the maritime environment, (2) using or against vessels or fixed platforms at sea or in port, or against one of their passengers or personnel, (3) against coastal facilities or settlements, including tourist resorts, port areas and port towns or cities.[39]

Maritime terrorism is thus distinct from piracy in that it includes attacks on port cities (although, as we saw earlier, the descent by sea provision for piracy also appears to countenance such attacks). Groups claiming responsibility for maritime terrorism include the Chechen rebels, who attacked Bosporus ferries in the late nineties; Al-Gama'a al-Islamiyya, which attempted to hijack passenger vessels; and a multiplicity of Palestinian groups including Hamas, the Palestinian Islamic Jihad, and, most famously, the PLF, which was responsible for the hijacking of the *Achille Lauro*.[40]

Such groups may seem at first distanced from conventional pirates (indeed that is the basis for maritime terrorism as a separate category), yet in reality the two are not as far apart as one might suppose. In 2002 members of al Qaeda intercepted the MV *Limburg* off the coast of Yemen and detonated an explosive, releasing or igniting some 297,000 barrels of crude oil. This single incident led to a brief collapse of international shipping business in the Gulf of Aden and a $0.48 increase in the price of crude oil per barrel. A statement from al Qaeda after the incident read as follows:

> By exploding the oil tanker in Yemen, the holy warriors hit the umbilical cord and lifeline of the crusader community, reminding the enemy of the heavy cost of blood and the gravity of losses they will pay as a price for their continued aggression on our community and looting of our wealth.[41]

Legal scholars would doubtless term this an act of maritime terrorism, which indeed it was. Yet it is significant that it occurred in precisely the same region, the Gulf of Aden, which has recently been plagued by Somali pirates. Moreover, the repercussions of the incident—as noted by the terrorists themselves—were precisely those of Somali piracy: the hindrance of trade and the rise of costs for transported goods.

This begs the question: can terrorists commit piracy? Some would say no, that the political motive of terrorism prevents the action from ever being piratical. This is an absurdity, and is made doubly so by the very real possibility of terrorists and pirates working together. In 2005, for example, the Joint War Council of Lloyd's Insurers declared the Malacca Strait as an "Area of Enhanced [Terrorism] Risk," in which it posited links between local Islamic militants and pirates.[42] A similar connection has also been made between the Somali pirates, insurgency groups, and terrorist organizations, including al Qaeda.

The concept of maritime terrorism is a viable one, and perhaps when it was formulated in the 1980s there were legitimate grounds for distinguishing it from piracy. But piracy itself has changed, and those grounds no longer exist. The difficulty with the Rome statute is shared by all international covenants on maritime terrorism: they lack the legal legitimacy given to piracy. As Wolfrum writes: "Whereas piracy is considered a truly international crime, an offense under the Rome Convention is not. The Rome Convention acknowledges only that several states may have an interest in prosecuting offenses under this agreement."[43] Similarly, such conventions also deal primarily with prosecution, not suppression. While laudable in its way, as Wolfrum points out, the Rome Convention is of little use when applied to suicide bombers.

Taken together, the insurers, IMB, and Rome definitions propose a version of piracy radically different from that of the 1982 UN Convention: the act no longer excludes allegedly political piracy, nor is it limited to areas beyond state jurisdiction. Thus the twin concepts of piracy and terrorism have, in the last fifteen years, moved closer and closer together.

A HEATED DEBATE

The ongoing tension in the law between limiting and expanding the definition of piracy with regard to political acts has also occasioned a great deal of scholarly debate. Such dialogues often do not make for riveting prose, and the reader may be forgiven for questioning why any consideration should be given to what appears—and indeed may often be—academic bloviation. But it is important, especially if one considers that international law is composed not merely of covenants and treaties, but customary law. And customary law derives in part from scholarly debate, much as domestic law derives from accumulated precedent.

Moreover, debates among scholars often serve as markers for the overall direction of the law: its limitations, its potential, and where it may be headed. In the contentious field of piracy law, two opposing poles can be discerned: conservative scholars attempting to preserve the traditional definition of piracy from extension to such "modern" crimes as hijacking and terrorism, and those who argue that the reality of piracy today necessitates such an extension, lest the definition slide into obsolescence.

It is interesting to note that the parameters for this debate were settled long before the issue of maritime terrorism arose. The reader will recall that the extension of piracy to states and insurgency groups under the Washington and Nyon agreements led to a scaling back in the law, ultimately resulting in the private/political distinction that survives today. This definition, however, was not in keeping with the general trend in the law. In 1934, one year after the Harvard Draft Convention, the English high court produced its own definition of piracy in *In Re Piracy Jure Gentium*, holding that frustrated attempts to commit piracy were still piratical, whether or not actual robbery occurred. Piracy, the justices concluded, applied to "an act of armed violence which is not a lawful act of war." This broad definition was reaffirmed by the Scottish Courts in 1971, in the case of *HMS Advocate v. Cameron and Others*.[44] The case involved the intentional ramming of one vessel by another, but no intent to board or steal. Concluding that this was indeed an act of piracy, the chief justice deferred to *In Re Piracy Jure Gentium* and cited a passage stating that "a careful examination of the subject shows a gradual widening of the earlier definition of piracy to bring it from time to time more in consonance with situations either not thought of or not in existence when the older jurisconsults were expressing their opinions."

The justice's mild language softens a critical point: definitions of piracy excluding political acts rely necessarily on an understanding of "political" limited to their era. Since such notions change over time (and never more so than in our own, with the advent of a state versus nonstate war on terror), a definition of piracy that presumes an understanding of "politics," absent any other description, is flawed and unworkable. Far better, as many scholars have advocated, to drop the political language altogether and simply distinguish piracy from acts committed by states.

This is precisely what numerous scholars have advocated since early in the last century. In *The International Law of the Sea*, authors Higgins and Colombo echo the English courts in terming piracy as "any armed violence at sea which is not a lawful act of war." Mindful that states can still engage in "illegal" warfare, J. L. Brierly in *The Law of Nations* offers a more precise definition: "Any state may bring in pirates for trial by its own courts, on the ground that they are *hostis humani generi.* . . . It is of the essence of a piratical act to be an act of violence, committed at sea or at any rate closely connected with the sea, by persons not acting under proper authority."[45]

The *Achille Lauro* affair of 1985 provided the impetus for a reconsideration of the entire subject. The UNCLOS definition of 1982 still defined piracy narrowly, but by this time the threat of aerial piracy, otherwise known as hijacking, had risen. After the *Achille Lauro*, and President Reagan's explicit use of the word *pirates* to describe the hijackers, scholars had to consider whether the conventional definition had merit or even relevance. Piracy and maritime terrorism looked almost exactly alike: should they not therefore have a joint definition?

This provoked a heated response from the traditionalists. Among the most reactionary was Alfred Rubin, whose text *The Law of Piracy* remains seminal in the field. Coming down hard on his progressive colleagues, Rubin took issue with J. W. Bolton's assertion that terrorism was the modern equivalent of piracy. Rubin waspishly responded, "Bolton seems to miss the point . . . that 'terrorism' cannot, by traditional forms of argument, be shown to be 'criminal' as a matter of international law whatever its quality might be in the municipal law of the state or group of states the 'terrorists' are trying to destabilize."[46] From its strident tone to its liberal use of scare quotes, this statement sums up the traditionalist perspective: Piracy has several thousand years of history and law, which we decline to prostitute or put to service newfangled and undefined notions like "terrorism."

Unfortunately for Rubin, events rapidly overtook such attitudes, making the traditional definition of piracy more arcane than ever. Terrorism proved to be more than a passing phenomenon. As early as 1991, Samuel P. Menefee argued for the melding of the two concepts in Natalino Ronzitti's *Maritime Terrorism and International Law*.[47] In contrast to Rubin's assertion that the history of piracy did not bear out analogies to modern terrorism, Menefee demonstrated that so-called insurgent passengers seizing control of their vessel (discussed at length earlier in this book) invariably raised questions of piracy. This not only provided the link between such cases and the *Achille Lauro* but for all other hijackings as well. Concluding, Menefee took specific issue with the limitations of the 1982 UN Convention:

> An argument may be made that the *Achille Lauro* insurgents were guilty of piracy under customary international law. This would mean, of course, that the definitions of the 1958 and 1982 Conventions were not exclusive. Such a view is not as unorthodox as it might seem. . . . The fact that piracy issues have been argued in *every* prior passenger takeover which has been investigated would suggest some justification for not recognizing the exclusivity of the Convention if its definition of piracy cannot be found to encompass the subject. This position would appear all the more true for 'third party attacks' [terrorist hijackings] a subject on which there seems to be general international consensus.[48]

Proponents for a reconsideration of piracy law received the greatest boost following the events of September 11, 2001. What the attacks accomplished was to present the world with a radically different conception of terrorism, even from that of the *Achille Lauro*. Terrorists were no longer peripheral figures waging quixotic battles against (or within) individual states. Terrorism went global, and a new understanding of what that meant was reflected in states' invocation of the right to self-defense. This was made explicit in resolutions passed by the UN Security Council and the Council of the North Atlantic Treaty Organization, which granted victimized states unprecedented freedom to pursue terrorist organizations *as if* they were aggressing states. One scholar, at least, recognized that something entirely new emerged from this prerogative: state versus nonstate warfare. He writes: "This interpretation of the right to self-defense reflects the fact that states have ceased to have monopoly on waging war. War-like activities with negative effects on peace and security may equally well be carried out by terrorists, especially if such terrorists are working within an international framework."[49]

But what did this mean for piracy and its cousin, maritime terrorism? In short, their combined law was revealed as even more archaic and out of step with current realities. Piracy had long been understood as state versus nonstate warfare, in the tradition of *hostis humani generi*. Yet modern piracy law ignores that potential, defining it so narrowly as to make it beyond anachronistic. As if that were not enough, most scholars and jurists refused to make the obvious link between piracy and maritime terrorism, despite the fact that by almost any reckoning the two were interchangeable—and, additionally, that such a melding would give maritime terrorism its proper (and much-needed) grounding in customary international law. There were, however, a few jurists who recognized both the threat and the potential. In a 2008 survey of the law entitled *Legal Challenges in Maritime Security*, Rudiger Wolfrum took up the banner of the legal progressives, critiquing the flimsy patchwork of maritime antiterror covenants and piracy laws, stating flatly, "New developments seem to indicate that these mechanisms do not embrace modern threats." He goes on: "The existing rules for the suppression of piracy are inadequate. They do not even provide an efficient regime against piracy narrowly defined."[50]

Nevertheless, the potential remains. The present reality of terrorism revealed the old political/private debate on piracy to be obsolete, even as it received one final airing. On May 25, 2007, a group of distinguished legal scholars held a panel discussion on piracy and maritime terrorism. Not surprisingly, the first issue on the agenda was the limiting language of the 1982 UNCLOS definition. The comments of the panel are indicative of how radically this discussion has changed. Samuel Menefee, who a decade earlier was almost alone in arguing for a reconsideration of the law, now found considerable support. "I do not think we can let terrorists define what the [political] 'ends' are," he declared. "One of the problems with the definition of piracy is that it stipulates private ends as opposed to public ones."[51]

Menefee's point is well taken. Nowhere in the 1982 convention does it state that terrorist organizations are political entities. Indeed, given the 1958 commission's fervor to distinguish piracy from acts committed by states, it is likely that terrorist organizations would *not* fall within the convention's definition of political. The imputation of political status is assumed, largely (as Menefee points out) by the terrorists' own declaration as political operatives. But it is not for them to define themselves thus; that is the task of states. And states have resolutely, and correctly, declined to grant terrorist organizations such legitimacy.

The best expression of the current thinking on piracy law comes from Professor William Baumgartner's reply to Menefee. Menefee had spent over a decade searching for loopholes in the political exclusion; Baumgartner suggested they move beyond it entirely, and in so doing signaled a profound shift in the dialogue on piracy. "We are making a very rash assumption by asserting that private ends are mutually exclusive with political ends," Baumgartner said.

This is a terrible mistake and is unnecessary in light of the history and background of piracy. I do not think that when the text was developed, a private terrorist, not looking to take over a state and not acting as an insurgent, would be exempt from the definition of piracy. I do not think that would have been envisioned. When you look at a private end, a state or state-sponsored end would certainly be a logical conclusion as the opposite of a private end.

Having succinctly disposed of the traditionalists' argument, he went on to offer a radically new perspective on the law:

This is something we repeat too often, that if it is political it cannot be private. I just do not think that is right, and we are jumping to a conclusion that is leading us to a place we do not want to go and it is illogical to go. We certainly do not give acts committed for terrorist purposes on land special status and accord them rights; quite the opposite . . . The private ends debate does not make any sense. We are not forced by the history, the text, or the context to let this idea dominate.[52]

Baumgartner's argument is an echo of Carol Hanisch: the personal *is* political. In the twenty-first century, geopolitics no longer remains the province of states but has been encroached upon by nonstate actors bearing certain similarities to states, yet operating entirely outside their normal parameters. What both Menefee and Baumgartner suggest is that by terming terrorists as political, it confers on them the legitimacy traditionally reserved for states. Yet while Menefee continues to work within the structure of existing law, Baumgartner suggests that current realities—unimagined even in 1983—have rendered any attempt to reconcile the private and political utterly futile. Better to abandon the debate entirely and accept that things have moved beyond such black-and-white distinctions. If we do so, says Baumgarter, we will finally see the obvious: that piracy and maritime terrorism are one and the same. It is ludicrous to distinguish between terrorism on land and terrorism at sea, or to maintain that piracy—which has always included myriad acts of violence—must be defined separately from maritime terrorism.

I propose to take this argument one step further. The current thinking is to include piracy among the list of terrorist offenses. While this is laudable, it is also quixotic: there is no definition of terrorism *per se*, and the crime lacks (as conservative legal scholars are quick to remind us) a comprehensive legislative history in both domestic and international law. It is piracy, not terrorism, that has over two thousand years of legal precedent behind it. Consequently, there is little to be gained by adding crimes of piracy to the already large and unwieldy list of terrorist offenses: it acknowledges that the reality of piracy has changed, but does not make capturing pirates any easier, or terrorists for that matter. I suspect that much of what underlies arguments to politicize piracy law is the desire to rescue it from senescence and demonstrate that it does have relevance in the modern world.

But the potential is considerably greater. Rather than defining piracy as terrorism, let us try the opposite: terrorism is piracy. This is a harder case, as it means that crimes of international terrorism (which may occur on land and involve nothing piratical except homicide or destruction of property) must nevertheless fit within the existing definition of piracy. I will not dwell too greatly on that argument here, as it comprises the entire second part of this book, but it is worth noting that it stems largely from the debates outlined above. The logical pattern looks something like this: (1) if *some* pirates are terrorists, and (2) *all* pirates are *hostis humani generi*, then (3) *some* terrorists must be *hostis humani generi* as well. Does it make any sense for some terrorists to be enemies of the human race and others not?

PIRACY RESURGENT: MALACCA STRAITS AND SOMALIA

For those who worried that maritime terrorism would supplant piracy, and piracy itself fade into oblivion, 2008 was a boon year. Yet the "new golden age of piracy," as some have termed it, has also put to rest once and for all the stale debate over political piracy. Over a decade ago prescient jurists warned that the private-ends limitation imposed on piracy would ultimately render all acts of modern piracy beyond definition. Now it has come to pass. For the Somali pirates, whose "takings" are usually confined to hijacking and ransom, and whose ransoms are put to the service of insurgency groups, are not pirates at all. Not, at any rate, under the 1982 UN definition.

This illustrates both how ridiculous the political exclusion has become and how potent a menace piracy can still be. Until late in the last decade we still spoke of maritime terrorism in terms of an isolated attack; as recently as 2007, the greatest piratical threat was presumed to be the seizure of a tanker filled with flammable material and its deliberate destruction or use against a port city, *vide* the attack on the Twin Towers. While that possibility remains (indeed, one of the findings released not long after 9/11 was the extreme vulnerability of our vessels and ports), piracy itself—in a more conventional, if still uniquely twenty-first-century iteration—has resurfaced with a vengeance. Its reappearance on the scene has forced states to confront the archaic nature of the law.

Another phenomenon is worth noting. In two apparently distinct geopolitical spheres, many of the same questions resonate: How do we achieve international consensus and cooperation to capture these criminals? Who should bear the burden of prosecution? Do we have the right to enter states and seize suspects therein, or launch attacks on pirate/terrorist camps located within sovereign territory? What domestic or international law covers these crimes and these suspects? Must our response always be reactionary, or can we eliminate the problem at its source?

The mere fact that piracy and terrorism share so many of these queries might in itself, absent any other linkages, suggest a connection between the two. Both stem from the same essential conundrum: the relative newness of state versus nonstate warfare. Just as our domestic and international laws lag behind the current reality, so too does our policy.

Yet the resurgence of Somali piracy may also present us with a unique opportunity to recognize the shared status of pirates and terrorists and to employ the longstanding precedent of piracy law (which itself has fallen somewhat into desuetude) against a new menace. But first we must consider how piracy returned, and what form it takes. Both of these are critical for understanding how we may proceed both in the Gulf of Aden against the pirates and around the world against international terrorists.

Before Somalia, there were the Malacca Straits. This narrow channel of water between Malaysia and Sumatra forms the link between the Indian and Pacific Oceans, and is thus one of the most frequently traversed passages for commercial vessels on earth. It has also been a hotbed for piracy since the Middle Ages. From the mid-1980s until the late 1990s, modern piracy was almost always associated with this region. Nor has it disappeared. In 2000, according to the IMB, there were seventy-five attacks against commercial vessels in this region. Targets range from fishing trawlers to giant chemical tankers, including the *Dewi Madrim* in 2003. In 2004 the BBC reported that incidents of piracy and violence on board captured vessels were on the rise, with a sharp spike in the number of crew murdered.[53] That same year IMB noted that while piracy around the world was in decline, it had increased in the Malacca Straits by 33 percent. Observers began to predict that piracy in Southeast Asia might one day attract terrorists, using the seizure of an oil tanker as means for either inflicting destruction or taking hostages.[54]

In fact, politics already underlay much of what was going on in the Straits. From 1976 to 2005, the island of Sumatra was engulfed in a civil war between Indonesian forces and the GAM (Gerakan Aceh Merdeka, or Free Aceh Movement). This conflict inevitably spilled over into the crowded sea lanes, as GAM members began employing piracy as a means of raising funds and awareness for their cause. In 2003 the IMB reported:

Several uniformed men suspected to be GAM rebels in a fishing boat hijacked . . . a fishing trawler and sailed it toward Indonesian waters, where Indonesian Marine Police confronted them. A shoot-out ensued in which two of the suspected GAM members on board the trawler were shot dead and another was injured.[55]

The scope of the attacks and targets only increased thereafter. One year later another vessel was captured by the GAM, its crew tortured, and a ransom of $132,000 demanded for their return.[56]

If the above reads remarkably like the current situation in Somalia, then it begs the obvious question: why has no one heard of it? Where were the news cameras and helicopters and international patrols then? One answer lies in the fact that despite their growing success, the Sumatran pirates never succeeded in capturing a prize as significant as the *Sirius Star*. Moreover, just as the political problems in Sumatra exacerbated the problem, their resolution in 2005—by a peace accord between the GAM and the Indonesian government—abated it. Piracy in the Malacca Straits was in steady decline since 2005, even as Somali piracy was on the rise.

The question of why Malacca Straits piracy rarely made the headlines is really another way of asking something far more profound: why has Somali piracy become so critical? The two are more congruous that most people realize: in both instances the modus operandi is more commonly hijacking and ransom, not actual theft; likewise, political motivations are the principal contributing factor. In August 2008, shortly after Somali pirates seized four vessels off the Horn of Africa, Reuters reported that the pirates were paying a significant portion of their ransoms to al-Shabaab, a Somali insurgency group identified by the US government as a terrorist organization with close ties to al Qaeda.[57]

Somali piracy has captured the attention of the world because the pirates' targets have become successively more ambitious. This, in turn, is due to the sluggish response of the international community—both its navies and its shipowners, who even today prefer to pay exorbitant ransoms rather than risk further injury to their ships or crews. As the pirates collected greater and greater ransoms, they furnished themselves with more sophisticated equipment and began extending their attacks over a much broader area.

Thus a combination of circumstances has contributed to the new golden age of piracy: the political situation in Somalia, the frequency and scope of attacks, the lackluster response by states, the difficulty in policing such a vast expanse of sea, conflicts between individual states' rules of engagement, the cowardice of shipowners, and the inability or unwillingness of states to prosecute (about which more later). Yet this apparent crisis also represents a great opportunity. Just as piracy once drove the nations of Europe to declare it beyond the pale of state behavior, so too has twenty-first-century piracy offered us a paradigm of how states can come together to combat an international scourge. Recently, the navies of over twenty different states have banded together and sailed in concert under a unified system of rules. The results have been extraordinary. The pirates have lost much of their seeming infallibility, and the United States and other nations have already sought UN permission to launch raids against the pirate bases on shore.

This kind of international comity is precisely what is needed to combat terrorism. Just as it was apparent that no one navy could adequately police the Gulf of Aden, so too must we now recognize that the United States cannot go it alone in its fight against terrorism around the world. But how do we gain that crucial cooperation? I would argue that here again the Somali precedent is instructive. Here we have seen how a relatively small band of criminals can have a vastly disproportionate effect on the global scene: the image of over fifteen arrested tankers all within sight of one another is as potent a metaphor as any.

The recognition needed here is more than just that pirates and terrorists have an equally detrimental affect on states; states must also recognize that, just as with pirates, the only way they can combat terrorism is by acting in concert. As the principle actor in the war on terror, that task begins with the United States.

CONCLUSION

In evaluating the relationship between piracy and terrorists, this quote from a Civil War case is particularly instructive. It is not enough for a group of persons to merely declare themselves a political entity; that recognition comes not from them but from states themselves:

> They carry on war, but it is not natural war; and they are not entitled to the benefit of usages of modern civilized international war. . . . If a number of persons, large or small, associate together, and undertake to establish a new government, and assume the character of a nation, and as such to issue military commissions, any other nation may . . . utterly refuse to recognize the existence of such assumed government and treat all who, acting under it, commit aggressions upon the ocean, as mere pirates.[58]

One might make precisely the same case for al Qaeda. The trend of piracy law has moved inexorably from an early understanding of sea robbery to a modern understanding of maritime terrorism. This is reflected in the municipal laws of England and the United States, the work of countless twentieth-century scholars, and even in the mangled machinations that produced the 1958 and 1982 conventions. As the nature of piracy itself evolved, the nature of its legal counterpart proceeded apace. By the early twentieth century, piracy for monetary ends was a peripheral problem, well within the jurisdictional and legislative purview of individual states. But piracy as an act of political coercion was coming into its own. As the number of unquestionably piratical acts receded, states began on their own initiative to stretch the definition to include newer forms of menace. This resulted in the Washington Agreement of 1922 and the Nyon Agreement of 1937.

By the end of the Second World War, the logical conclusion to this evolutionary process could be easily anticipated; a new politicized definition of piracy that would replace its obsolete precedent, sea robbery. Yet with the advent of the Cold War, the evolution was sidetracked. Bipolar politics introduced a retrogressive element: as the Eastern Bloc sought to hasten the definition of piracy to its fully political end, their Western nemeses clung with increasing desperation to its traditional, irrelevant, ossified antecedent. This can only account for the strangely limited and arcane definition that the crime of piracy holds today. It is the product not of dispassionate legal inquiry but a realpolitik evaluation of lesser evils. Piracy was thus allowed to become marginalized in the law to prevent it from becoming a tool against insurgent (perhaps democratic) governments.

There is a middle ground between the Nyon Agreement and the 1982 convention, and it lies in the arguments advanced on both sides of much-debated issue of political piracy. One position, briefly stated, would expand the definition of piracy to include virtually any act of armed violence at sea. This would probably (though not certainly) exclude warships, but would most certainly include rebel vessels or those of revolutionary governments. The other position, also oversimplified, states that all inquiry into the political dimensions of piracy necessarily produces a maelstrom of vagaries between political and private acts. Piracy, therefore, must be wholly divorced from such debates and limited exclusively to acts committed for private (i.e., pecuniary) gain.

The middle ground between these two definitions is, appropriately, the specter of maritime terrorism. Although both the 1958 and 1982 conventions expressly exclude political piracy, they limit their definition of *political* to a conventional idea of state versus state or, alternately, civil war. This is consistent with recorded history to that time, where the pattern of conflict had been exclusively between states or within states. It is not, however, applicable to the current war on terrorism. Organized terrorism presents a third, hitherto unknown form of conflict: state versus nonstate. Unlike the others, it is not waged *within* a given territory nor *over* that territory. Instead, contemporary terrorism—like piracy—is waged all over the world against a multitude of states. These states, the terrorists' "enemies," share no necessary commonalities among themselves except loss of life and property. As the aims of terrorist organizations vary widely between quasi-legitimate governmental objectives (such as the establishment of territorial boundaries and the enfranchisement of minorities) to seemingly apolitical, cultural, or religious ambitions, so too do the terrorists' motivations vary in determining their enemies. A state may have only peripheral contact with the issue in dispute (as in ex–colonial nations), a past history of diplomatic involvement in the disputed area (as with the United States in Afghanistan), or cultural practices, religious observances, and governmental regimes that are anathema to the terrorists. The "enemy" state might even have no appreciable connection to the terrorists whatsoever. This situation is markedly different from that envisioned by the drafters of the 1958 and 1982 conventions. As the world has moved beyond the Cold War into a new century and new political realities, so too must piracy law adopt these realities within a new, unabashedly political definition.

This requires virtually no alteration of the existing law, only recognition of its logical limitations. By their express language, the 1958 and 1982 conventions limit their understanding of "political" to state conflict and civil war. Without denigrating that definition, international jurists can stress its corollary: that other forms of violence (1) otherwise falling within the definition of piracy, (2) committed by private organizations (that is, nongovernmental, nonmilitary, and having no direct affiliation with a revolutionary government), and (3) whose only ground for denying jurisdiction is the self-professedly political ends they wish to achieve are nevertheless piracy under international law.

There is inferential support for this interpretation throughout modern international and municipal piracy law. The most obvious source is the repeated affirmation that piracy encompasses acts of violence, such as homicide and destruction, that are committed for private ends other than pecuniary gain. The solution to the private/political dichotomy lies in considering the logical extremities of these private ends. Suppose a band of pirates boards a vessel, lulls its crew, and burns it to the keel. Captured as pirates, they advance the argument that they did so to protest the imprisonment of certain key Palestinian rebels. Would they then be entitled to release simply because they claimed a political motive? Certainly not—the result would be akin to that in Gilbert and Sullivan's *Pirates of Penzance*: the good-natured pirates release anyone claiming orphanage; therefore, every person captured immediately swears himself to be an orphan. The legal limitation of piracy to nonpolitical acts clearly presupposes more than a mere assertion of a political objective. Some appreciable nexus to a government, whether existing or insurgent, must be required to separate the wheat from the chaff.

One might argue, in contrast, that an organization such as al Qaeda becomes a de facto political entity by virtue of its size, complexity, and objectives. But this argument fails to account for the crucial difference between a revolutionary government—however disorganized—and a terrorist organization. The difference lies in objective and means: the revolutionaries seek to replace the existing government with their own, directing their attacks solely at that government; a terrorist organization has no such limitations on its agenda, nor on the scope of its attacks. Regime change may or may not coincide with a plethora of other initiatives, and the weapon of terror may be inflicted against any state or its citizens. It is this lack of limitation that distinguishes the terrorist from the revolutionary. For a terrorist organization to represent itself as a belligerent or revolutionary organization within the meaning of the law, it must (1) confine its attacks to within the jurisdictional and/or territorial boundaries of a single state, (2) have no political objective beyond regime change, and (3) represent itself as the alternative governmental regime.

Pirates who do not confine themselves to the above-mentioned quasi-governmental limitations fall outside the "political" exemption and become *hostis humani generi*. So too must terrorists. It should be of no greater account whether the terrorist band is comprised of ten members or one hundred thousand than it would if the pirates attacked by a phalanx of ships or an inflatable life raft. The law rightly concerns itself only with determining whether this is a crime or an act of war, and beyond that it does not inquire.

Having demonstrated that the political dimensions of modern terrorism are not inconsistent with piracy law, it remains to demonstrate that acts of terrorism are likewise amenable. We have already seen that the current definition of piracy encompasses a number of acts that coincide with terrorism, most notably murder and destruction of property. If the same act can be termed both an act of piracy and an act of terrorism, the two definitions meld.

This leaves us with the question of locus. Can piracy occur on land? By most modern definitions, the answer is yes. Both the 1958 and 1982 conventions recognize the possibility of piracy in territories outside of any state jurisdiction. The 1932 Harvard Draft Convention goes even farther, allowing for acts of piracy committed on land "by descent from the sea." This idea is reaffirmed by the municipal laws of both the United States and Great Britain. As the 1958 and 1982 conventions do not specifically discount this possibility, nor offer an alternative definition for it under international law, the possibility of sea descent may be considered still valid under international customary law.

Within this nebulous concept of "descent by sea" lies an exciting possibility. The law does not specify how this descent should occur, nor where, nor whether the pirate must begin the act of piracy immediately after landfall. And although it implies that such descent "by sea" should be from an ocean vessel, it does not say so explicitly—and the recognized possibility of aerial piracy argues strongly for an extension of definition. Acts of aerial piracy have enjoyed long recognition in international law. Thus it is likely that a definition of "descent by sea" might—

in fact, must—include descent by sea from the air; that is, the landing of an overseas airplane. This can occur anywhere—even in landlocked countries—provided that the plane crossed over some form of ocean during its flight path or originated from another country. There is no requirement that this plane land in a coastal city for it to remain piratical. Therefore the pirate still descends by sea wherever he lands, even if it is inland. Finally, there is no time limitation imposed by the law. The pirate need not commence sacking and pillaging immediately; it is sufficient for him to have engineered the idea prior to arrival. Thus, if one defines this act of descent in the broadest possible terms, it may be applied to any person—other than a citizen—who arrives at the victimized state from overseas with the specific intent of committing an act of terror while within that state. This means that any terrorist arriving from abroad with the prior intent of committing an act of terror may be classified a pirate under international law, specifically the uncontested descent by sea provision of the Harvard Draft Convention.

While this may be something of a stretch from the meaning of sea descent in common parlance, it is quite consistent with the underlying objective of the provision. Whether the pirate arrives by ship or by plane, whether he touches down on the coast or inland, and whether he begins to wreak havoc immediately or waits for his plans to mature, are all irrelevant considerations. To remain true to the spirit of the law, one must only determine whether he arrived from overseas with the prior intention of committing an act that falls within the definition of piracy.

A crime, in municipal or international law, has three elements: the *mens rea*, the *actus reus*, and the *locus*. For terrorism to fall within the common definition of piracy, it must therefore be consistent in its requisite mental state, actions, and place of occurrence. The *mens rea* of piracy is the desire to inflict death, destruction, or deprivation for private ends. Recognizing the difference between the political ends of a revolutionary government and those of a terrorist organization, we can now conclude that international terrorism falls outside the political exemption and thus within the common understanding of piracy. Second, the *actus reus* of piracy, which includes acts of homicide and destruction absent actual robbery, is synonymous with the *actus reus* of most forms of modem terrorism. Third, the *locus* of piracy, while traditionally confined to the high seas or other territories outside state jurisdiction, has been expanded to include acts of piracy committed on state territory by descent from the sea; a provision that, as outlined above, may likewise apply to nearly all acts of terrorism.

Since piracy and terrorism share a *mens rea*, *actus reus*, and *locus*, we may conclude that they are, in effect, the same crime. They must also, accordingly, share a legal definition. Terrorists, like pirates, are *hostis humani generi* under international law.

NOTES

1. Alfred Rubin, *The Law of Piracy* (Irvington-on-Hudson, NY: Transnational Publishers, 1985), p. 231.

2. Ibid., p. 229. Interested readers should examine the chapter titled "British Practice in the Nineteenth Century," pp. 221–310, for a complete account of British imperial policy on the pirates.

3. Ibid., p. 262. See also Peter Earle, *Corsairs of Malta and Barbary* (London: Sidgwick & Jackson, 1970).

4. See Philip Buhler, "New Struggle with an Old Menace: Towards a Revised Definition of Maritime Piracy," *Currents International Trade Law Journal* 8 (1999).

5. *In Re the Magellan Pirates*, 1 Spink Ecc. & Ad. 81 (1853).

6. Ibid.; see also Rubin, *Law of Piracy*, p. 261, for analysis of this case.

7. Legal Report rendered to Foreign Secretary George W. F. Villiers by the Law Officers of the Crown, "Pirate Vessels under British and Other Flags," F. O. 83.2209.

8. P. W. Birnie, "Piracy Past, Present and Future," in *Piracy at Sea*, ed. Eric Ellen (London: International Maritime Bureau, 1989), p. 137.

9. Barry Hart Dubner, *The Law of International Sea Piracy* (Boston: Martinus Nijhoff, 1980), p. 116.

10. Quoted in ibid., p. 37.

11. *US v. Smith*, 5 Wheaton 153 (1820), cited in ibid., p. 761.

12. Harvard Draft Convention, pp. 773–75.

13. *In Re Piracy Jure Gentium*, A. C. 586.

14. Harvard Draft Convention, p. 786.

15. Cited in ibid., p. 777.

16. Cited in ibid., p. 779.

17. Reply of Rumania, November 20, 1926, cited in Harvard Draft Convention, p. 781.

18. Ibid., p. 809.

19. Ibid., p. 781.

20. Cited in ibid., p. 776.

21. Cited in ibid., p. 781.

22. Ibid., p. 857.

23. Birnie, "Piracy Past, Present and Future," p. 138.

24. Ibid.

25. Remarks of Sir Gerald Fitzmaurice, par. 92, app. 4, in Discussions of the 327th meeting, July 5, 1955, 1 *Yearbook of the International Law Commission* 266, 267 (1955).

26. Remarks of Mr. Hsu, par. 5, app. 5, in ibid., p. 286.

27. Dubner, *Law of International Sea Piracy*, pp. 110–13.

28. Remarks of Mr. Zourek, para. 37, app. 12, in 1 *Yearbook of the International Law Commission* (1955): 46–48.

29. Remarks of Sir Gerald Fitzmaurice, par. 44, app. 12, in ibid, p. 267.

30. Ibid., p. 287.

31. 2 *Yearbook of the International Law Commission* 282, art. 39, comment 3 (1956).

32. Birnie, "Piracy Past, Present and Future," p. 139.

33. International Law Association, 54th Report, The Hague, 1970. See also D. H. N. Johnson, "Piracy in Modern International Law," *Grotius Society Transactions* 43 (1957): 63.

34. United Nations Convention on the Law of the Sea, Montego Bay, December 10, 1982, ILM 21 (1982), art. 101.

35. Buhler, "New Struggle with an Old Menace," p. 68.

36. Quoted in ibid.

37. Rudiger Wolfrum, "Fighting Terrorism at Sea," in *Legal Challenges in Maritime Security*, by Myron Nordquist et al. (Boston: Martinus Nijhoff, 2008), p. 13.

38. Amendment to the Rome Convention for the Suppression of

Unlawful Acts against the Safety of Maritime Navigation, 27 ILM 672 (1988), adopted October 14, 2005.

39. Quoted in Michael Greenberg et al., *Maritime Terrorism: Risk and Liability* (New York: Rand, 2008), p. 9.

40. Ibid., p. 19.

41. Quoted in Russell Herbert-Burns, "Terrorism in Early Twenty-first Century Domain," in *The Best of Times, The Worst of Times: Maritime Security in the Asia-Pacific*, by Joshua Ho et al. (Singapore: Scientific World, 2005), p. 157.

42. Greenberg et al., *Maritime Terrorism*, p. 14.

43. Nordquist et al., *Legal Challenges*, p. 18.

44. *Scots Law Times* 2 (1971): 206.

45. P. R. Brierly, *The Law of Nations* (Oxford: Oxford University Press, 1928), p. 154.

46. Rubin, *Law of Piracy*, p. 378.

47. Samuel Menefee, "Piracy, Terrorism and the Insurgent Passenger," in *Maritime Terrorism and International Law*, by Natalino Ronzitti (Boston: Martinus Nijhoff, 1991), p. 43.

48. Ibid., p. 61.

49. Wolfrum, in Nordquist et al., *Legal Challenges*, p. 32.

50. Ibid., p. 6.

51. "Edited Transcripts from Question-and-Answer Session: International Maritime Security Needs and Initiatives and Piracy," in ibid., p. 501.

52. Ibid., p. 502.

53. *BBC World*, "Killings by Pirates on the Rise," July 26, 2004.

54. ICC International Maritime Bureau, Piracy and Armed Robbery against Ships: Annual Report, 1 January–31 December 2003.

55. Ibid., sec. 91.

56. Samuel Menefee, "An Overview of Piracy in the First Decade of the Twenty-first Century," in Nordquist et al., *Legal Challenges*, p. 448.

57. *Reuters*, "Piracy Ransoms Funding Somalia Insurgency," August 24, 2008.

58. 30 Fed. Cas. 1049, no. 18, 277 (October 1861).

Part 2
TERRORISM IS PIRACY

Chapter 4

THE PIRATE MUSE

He looked too small to be allowed. The Somali pirate accused of leading the hijacking of the *Maersk Alabama*, threatening Capt. Richard Phillips at gunpoint, grappling with the ship's crew, and boasting that he had led many other successful sorties, stood just over five feet tall and weighed less than one hundred pounds. His meager frame seemed lost in his orange jumpsuit, and when he flashed a smile for the cameras—a show of bravado—it was painfully reminiscent of the faces in an Oxfam poster.

The Federal Court for the Southern District of New York, in contrast, loomed with impressive majesty. It was there, behind a row of Doric columns, that John Gotti and Bernie Madoff received their sentences. With its high walls, dark paneling, and flags, the courtroom seemed to almost encourage displays of broad-shouldered, Miltonesque defiance. Yet Abduwali Abdukhadir Muse sat silent, staring into his lap, as the charges were read against him. One of his hands was heavily bandaged, legacy of a desperate fight on board the *Maersk Alabama*. Defense attorneys had already begun the difficult task of recasting their client as an innocent waif caught up in machinations beyond his understanding. "He's confused. He's terrified," one of them said. "As you can imagine, he's a boy who fishes, and now he's ended up in solitary confinement here. He's having a very difficult time."[1]

This was Abduwali Muse's second appearance in court. His first produced an hour-long wrangle over the defendant's alleged age (variously given as fifteen, sixteen, eighteen, and twenty-six) and the ultimate decision to try him as an adult. Now Justice Loretta A. Preska asked him, "How do you plead, sir?" Through his interpreter, Muse answered, "Not guilty."

The grand jury had returned with twelve indictments. The first was seminal:

> From on or about April 9, 2009, up to and including April 12, 2009, on the high seas, the defendant . . . *committed the crime of piracy as defined by the law of nations*, and was afterward brought into and found in the United States, to wit, the defendant unlawfully, willingly and knowingly seized and robbed, and aided and abetted the seizure and robbery, of a US flagged ship, the *Maersk Alabama*, while the ship was navigating in the Indian Ocean beyond the outer limit of the territorial sea of any country.[2]

There was little reaction from the defendant or the court as this was read, no recognition that history had been made. And yet it had: the first piracy trial convened in the city of New York in almost two centuries, the first such trial in the United States since 1885.

Other aspects of the indictment were more familiar. It had only been a few years since several al Qaeda operatives had sat behind the same desk as the defendant Muse. The physical contrast could hardly have been more obvious, yet his indictment raised echoes of the tragedy that had occurred only a few blocks away, eight years before. "The defendant," the second count began, "knowingly . . . seized and exercised control over a ship by force and threat of force, and attempted to do the same, to wit, the defendant, armed with a firearm, attempted to hijack, hijacked and aided in the hijacking of the *Maersk Alabama*."

The facts of the case, as alleged by the prosecution, made for thrilling reading.[3] At 4:30 a.m. on April 9, 2009, the US-flagged container ship *Maersk Alabama* was 240 nautical miles southeast of the Somali city of Eyl when a crewmember spotted a light on the port side of the ship. It appeared to be coming closer, then disappeared. Two hours later, Muse and three other pirates, in ages ranged from seventeen to nineteen, secured a grappling ladder to the side of the *Maersk Alabama* and boarded her. The master of the *Maersk Alabama*, Captain Phillips, desperately fired flares at the oncoming pirates to stave off the assault. Muse fired several shots at the bridge with an automatic weapon and secured Phillips as a hostage. The captain was instructed to radio his crew to join him on the bridge, where they too would be taken prisoner.

Some, however, had other ideas. Several crewmembers secured themselves in a "safe room," while another hid on one of the ship's cranes, from which he observed, through the plate glass windows of the bridge, Muse and other pirates threatening Captain Phillips at gunpoint. The failure of the crew to submit caused consternation among Muse and his confreres, and they finally decided that he should hunt the missing men down. He took a member of the *Alabama*'s company as a guide and began searching the ship, deck by deck.

Gradually, Muse and his captive drew closer to where one crewmember, the same man who had observed the scene on the bridge, was hiding. Muse still held the automatic weapon, cocked and ready. As his shadow passed, the crewmember suddenly leaped from his concealment and tackled Muse. His colleague joined in, and after a short struggle the two men disarmed the pirate and secured his wrists with wire.

The situation on the bridge, meanwhile, had become increasingly tense. When the pirates discovered that one of their own—their alleged leader—had been overcome, they offered a trade: they would leave the ship, if Muse was returned. This was agreed. As security, however, they took with them Captain Phillips and escaped in a twenty-eight-foot lifeboat.

The events that followed were monitored by news agencies throughout the world and scarcely need repeating here.[4] After several days' standoff between the pirates and the US Navy, it had become clear that Phillips' life was in imminent danger. He had eluded his captors once, jumping into the sea and swimming for freedom, only to be hauled back aboard, beaten, and secured. The pirates knew their options were dwindling. The same thought ultimately compelled the master of the destroyer USS *Bainbridge* to intervene. A sniper positioned on the destroyer's fantail fired a volley of shots in quick succession. Muse's three compatriots were killed instantly; he was slightly injured. Shortly thereafter both he and his former hostage were taken aboard the *Bainbridge*, where they received medical attention.

The safe return of Captain Phillips brought a joyous close to the incident for most people, but from the legal standpoint it had just begun. The capture (and survival) of Abduwali Muse now presented the United States and the international community with a unique challenge: the first piracy trial on American soil in decades.

"Count 3: Defendant and others . . . combined, conspired, confederated and agreed together and with each other to violate Title 18, US Code, Section 2280 (a) (1) (A)." Behind this dry indictment lay a legal tussle. Not long after Muse arrived in the United States, his mother made a personal plea for clemency to President Barack Obama. The boy, she claimed, was only sixteen. His father put it even lower, at fifteen. Muse himself had told FBI agents that he was sixteen, then amended it later to seventeen. The claim was plausible: in fact, he looks younger still. The legal age of adulthood for trial in a Federal Court is eighteen.

As this matter was debated, others roiled. The first and most obvious question was whether the United States should exercise jurisdiction at all. Trying pirates was a political hot potato: despite the presence of at least fifteen different states' navies in the Gulf of Aden, thus far only Kenya had agreed to prosecute any of those captured. For most nations, the lacunae of multiple nationalities, charges, and applicable legal systems was too much for their courts to unravel. Some countries adopted a bizarre "catch and release" policy, setting free captured pirates rather than face the daunting task of extraditing or prosecuting them. One day before Abduwali Muse's appearance in Federal court—April 20, 2009—word came that the Dutch Navy had released seven Somali pirates captured while attempting to attack a petroleum tanker. The Dutch confiscated their weapons and freed twenty Yemeni hostages. However, as they were technically part of a NATO exercise and not the EU force tasked with piracy patrols, the Dutch government claimed it had no jurisdiction to prosecute. To this appalling statement, US Secretary of State Hillary Clinton commented mildly, "It sends the wrong signal."[5]

Nor could the Somali government offer any assistance. The legal system of the state had broken down in the mid-1990s, and the situation had only deteriorated thereafter. The Somali Mission to the United Nations, too, passed the buck to the United States, as an official, Idd Beddel Mohamed, commented, "Overall, we have full confidence in the American legal system, and I think in due course, justice will be served on both sides."[6]

Nevertheless, the decision to exercise jurisdiction against the defendant Muse was a considerable undertaking for the US Federal court. American piracy law had not been updated in well over a century, and still (as the indictment indicates) deferred to the law of nations in determining which acts were piratical. In some ways it would have been much easier to abandon the piracy charge altogether and concentrate instead on maritime terrorism, which did have a respectable though limited body of statutes. Title 18 of the US Code, Section 2280 dealt with "maritime violence" and was formulated specifically in response to the *Achille Lauro* hijacking twenty-four years earlier (quoted earlier in this book). Muse's actions on board the *Maersk Alabama* clearly fell within its purview, and the entire trial could easily have been conducted on this single charge, thereby eschewing all attempts to link such crimes with their more arcane and anachronistic predecessor.

Yet, on the other hand, could prosecutors really afford *not* to charge Muse with piracy? The word was ubiquitous, so much so that when Muse appeared in federal court on April 22, the *New York Times* ran an article titled "When the City Held Pirates in High Regard," detailing the close relationship between Governor Benjamin Fletcher and the New York pirates in the 1690s. A second "pirate fever" had gripped both the city and the nation. After reading extravagant tales of hijacking, ransoms, and mid-ocean rescues, to redefine the whole incident as "maritime violence" seemed almost a comical understatement.

The prosecution compromised by charging Muse with both offenses as separate counts. Then they added a third, not specifically defined but laden with meaning:

> Count 7: Defendant seized and detained and threatened to kill, injure, and continue to detain another person, namely, a national of the United States, in order to compel a third person and a governmental organization to do or abstain from doing an act as an explicit and implicit condition for the release of the person detained.

The language "in order to compel a . . . governmental organization to do or abstain from doing an act" is significant. It is taken in part from the language of Section 2280, which grants jurisdiction to cases arising from "an attempt to compel the United States to do or abstain from doing any act." Yet both phrases emerge from a single source: ongoing attempts to define terrorism. As recently as 1999, the Terrorist Financing Convention prohibited the financing of "any other act intended to cause death or serious bodily injury to a civilian . . . when the purpose of such act, by its nature or context, is to intimidate a population or compel a government or an international organization to do or to abstain from doing any act."[7]

Clearly the prosecution team recognized what had been obvious since the last century: the crimes of piracy and terrorism are intertwined. Joseph M. Demarest Jr., the director of the New York FBI, told reporters: "Modern-day pirates bear little resemblance to the swashbuckling antiheroes of popular fiction," and referred to Muse and his confreres as "armed hijackers who robbed the ship, threatened the crew, and held the captain hostage at gunpoint."[8] Nowhere was the linkage between the two crimes more apparent than in the original charges against Muse, filed by prosecuting attorneys Michael Farbiarz and Brendan McGuire in federal court on April 21, 2009. The basis of jurisdiction was cited in three precedents: *US v. Yousef*, *US v. Bin Laden*, and *US v. Lei Shi*.

It is worth pausing a moment to consider the significance of these three cases. *US v. Yousef* [9] was the famous trial of Ramzi Ahmed Yousef, a member of al Qaeda responsible for the 1993 bombing of the World Trade Center. Yousef and three other accomplices were also tried for conspiracy to detonate bombs aboard twelve US commercial airliners in Southeast Asia. Yousef, an Iraqi citizen, was apprehended in Pakistan and extradited to the United States to face charges of homicide, concealed weapons, hijacking, and conspiracy. Yousef did not challenge the US government's right to try him for the attempt on the World Trade Center, but countered instead that it had exceeded its jurisdiction in trying him for the airline plot. This, he said, violated customary international law limiting a state's ability to prosecute crimes committed outside its borders, and thus the entire trial violated his right to due process under the Fifth Amendment of the US Constitution. Specifically, he claimed that the applicable statute, Title 18, Section 32, did not apply to acts committed outside the United States. The statute reads in part:

a) Whoever willfully—

1) sets fire to, damages, destroys, disables, or wrecks any aircraft in the special aircraft jurisdiction of the United States or any civil aircraft used, operated, or employed in interstate, overseas, or foreign air commerce;

2) places or causes to be placed a destructive device or substance in, upon, or in proximity to, or otherwise makes or causes to be made unworkable or unusable or hazardous

to work or use, any such aircraft, or any part or other materials used or intended to be used in connection with the operation of such aircraft, if such placing or causing to be placed or such making or causing to be made is likely to endanger the safety of any such aircraft.

In essence, Yousef based his claims on the assertion that terrorists were not *hostis humani generi*. Only pirates, defined as such, merited universal jurisdiction. The district court disagreed, contending that universal jurisdiction was implied in acts of international terrorism. In affirming this judgment, the US Court of Appeals defined the jurisdiction of the United States somewhat more narrowly, avoiding the question of universal jurisdiction and deciding the case on the basis of the *aut dedere aut judicare* principle created by the Montreal Convention and implemented in Title 18, Section 32 and Title 49, Section 46502 (aircraft piracy).

The precedent set in *US v. Bin Laden*[10] was even more extraordinary. In a case that began a year before the attacks of 9/11, Osama bin Laden was charged in absentia with conspiring to detonate bombs in US embassies and other targets around the world. After 9/11, the attacks against the World Trade Center, Pentagon, and civilian aircraft were added. Among the many issues raised in this broad prosecution was whether the CIA acted improperly in searching bin Laden's home in Kenya without a warrant, under the Foreign Intelligence Surveillance Act of 1978. In deciding for the prosecution, the court denied that the warrantless search was improper, as terrorist organizations like al Qaeda could be defined as "foreign powers" for the purpose of the law.

These two cases present us with an encapsulated view of how terrorism is perceived under US law, and it is doubly significant that they are raised as bases of jurisdiction in a piracy case. Both extend US jurisdiction broadly to international terrorists, implying if not explicitly granting universal jurisdiction for their crimes. The bin Laden case goes even further: by defining terrorist organizations as akin to states, the court recognizes their unique status under the law. But the precedent is a dangerous one. Al Qaeda is not a state, and does not obey states' rules. Even granting it status as such for the purposes of FISA was a questionable decision, as it could be equally used to exempt the organization from other charges arising in other contexts.

Nevertheless, the fact that both cases were raised to justify jurisdiction over a Somali pirate is, at the very least, suggestive. It indicates that the argument of this book exists in some fashion already in the minds of the prosecutors and, therefore, in the law. *US v. Yousef* demonstrates that terrorism shares certain elements with piracy; *US v. Muse* appears to argue the inverse.

Given the weighty subject matter of the first two precedents, the last case cited, *US v. Lei Shi*,[11] initially seems undersized. The defendant is not an al Qaeda mastermind, but a Chinese cook aboard a fishing vessel. But in the context of defining piracy as terrorism, this case may well be the most important.

The facts are these. In March of 2002 the defendant Lei Shi, a cook aboard a Seychelles-registered fishing vessel sailing off the coast of Hawaii, became enraged and stabbed both the ship's captain and first mate to death with knives from the ship's galley. He then ordered the second mate to "drive the ship," instructing the other crew that he would execute anyone who disobeyed him. For two days the fishing trawler was under his command, after which time its owners notified the US Coast Guard, which intercepted the vessel sixty miles from Hilo, Hawaii. Meanwhile, the remaining crew had succeeded in overpowering Shi and incarcerating him in a storage compartment. The Coast Guard arrested Shi for violating Title 18, Section 2280, the same "violence against maritime navigation" statute cited in the Muse case, and he was duly charged with one count of seizing control over a ship by force and two counts of performing an act of violence likely to endanger the safety of the ship. After a jury trial, Shi was convicted and sentenced to thirty-six years in prison.

Shi appealed, challenging the district court's jurisdiction. But the Ninth Circuit Court of Appeals confirmed the conviction, Justice O'Scannlain citing Article I, Section 8, Clause 10 of the

Constitution, which empowers Congress to "define and punish Piracies and Felonies committed on the high Seas, and Offenses against the Law of Nations." The United States had every right to prosecute Shi, O'Scannlain wrote, as pirates are subject to universal jurisdiction.

This was an incredible judgment, and a yardstick of how far we have come since twentieth-century debates over the political exclusion for piracy. The significance lies not in Justice O'Scannlain's definition of piracy, but its application. The defendant Shi was not a pirate. He did not board the vessel from a second ship, nor attempt to purloin its fixtures or its catch. Moreover, he was not even charged with piracy, but rather an offense to maritime navigation under Title 18, Section 2280. One might conjecture that the federal government consciously declined to include a piracy charge, on the very grounds that it would be almost impossible to prove on its merits.

But the judge found it, nevertheless. Was this simple error? It is unlikely. The language of the decision suggests something else: that Justice O'Scannlain properly understood Title 18, Section 2280 as applicable to piracy cases. In other words, he declined to distinguish between violence against maritime navigation and piracy; they were, in his opinion, the same crime. It is worth recalling the extensive work done by Samuel Menefee on previous insurgency cases, which likewise were defined in US law as "piracy."

If insurgency is piracy, then there can be no distinction between what occurred on board the Taiwanese vessel or the commercial airliners of 9/11. Moreover, its application by prosecutors to the incidents of the *Maersk Alabama* suggests that they, too, recognize a new and very different definition of piracy. Indeed, if the Muse case demonstrates nothing else, it proves beyond dispute that piracy is, in the twenty-first century, a form of terrorism. The two crimes have coalesced in fact and in law, and they have been recognized as such.

But this is only half the recognition needed to transform the fight against terrorism. The prosecution of Abduwali Muse occurs at a time when the United States has reached a pivotal crossroads. Having tried and failed to define its "war on terror" for almost a decade, the US government has fallen back on regarding terrorists as quasi military combatants. But this definition, as we shall see, has merely isolated the United States from its erstwhile allies, encouraged its enemies, and mired it further in the swamps of legal, political, and procedural confusion. Time and again judges have tried to reach consensus on what a terrorist is—that strange hybrid of ordinary criminal and political actor—only to fall short. The current definition, if one can call it such, is aptly summed up by an earlier Supreme Court justice's definition of pornography: he couldn't define it, he said, but he knew it when he saw it.[12]

That might be good enough for pornography, but it cannot meet the case here. The confusion over definition has already led to excesses and even atrocities. The United States has suspended habeas corpus, created extralegal prison camps to hold detainees without charge (an act whose most recent precedent was the infamous Japanese internment camps during the Second World War), and violated suspects' dignity and human rights. It has also attempted to employ military commissions to try suspected terrorists, yet adopted the bizarre double standard of convening the commission yet denying that it operates within the code of military justice. These commissions, as the Supreme Court recently ruled, were nothing more than kangaroo courts.

These ad hoc and illegal measures, while granting the United States relative impunity, have damaged its overall ability to frame the fight against terrorism and wage it effectively. Broadly speaking, the crucial difference between a state and a terrorist organization is that the former operates within a sphere of law, while the latter does not. It is from the law that states derive their legitimacy. Therefore, if a state refuses to operate within its own laws or bends and confounds those laws to suit its purpose —however justified its leaders may feel in so doing—it has abolished the ethical distinction between itself and its enemies. Whatever the short-term gains, the long-term result is the deni-

gration of a justified police action into a political miasma, with
both sides claiming the moral high ground.

It is no accident, therefore, that even as Abduwali Muse was
held in confinement, awaiting a January 12 court appearance,
New York police raided a Queens apartment and arrested a
young Afghani shuttle bus driver and accused him of assembling
bomb materials for an impending attack on the city. The fight
against terrorism is ongoing, and in the absence of recent piracy
cases it is no surprise that prosecutors chose to employ two of
the most famous terrorist cases in recent history, *Yousef* and *Bin
Laden*, to argue jurisdiction against the pirate Muse.

It is impossible to speculate whether the link between piracy
and terrorism would ever have been presented to us so cogently,
absent the rise of the Somali pirates. Certain trends in the law,
most particularly the development of maritime terrorism as a
discrete crime, suggest that it might. But if piracy and terrorism
were ultimately joined in definition, piracy would almost certainly have been the subordinate: modern piracy would be
joined with maritime terrorism as elements of a much larger
crime, international organized terrorism. Thus the fears of legal
conservatives might well have come to pass. Traditional piracy,
with all its restrictions, two-ship provisions, and private versus
political exclusions, would probably have disappeared altogether. Even as recently as 2005, most prognostications of
future piracy concerned the use of flammable tankers being
hijacked by terrorist organizations and launched against port
cities, much like the commercial airliners of 9/11.

With the advent of Somali piracy, however, that alternative
future has faded. Piracy, in this new yet recognizable form, has
reemerged as a menace in its own right. Its twenty-first-century
iteration is a unique melding of past and present, of pecuniary
and political goals, of traditional two-ship boarding and contemporary hijacking and ransom. This current reality cleaves
through hidebound distinctions between piracy and terrorism
once and for all.

All this is reflected in the trial of Abduwali Muse. The charges against him include the traditionally piratical (count 1), maritime terrorism (count 3), and outright terrorism (count 7). It bases itself on both the right to universal jurisdiction given to all pirates under the law of nations (and recognized by US Law) and the extension of that law to crimes of terrorism under *Yousef* and *Bin Laden*. Finally, it presents the court with a broadened notion of what piracy consists of, and the prerogative of the state to extend it to felonious crimes, under *US v. Lei Shi*. The implication is clear. Whether Abduwali Muse is a pirate, a maritime terrorist, or a terrorist outright, the United States may prosecute him for all crimes jointly and exercise that right under universal jurisdiction. The Muse trial, therefore, has implications not only for the future of piracy under law but also for the future of terrorism as well.

This brings us to a contentious proposition. The first part of this book was devoted to demonstrating that piracy is a form of terrorism. That proposition has been proved, and it is demonstrated in the real-world example of Somalia. The much more difficult task, however, lies in proving the inverse, that terrorism is a form of piracy. Instantly the objections appear: pirates have different motivations than terrorists; piracy involves a specific list of offenses, while possible terrorist acts are considerably broader; terrorist acts do not always (or even frequently) occur at sea. The first and second of these have already been challenged in the first part, where we considered the frequently political motives of pirates, especially in the last century. We also explored how the list of piratical offenses has expanded greatly over time to include nearly all the elements comparable to terrorism: not merely robbery and homicide but hijacking, insurgency, ransom, conspiracy, destruction of property without actual taking, and (in the case of states) offering safe haven for those who plan or commit those crimes.

The final objection, however, appears to be a stumper. However much piracy has expanded, it remains indubitably a maritime crime. It was precisely this quality that distinguished it from land-based felonies in the seventeenth and eighteenth centuries. The sea confers a special status on pirates, separating them physically and symbolically from their states and rendering them free agents, nonstate actors who nevertheless possess some elements of states.

It would be easy to maintain that if we simply remove the maritime component, this precise recognition could be instantly perceived in terrorist organizations. They too gather in extraterritorial enclaves, employ cellular structures dispersing themselves throughout the world, and use their extranationality as a weapon against states. In this conception, the sea loses its territorial qualities and instead becomes that which it was perceived in law since Roman times: the blank space between states. It was not because the sea was blue or wet that jurists chose to distinguish crimes occurring thereupon, but because it lay outside the jurisdiction of any one state. Oceans were, in that sense, the legal domain of pirates. Hence pirates were understood as quasi states whose dominion was the sea itself, and any state was justified in capturing them in "their" territory.

The same is true of terrorist organizations, which exist within not one but many states and often plan attacks against one state while within the boundaries of another. If one considers an organization like al Qaeda not as a collection of individual cells or operatives but a corporate whole, it is in every way as extraterritorial as a pirate band. Recently, scholars have remarked on this quality, comparing terrorist organizations to multinational corporations. But a corporation is still registered under the laws of one particular state; a terrorist organization, for obvious reasons, is not. Like the sea, it touches many nations but binds itself to none; terrorists themselves move fluidly in the gray, amorphous space between.

It is precisely this quicksilver quality that has confounded our attempts to define and even understand international terrorist groups. Domestic criminal law reaches only the crimes that occur within a state; it has no conception of crimes that transcend states. That is the province of international law (and, indeed, the reason why such laws exist), yet international law traditionally concerns itself only with the actions of states and their representatives. Hence a dichotomy exists, states on the one side, ordinary criminals on the other. International terrorists (as distinct from domestic ones) fall exactly halfway in between the two. In recorded history, only one other person has ever occupied that same position: the pirate.

Therefore it will be the task of this part to prove that terrorism, in its essential qualities, is the inheritor of the law of piracy. This does not mean that terrorists necessarily need to *look* like pirates, nor even that their crimes are exactly analogous—although, as we have seen, they often are. The critical question is not whether they are identical, but instead whether the threat they pose merits the same legal response: universal jurisdiction and definition as *hostis humani generi*.

Fortunately, there is already a body of recent precedent to support this proposition. The US federal courts have expanded the concept of universal jurisdiction to cover crimes previously unimagined by scholars even as recently as two decades ago. Since the Second World War, universal jurisdiction has been extended beyond mere piracy to a host of other crimes: genocide, slavery, war crimes, and crimes against humanity. The principle underlying this extension is that such crimes exceed the parameters of domestic criminal law; hence, judges have traditionally distinguished between international crimes as ordinary felonies (much as the English courts once distinguished piracy and felony on the same grounds). One of the stumbling blocks for gaining international cooperation in the pursuit and capture of terrorists is that their crimes mostly fall within the category of felonies: murder, destruction of property, and so on. The larger and more nebulous crime of belonging to a terrorist organization—which the United States has recently tried (and failed) to define as felonious conspiracy—does not fall within domestic criminal law. Without universal jurisdiction, the United States can only pursue terrorists suspected of planning and perpetrating actual attacks against its citizens and must pursue them using the conventional channels of extradition.

Of course, the United States has not done this. It has repeatedly entered sovereign territory, often in hostile states, and seized suspected terrorists. These captures are euphemistically termed "renditions," and have become a serious sticking point between the United States and other nations. Covertly encroaching upon another state and removing its citizens is not merely an example of US unilateralism; it is an act of war. Just as our government has thus far failed to craft a working definition of terrorism for its own courts, it has likewise failed to offer justification for these renditions.

Yet in this instance the federal courts have advanced quicker than the legislature. Two recent cases, both decided in 2009, have opened an exciting possibility. *US v. Alberto Angulo-Hernandez et al.*[13] and *US v. Marco Antonio Salcedo-Ibarra*[14]—the former decided in conjunction with four other cases before the United States Court of Appeals—concerned Mexican drug smugglers caught by the US Coast Guard outside the national waters of the United States. The defendants claimed the United States had no jurisdiction, as no felony had been committed in its territory. Both the District Court and the Court of Appeals disagreed, holding instead that the United States could capture suspected smugglers on the grounds of universal jurisdiction. This is the first time that a US court—much less two courts, independent of one another—has specified that crimes committed by nonstate actors other than pirates could warrant universal jurisdiction. Moreover, the crime of which the defendants were accused was conspiracy to commit a felony; conspiracy and felony are domestic crimes, and so this was also the first time that such crimes could be construed as meriting universal jurisdiction.

If the United States can seize and prosecute drug smugglers outside its borders on the grounds of conspiracy, it is even less of a stretch to posit a similar extension of universal jurisdiction to conspiracy to commit acts of terrorism, or indeed membership in a terrorist organization. In fact, a precedent exists for that as well. In 1991, the United States Court of Appeals for the District of Columbia Circuit heard the petition of Fawaz Yunis. Yunis, also known as Nazeeh, was a member of Hezbollah and leader of a team of hijackers responsible for capturing Royal Jordanian Flight 402 in June 1985. Two years later, Yunis was lured onto a yacht in international waters by agents of the FBI posing as drug smugglers. He was arrested and brought back to the United States, in one of the first-known "renditions" against a foreign national. The fact that the sting operation occurred at sea was not an accident; the FBI deliberately staged it outside the jurisdiction of any state to avoid charges of violating that state's sovereignty. Yunis was tried in federal court[15] and convicted on charges stemming from the fact that four of the plane's passengers were American citizens.

Yunis appealed, citing his "illegal" capture and maintaining that the United States had overstepped its bounds in prosecuting him for a crime occurring outside its jurisdiction. The Court of Appeals disagreed, and Chief Judge Mikva ruled instead that "under the universal principle, states may proscribe and prosecute certain offenses recognized by the community of nations as of universal concern, such as *piracy*, slave trade, attacks on or hijacking of aircraft, genocide, war crimes, and perhaps certain *acts of terrorism, even absent any special connection between the state and the offense.*"

This was revolutionary, as it cleared the way for the United States to apply universal jurisdiction to all acts of terror, even those not specifically targeted at Americans. Strangely, the precedent was ignored (perhaps because it came a decade before the events of 9/11, and thus was largely forgotten). But if one combines the *Yunis* case with the more recent drug smuggling cases, it becomes apparent that US law *already considers* acts of terror to warrant universal jurisdiction, as if they were piracy. Moreover, under *Angulo-Hernandez* and *Salcedo-Ibarra*, American courts can exert jurisdiction over nonfelonious crimes or conspiracy to commit felonies in the United States.

What this means in practice is that our legal system is already positioned to hear cases against members of terrorist organizations that (a) committed attacks against the United States; (b) committed attacks against other nations; (c) conspired to commit such attacks against the United States and/or other nations; and/or (d) were members in a criminal organization that planned or executed such attacks. In other words, the precedent is there to put every single member of al Qaeda on trial. Moreover, the principle of universal jurisdiction conveys not only the right to prosecute but also the right to capture suspects wherever they may be found.

All that is lacking, in fact, is the explicit statement in US law that terrorists are *hostis humani generi*. It is not enough to imply that they are or rely on case law; both measures still force the United States to examine each new case afresh. The principle must be articulated in statutory law, based on the legal linkages discussed in the first part and the weight of precedent emerging from this century.

If we define terrorists as pirates—or, more accurately, as *hostis humani generi* warranting universal jurisdiction—then the potential exists to transform the fight against terror, not only within our own country but also around the world. As we shall see, both the United States and the international community have failed to define terrorism. This failure has crippled our efforts to respond to it because almost a decade after the war on terror began, we still do not fully comprehend what or whom we are fighting. Terrorism is conflated with domestic extremism, religious fundamentalism, Islamic militarism—elements that it may or may not share, but that do not together or separately provide any full understanding of what terrorism *is*. Jurists have also tried approaching the problem from the procedural standpoint, enumerating a list of offenses and labeling them as terrorist. But terrorism is greater than the sum of its offenses. It represents not merely a challenge to persons or property but to the state itself. Just as a virus shares certain qualities with the cells it destroys, the elements of a terrorist organization that remove it from domestic criminality—its statelike qualities—are precisely those that make it most dangerous.

It is those elements, I will argue, which merit a joint definition of piracy and terrorism. Piracy, the original war against all the world, represents the only known precedent for the hybrid state versus nonstate war of today. In addition, by defining the crime and giving it a body of precedent, the United States lays the groundwork for true international cooperation. The ultimate aim of the war on terror is not indefinitely prolonging the next attack, but striking terrorism at its source: the safe havens where terrorist groups are allowed to congregate, train, and plan. If we present ourselves as good-faith partners in the fight to rid the world of an international scourge, the combined effort of the United States and her allies may compel otherwise hostile states to relinquish the terrorists within their borders. Otherwise, under the doctrine of universal jurisdiction, the United States may enter those states and capture the suspects, without violating that state's sovereignty.

This part is divided into two sections. The first will consider attempts to define terrorism in the last century and the reasons it has proved so difficult. The second will go on to present a model definition for the crime of terrorism, drawn from both contemporary attempts at definition and the existing law of piracy. Finally we shall consider the importance of this law, and how it might best be presented to the world.

NOTES

1. *New York Times*, "Somali Piracy Suspect Pleads Not Guilty," May 22, 2009.

2. *US v. Muse*, Indictment before Judge Andrew J. Peck, United States Federal Court for the Southern District of New York, May 19, 2009.

3. See original charges against defendant Abduwali Abdukhadir Muse, submitted by US Attorney for the Southern District of New York, April 22, 2009.

4. See, for example, Associated Press, "Pirate Comes to New York, World Away from Home in Africa," April 22, 2009.

5. *New York Times*, "Pirate Suspect to Be Charged as Adult in New York," April 22, 2009.

6. *New York Times*, "Not Guilty," May 21, 2009.

7. United Nations General Assembly, Measures to Eliminate International Terrorism: Working Group Report, October 26, 1999.

8. *New York Times*, "Pirate Suspect to Be Charged as Adult in New York," April 22, 2009.

9. *US v. Yousef*, US F.3d 56 (2003).

10. *US v. Bin Laden*, 126 F. Supp. 2d 264 (2000).

11. *US v. Lei Shi*, 317 F.3d 715 (2004).

12. Opinion of Justice Potter Stewart, *Jacobellis v. Ohio*, 378 US 184, 197 (1964).

13. *US v. Alberto Angulo Hernandez*, 576 F.3d 59 (2009).

14. *US v. Marco Antonio Salcedo-Ibarra*, US Dist. 62096 (2009).

15. *US v. Yunis*, 924 F.2d 1086 (1991).

Chapter 5

TRIAL AND ERROR

The Definition of Terrorism

If the prosecution of Abduwadi Muse shows us how far the law's potential can reach, another case, decided three years earlier, revealed its limitations. Yet this case, too, is pivotally important in understanding the need for a working definition of international terrorism. In the law failures can be successes in their own right, for by closing down false paths, the proper route may finally be achieved. Let us begin, then, with a notable failure.

In historical retrospect, the events that led to the Supreme Court decision in *Hamdan v. Rumsfeld*[1] will be regarded as an example of executive overreach, an attempt to conceal naked power behind the flimsiest fig leaf of constitutionality. Salim Ahmed Hamdan was a Yemeni citizen captured by the United States during its invasion of Afghanistan and accused of conspiracy to commit terrorism as a member of al Qaeda. Hamdan was detained without charge at Guantanamo Bay, Cuba, and finally brought before a military commission convened under Military Commission Order no. 1, of March 21, 2002. This commission proposed to treat members of terrorist organizations, for the purposes of capture and prosecution, as enemy combatants at war with the United States. Hamdan challenged the validity of the commission, claiming (among other charges) that his right to habeas corpus had been violated, and his prosecution by military commission violated his rights under the Geneva Convention.

The military commissions themselves were built upon a tenuous premise, that members of al Qaeda were legally akin to soldiers acting under a state authority. The problem with this definition is that there was no "state," and therefore no recognized body issuing orders. Moreover, under the Geneva Convention, enemy combatants are granted certain rights as prisoners of war. These rights presume that the soldier is following orders from a superior officer or governing body and is a recognized agent of that body. If he or she is tried for war crimes in the capturing state, that trial must be conducted upon rigorously delineated grounds regarding evidentiary proof and equitable procedure.

The right to a fair trial was the last thing that the Bush administration wished to grant to al Qaeda. Justice Antonin Scalia summed up the government's position months before he sat in judgment over the *Hamdan* case: "I'm not about to give this man who was captured in a war a full jury trial. I mean it's crazy."[2] This policy amounted to having their cake and eating it too: terrorists were "enemy combatants" engaged in a "war," yet without any of the rights customarily awarded to enemy soldiers.

It is hard to pinpoint exactly where this perception of terrorists as combatants took hold. Since the attacks of 9/11 the Bush administration had spoken of a "war on terror," but this was a catchphrase not unlike the Reagan administration's "war on drugs." Then came the invasions of Afghanistan and Iraq, and the "war" took on a new and different meaning. Eager to gather their enemies together on one side of an ideological pole, the American government willingly conflated Taliban sponsorship of al Qaeda, Iraqi WMD's, and sundry other incidents throughout the Arab world as equal facets of the war on terror. By the time of Hamdan's trial, July 2004, the idea of a worldwide war against al Qaeda operatives had given way to a much more localized conception of a war against the leaderships of Iraq and Afghanistan.

But clearly there needed to be some means of distinguishing between ordinary soldiers of the Iraqi Republican Guard and members of al Qaeda, in law if not in propaganda. Hence the Bush administration coined the term *"unlawful* enemy combatant"* (citing a single source, the 1941 saboteur case of *ex parte Quirin*)[3] and claiming it had the right under the 2001 Authorization for Use of Military Force (AUMF) to define certain persons as such and try them under military commissions. The AUMF, passed by Congress in the heady days immediately following the attacks of 9/11, granted President Bush the power to use "use all necessary and appropriate force against those nations, organizations, or persons he determines planned, authorized, committed, or aided the terrorist attacks that occurred on September 11, 2001."[4] President Bush, who was never slow to capitalize on an opportunity to enhance the executive, transformed this power into an order for suspected al Qaeda members "to be detained, and, when tried, to be tried for violations of the laws of war and other applicable laws by military tribunals." These persons were defined as "unlawful enemy combatants."[5]

These military tribunals had been up and running for over two years by the time the defendant Hamdan appeared before them. Human rights organizations decried their existence, but such challenges met with scant success in the legal system. Hamdan's habeas petition was affirmed by the United States District Court for the District of Columbia but unanimously overturned by the three-member panel of judges on the Court of Appeals. Its chances were not rated for much with the Supreme Court, which thus far had been unwilling to check the executive's power in a time of considerable unrest and fear. Chief Justice Roberts had, in fact, been a member of the Court of Appeal panel that upheld the conviction. When certiorari was surprisingly granted, most pundits believed it was merely for the

Supreme Court to formally legitimize the commissions and thereby uphold the government's power.

In oral argument, Hamdan's attorney Neal Katyal claimed that the government's position was contradictory.[6] Either men like Hamdan were ordinary criminals or they were enemy combatants, but they could not be both—they had to be one or the other. If they were ordinary criminals, they were entitled to a jury trial for felonies arising from membership in a terrorist group. They could also be tried for conspiracy. If they were enemy combatants, they were entitled to a military tribunal conducted under the auspices of the Geneva Convention. Either avenue of prosecution, civilian or military, needed to be convened under existing law. But what the Bush administration had achieved with its unlawful combatant tribunals was to conceive a court "literally unbounded by the laws, Constitution, and treaties of the United States."[7]

Moreover, Katyal argued, the additional charge of conspiracy against Hamdan—an essential charge, as he had not actually engaged in any criminal activity but was simply a member of al Qaeda—was not recognized as a war crime under any known military commission. Criminal conspiracy was a felony charge, appropriate only for domestic criminal courts. The reason was obvious: military commissions dealt with the agents of states, and states cannot engage in conspiracies. "Conspiracy has been rejected as a violation of the laws of war in every tribunal to consider the issue since World War II," Katyal told the court. "It has been rejected at Nuremberg, it's been rejected in the Tokyo tribunals, it's been rejected in the international tribunals for Rwanda and Yugoslavia, and, most importantly, it's been rejected by the Congress of the United States in 2005."[8] The idea of a criminal conspiracy suggested something else, even more inimical to the administration's attempts to define terrorists as quasi military combatants. Members of an army cannot be prosecuted for simply belonging to that army; they can only be tried for specific crimes that they themselves engaged in. If the United States wanted to put people on trial for passive membership in al Qaeda, military tribunals were not the way to go. Yet without the ability to make membership in a terrorist organization itself a crime, the United States could never hope to strike at the heart of organizations like al Qaeda.

The untenable quality of the government's position became glaringly clear when the solicitor general, Paul Clement, rose to defend it. The Bush administration had circumvented the Geneva Convention by claiming that when it was written, conflicts like the war on terror had not been envisioned. Katyal slammed this argument, claiming that if the United States was going to call it a war, it was bound to conduct it as such. As Clement began to outline the government's case, Justice Stevens interrupted to ask what sorts of laws these military commissions were designed to enforce. "Well, what I would say, Justice Stevens," Clement answered, "is, they basically enforce the laws of war."

Justice Souter then asked whether the Geneva Conventions were an essential part of the laws of war, and if so, why were they irrelevant? "We're not trying to have it both ways, Justice Souter," Clement said. "The fact that the Geneva Conventions are part of the laws of war doesn't mean that Petitioner is entitled to any protections under those Conventions."[9]

In the end, by a 5–3 decision, Hamdan's conviction was overturned and his petition for habeas corpus upheld. Justice Stevens, writing for the court, went much further than anyone—even Hamdan's lawyers—anticipated. The executive branch had exceeded its authority (as, arguably, had the legislative) and the judicial branch issued a sharp rebuke. "Unlawful military combatant" had no meaning under law: enemy combatants were entitled to tribunals convened under Article III of the Geneva Conventions and "the danger posed by international terrorists, while certainly severe, does not by itself justify dispensing with the usual procedures." Stevens also agreed with Katyal that no military tribunal could convict a defendant on conspiracy, as "no treaty or domestic statute makes conspiracy a war crime, and the historical materials from this country as well as international sources confirm that it is not a war crime under the common law of war."[10]

The Bush administration's most committed attempt to define the crime of international terrorism had met with complete disaster. The military tribunals would continue to be convened, but only against terrorists accused of actually planning or perpetrating crimes against the United States. Moreover, many of the elements that had violated the Geneva Convention—including suspending habeas corpus, controlling witness testimony, and submitting evidence obtained under torture—were gradually revoked. Such commissions continue to this day, although under considerably more equitable conditions.

Nevertheless, these do not represent any real gains in defining terrorism, but rather short-gap measures allowing some justice to be administered by the usual legal channels. They do not address the critical question: are terrorists combatants, criminals, neither, or both?

That question remains unanswered to this day.

ATTEMPTS AT DEFINITION

What is terrorism? The short answer is: we don't know. And not knowing is, as the *Hamdan* case makes clear, a serious problem. Ben Saul recently commented: "Despite the shifting and contested meanings of 'terrorism' over time, the particular semantic power of the term . . . is its capacity to stigmatize, delegitimize, denigrate and dehumanize those at whom it is directed. . . . In the absence of a definition of terrorism, the struggle over the representation of a violent act is a struggle over its legitimacy."[11]

The word *terror* took on political meaning in the eighteenth century, when the horrors of the French Revolution were termed by English commentators the "Red Terror" or "Reign of Terror." For much of its subsequent history, the term denoted illegal brutality by states, until anarchist attacks against world leaders in the nineteenth century were branded terrorism.[12] Gradually this developed into a contemporary understanding of terrorism as violence committed by private individuals to further a political cause, as expressed in the Third Conference at Brussels in 1930:

> The intentional use of means capable of producing a common danger that represents an act of terrorism on the part of anyone making use of crimes against life, liberty or physical integrity of persons or directed against private or state property with the purpose of expressing or executing political or social ideas will be punished.[13]

Thus terrorism as a concept has existed, but that is not the same as a definition. And here we must ask the question of *why*; why should a seemingly simple and easily identifiable act present such a formidable obstacle to international law? The most common response is that terrorism, like piracy, is context specific. Recalling the common adage that "one man's terrorist is another man's freedom fighter," this argument suggests that there simply is no way of providing a definition for acts ranging from ordinary homicide to a convoluted morass of political motivations.[14] This might be termed the cultural relativist argument, and it is not surprising that its most ardent advocates often emerge from the same cultural antecedents as the terrorists themselves. At the opposite end of the spectrum are the universalists, those who would dodge the problem of definition altogether in favor of quick and decisive action. Yet even the best intentioned efforts to define the crime are thwarted by its bogeyman qualities; thus, as Saul notes, in the wake of 9/11 we have seen the term ubiquitously and indiscriminately applied in such instances as "cyberterrorism," "ecoterrorism," "narcoterrorism" and even "agroterrorism."[15] Little wonder that no consensus has yet been reached.

In between these dichotomous positions—one arguing the impossibility of definition and the other its irrelevance—lie the well-intentioned efforts of international law. Beginning with the Convention against Terrorism of 1937 by the League of Nations and extending to the 1996 UN Resolution 51/210 (establishing an ad hoc committee to draft *inter alia* a terrorism convention)—and most recently to the flurry of debate surrounding its exclusion from the justiciable crimes of the International Criminal Court—terrorism's long struggle for definition reflects competing notions of justice, sovereignty, self-determination, diplomacy, universal jurisdiction, *hostis humani generi*, and the law of nations. This chapter is devoted to raising, and answering, the many questions surrounding the recognition of terrorism as an international crime. Such recognition is not only appropriate but vital. The question is how to reach it. Problematically, there are as many different and divergent approaches to dealing with the crime of terrorism as there are to defining it. Often the two are intertwined. There are those, for example, who advocate the inclusion of terrorism in the ICC as a crime against humanity or, alternately, genocide.[16] Others, wary of this attempt to pack and stuff terrorism into crimes that are patently distinct from it, argue instead that terrorism should be a separate category altogether.[17] But this approach raises the old problem of applying a definition for this "new" crime; a problem that the former approach, however contrived, managed to avoid. Although each attempt provides further insight on the crime of terrorism, all fall victim to their own deficiencies. Those who tackle the problem head-on by advocating a new body of terrorist law become ensnared by heterogeneous definitions and political disputes; those trying to avoid the problem by fitting terrorism within existing international law often seem to be pounding a square peg into a round hole. Both endeavors are thwarted by the same paradox: *nulla poena sine legis*, a crime cannot be proscribed until it is defined. As there is no universal definition of terrorism, there can be no universal response.

The second goal of this chapter is to examine the existing international law on terrorism from an evolutionary perspective, with the intention of using its previous course as a yardstick for future progress. Despite the lack of consensus on definition, there have been no less than eighteen international conventions on terrorism since 1963, not to mention a multitude of regional and bilateral agreements. The most startling aspect of this body of law is its scattered, almost slapdash quality; conventions exist covering nearly every aspect of organized terrorism from hijacking to finance, yet none have categorically classified terrorism itself as an international crime. Nevertheless the existing covenants, taken together, may provide the basis for such a classification. Likewise, their lists of proscribed terrorist acts offer a collective definition for terrorism itself, not explicit but rather inferred. The third and final goal of this chapter is to suggest an approach for incorporating the crime of terrorism within international law, an approach (1) built upon the framework of current international law and (2) avoiding the Scylla of culturally relative (and thus ineffectual) legal definitions and the Charybdis of attempting to force nonsynonymous concepts into existing law. This solution is based upon the law of piracy. Rather than trying to place terrorism within the framework of genocide or crimes against humanity—both of which are centered almost exclusively on crimes committed by states, governments, or their representatives—the crime of piracy provides an ideal historical precedent embodying the same tenets of universal jurisdiction, law of nations, and *hostis humani generi* against private individuals without any government nexus. Piracy is, in fact, the *only* crime that applies such principles against private persons. While the attempt to sneak terrorism though the back door to universal jurisdiction by way of genocide or crimes against humanity is laudable, it is also fraught with inconsistencies and an overall sense of illegitimacy. Similarly, regarding those advocating the creation of a new crime of terrorism, piracy law provides the definition and the precedent to buttress such a law and removes it from the miasma of cultural relativism. In short, this chapter advocates a middle ground between the two approaches, one that recognizes the need to incorporate terrorism within existing law yet also appreciates its significance as a crime *sui generis*.

TERRORISM AND THE LAW: 1937 TO THE PRESENT

Aut dedere aut judicare; either extradite or prosecute. This is the fundamental principle that has governed international criminal law since its inception.[18] It places the obligation upon states capturing or harboring international criminals to either prosecute the malefactors themselves or extradite them to another country for prosecution. Until the creation of the ICC in 1998, *aut dedere aut judicare* was found primarily in bilateral or multilateral treaties between states.

The existence of a permanent international criminal court, however, removes the obligation (or, in some circumstances, privilege) of prosecution and extradition for states, extending its jurisdiction over certain international crimes for which state prosecution is considered inadequate.[19] Yet as terrorism does not yet fall within the jurisdiction of the ICC, and most of the conventions regarding it predate the court's inception, the principle of *aut dedere aut judicare* remains in force. The inherently political nature of terrorism confounds a just application of this doctrine, most particularly where the terrorists enjoy the protection of a harboring state. Indeed, regardless of whether the organizations' acts were state sponsored or not, it would be remarkable if its aims did not coincide with those of some rogue government willing to protect it.

Among the most egregious examples of this was the long, difficult process of adjudicating the terrorists responsible for the crash of Pan Am flight 103 over Lockerbie, Scotland. Libya's initial refusal to extradite the accused terrorists, and its persistent delaying tactics after such extradition was eventually achieved, highlight the problems manifest in applying *aut dedere aut judicare* to international terrorism and argue strongly for jurisdiction over terrorists in the ICC.[20] Nevertheless it remains the governing principle of current terrorist law, and as such forms the foundation of our subsequent inquiry into that law's history.

Following the assassination of Alexander I of Yugoslavia by

a Macedonian nationalist in 1937, the League of Nations responded by formulating a Convention for the Prevention and Punishment of Terrorism. It was never entered into force, however, since it only had one signatory, India. The first international convention against terrorism was drafted not long thereafter by the United States and six Latin American nations, with the cumbersome title of the Convention to Prevent and Punish Acts of Terrorism Taking the Form of Crimes against Persons and Related Extortion. While the convention had relatively little effect on deterring terrorism in Latin America, it did facilitate extradition and represents an important development in international customary law.[21]

The UN conventions on terrorism are manifold but are drafted to address the individual threats of terrorist activities, not the crime itself. Beginning with the Convention on Offenses and Certain Other Acts Committed on Board Aircraft of 14 September 1963, they represent a patchwork of individual offenses without any coherent pattern or whole.[22] They seem, indeed, to emerge as responses to individual acts, much as the 1937 convention came in response to an assassination. There are a total of twelve such conventions passed between the years of 1963 to 1999, with relatively high concentrations of activity in the early 1970s and late 1980s. Jennifer Trahan, in her article "Terrorism Conventions: Existing Gaps and Different Approaches," writes that there are "ten multilateral conventions and two protocols addressing a variety of terrorist acts, but no convention covering terrorism generally."[23] Referring to such coverage as "piecemeal," she goes on to classify its breadth and scope. As the elements to the crime of terrorism are of particular relevance to our discussion, this excellent analysis is worth quoting in full:

> *Airplane hijacking and airports.* Airplane hijacking is covered by three conventions, known as the Tokyo, Hague, and Montreal Conventions. The conventions apply to acts occurring while a civilian aircraft is in flight, destroying or endangering the safety of such an aircraft, or damaging or destroying inter-

national air navigation facilities. An additional protocol to the Montreal Convention covers acts against persons at airports, airport facilities, and aircrafts not in service.

Attacking "internationally protected persons." The Convention on the Prevention and Punishment of Crimes against Internationally Protected Persons, Including Diplomatic Agents covers terrorist acts against (a) a head of state, a head of government or a minister of foreign affairs, whenever such person is in a foreign state, as well as any accompanying family members, and (b) any representative or official of a state or international organization of an intergovernmental character, who is entitled to special protection from attack under international law.

Theft of nuclear materials. The Convention on the Physical Protection of Nuclear Material covers unlawful receipt, possession, use, transfer, alteration, disposal, dispersal, theft, embezzlement, or fraudulently obtaining nuclear materials; demanding such materials by use of force; and threatening to use such materials.

Taking hostages. The International Convention against the Taking of Hostages covers "any person who seizes or detains and threatens to lull, to injure, or to continue to detain another person . . . in order to compel . . . a State, an international intergovernmental organization, a natural or juridical person, or a group of persons, to do or abstain from doing any act as an explicit or implicit condition for release of the hostage.

Unlawful acts against maritime navigation and fixed platforms on the continental shelf. The Convention for the Suppression of Unlawful Acts against the Safety of Maritime Navigation covers acts committed on board a ship, destroying a ship, endangering persons on the ship, or destroying or seriously damaging maritime navigation facilities. A protocol extends coverage to fixed platforms on the continental shelf.

Terrorist bombing. The International Convention for the Suppression of Terrorist Bombings covers a person who "unlawfully and intentionally delivers, places, discharges, or detonates an explosive or other lethal device in, into, or against a place of public use, a State or government facility, a public transportation system or an infrastructure facility."

Financing terrorism. The International Convention for the Suppression of the Financing of Terrorism covers "directly or indirectly, unlawfully, and willfully" providing or collecting funds to terrorist organizations or persons engaged in terrorism.

Marking plastic explosives. The Convention on the Marking of Plastic Explosives for the Purpose of Identification obligates states to mark plastic explosives with certain detection agents, and destroy existing stockpiles of explosives that lack those detection agents.[24]

The most striking aspect of this list is the breadth of activities that fall within the rubric of terrorism. Terrorism may well be the most codified and comprehensive crime outside the jurisdiction of the ICC—a potent reason for inclusion in itself. Yet this argument can be reversed; one might equally say that terrorism's multitudinous character makes it impossible to define singly, thus impossible to classify as an international crime. The approach of international jurists heretofore has been to proscribe individual terrorist offenses while avoiding the central question of terrorism itself, thus striking at the beast's limbs instead of its heart.

To further this end, most international conventions on terrorism not only outlaw the activities but obligate states to draft appropriate punishments, search diligently for terrorists within their borders, notify the UN secretary-general of such efforts and, of course, extradite or prosecute.[25] Additionally, many conventions also provide for an extension of state jurisdiction "in certain contexts," tantamount to establishing a principle of universal jurisdiction for some acts of terrorism.

Despite its apparent stringency, the "piecemeal" approach has glaring flaws. First, by continuing to establish conventions in response to new terrorist threats, the law remains always one step behind the terrorists. It cannot be preemptive, nor deterrent. Terrorist organizations have flourished in the later twentieth and early twenty-first century despite such laws and have now become hydras furnishing a new head for each one the law destroys. Second, just as the responsive approach fails to address future possibilities, it leaves fatal gaps in coverage under existing conditions. Trahan points out, for example, that the three conventions addressing aerial terrorism concern acts undertaken "in flight," but contain no reference to such activities on the ground.[26] Furthermore, terrorist attacks in civilian locations are not covered, unless the act occurs in an airport or, bizarrely, a "protected person" is involved. In sum, says Trahan, "addressing terrorism topically is necessarily a responsive approach in that it responds to the types of terrorist methods currently in use or used in the past but fails to address new methods of terrorism."[27] She identifies five major problems: (1) the conventions deal with only "a piecemeal variety of topics"; (2) their focus is primarily on prosecution, not prevention; (3) they exclude from consideration acts occurring within a single state; (4) the obligations they impose on states are insufficient to deter domestic terrorism; (5) they are inconsistent on the question of extradition for terrorism suspects in allegedly political crimes.

The ramifications of these gaps are potentially devastating. The 9/11 attacks, for example, fall outside the purview of the Montreal Convention because the planes were registered in the United States and the attacks made on US soil—thus a "single state" act of terrorism. Even more repugnant is the possibility that terrorists may escape jurisdiction by claiming political motives. Earlier terrorist conventions, like their cognates in piracy, explicitly exclude political acts of terrorism, but provide no real guidance on determining such acts. Encouragingly, later conventions, such as the International Convention for the Suppression of the Financing of Terrorism, seem to have perceived the ludicrous nature of nonpolitical terrorism. This is reflected in the following provision excerpted from that document:

> None of the offences shall be regarded for the purposes of extradition or mutual legal assistance as a political offence or as an offence connected with a political offence or as an offence inspired by political motives. Accordingly, a request for extradition or for mutual legal assistance based on such an offence may not be refused on the sole ground that it concerns a political offence or an offence connected with a political offence or an offence inspired by political motives.[28]

A provision that states that political terrorism will not be construed as political is perhaps not the most logical approach to the problem; it is rather like saying that if it looks like a duck, acts like a duck, and sounds like a duck, it is not for this purpose a duck. Nevertheless, this tautological approach reflects a cognizance among international jurists of the inherently political nature of terrorism, however loosely one may define either term. It also brings us closer to recognizing its similarities to that other quasi-political crime, piracy.

An attempt was made in the late 1990s to correct the flaws of existing terrorist law by formulating a comprehensive terrorism convention, complete with a universal definition. In 1996 the United Nations General Assembly approved Resolution 51/210, creating an ad hoc committee to draft such a convention. The dimensions of the proposed convention, as reflected in a draft copy, were revolutionary. Its stated aims included: (1) defining the crime of terrorism; (2) requiring states to criminalize it accordingly; (3) defining the parameters of state and international jurisdiction over terrorists; (4) requiring states to investigate and, if possible, capture suspected terrorists within their borders; (5) reinstating the principle of *aut dedere aut judicare* for captured terrorists; (6) obligating states to collectively and individually assist each other in their investigations or extradition of suspected terrorists; and (7) mandating that the offense be covered in any and all extradition treaties between states.[29]

Three years in advance of 9/11, this proposed convention would have effectively made terrorism an international crime, perhaps even opening the road to universal jurisdiction. It was not coincidental that this debate ran concurrent to the ratification of the International Criminal Court. There was considerable pressure on member states to include terrorism within the list of the court's juridical crimes. The stage seemed to be set, prior to 9/11, for the creation of a new international crime of terrorism. Yet the debate broke down over the familiar bugbear of "political" terrorism, and no universal definition could be agreed upon.[30] As of this writing, neither the proposed convention nor the proposed ICC jurisdiction have emerged. Instead, the General Assembly adopted in 1997 an International Convention for the Suppression of Terrorist Bombings, which bears superficial similarities to the proposed comprehensive convention in that it too provides for prosecution or extradition. Yet it entirely lacks the cohesiveness and definition of the former, and is thus little more than an addition to the piecemeal list of terrorist crimes. It entered into force on May 23, 2001.

Another source of international terrorist law is the UN Security Council. In a measure designed to reinforce state obligations to fight and prevent terrorism, the Security Council passed Resolution 1373 less than three weeks after the 9/11 attacks, on September 28, 2001. This resolution required member states to undertake numerous measures to combat terrorism and established a Counter-Terrorism Committee to monitor their progress.[31] Significantly, although Resolution 1373 does not provide a definition of terrorism, it mandates state compliance with all existing terrorist conventions. Moreover, it states that it applies to all "terrorist acts," not merely those recognized by existing conventions.

By this extraordinary statement, the Security Council recognizes the limitations of the piecemeal approach, acknowledges the deficiencies of current terrorist law, and allows for both states and the United Nations itself to extend the definition of terrorism to include present realities and future potentialities—

in short, to any act that is or could be recognized by either party as terrorism. In absence of a concrete definition of terrorism, this fluid approach suggests that terrorism may mean whatever acts are mutually agreed upon to be terrorist at a given point in time. The provisions of Resolution 1373 require that states: (1) do not provide any support, financial or otherwise, to terrorist groups; (2) take all possible steps to deter terrorist acts, including the establishment of an early warning system; (3) refuse to grant sanctuary to terrorists or their accomplices; (4) ensure through domestic laws that terrorists and their accomplices are brought to justice; (5) give each other "the greatest measure of assistance in connecting with criminal investigations or criminal proceedings."

Thus Resolution 1373 attempts to fulfill the function of the proposed comprehensive terrorism convention without concerning itself with the problem of definition. Its relation to preexisting UN law is analogous to that between the Monroe Doctrine and the Roosevelt Corollary in the United States; the former as an expression of policy, the latter of the will to enforce it.

The current attitude of the United Nations toward organized terrorism could be expressed thus: Terrorism is any act that we have heretofore declared it to be, as well as any act that we may in future decide to include; all states carry the obligation to prevent and punish these acts equally. While this approach has the virtue of adaptability, it is far from ideal. The persistent difficulty of formulating a definition for terrorism cannot be ignored, nor sidestepped. The attitude of the Security Council is dangerously close to the aforementioned judge who declared he couldn't define terrorism, but knew it when he saw it. The problems inherent in this approach are manifest. Rigid legal definitions become archaic over time as new realities emerge, and must be adapted to fit changing circumstances; the common-law system, recognizing this fact, provides within its apparatus a means for the law to evolve.

International criminal law is engaged in a similar process of evolution, building upon the precepts established under the law of nations regarding piracy, responding to new atrocities with new forms of criminal conduct after Nuremberg, culminating in the creation of an International Criminal Court in 1998. Just as the ICC was established to replace individual ad hoc tribunals, the recognition of certain international crimes evinces a desire to transcend mutable lists of proscribed offenses in favor of universal, immutable definitions. Of these, customary law furnished the crime of piracy, while Nuremberg supplied war crimes, aggression, and crimes against humanity. Even absent all argument of terrorism as a form of piracy, the paramount menace it poses to contemporary society alone provides sufficient grounds for inclusion. In defense of the Security Council, it could be argued that the date of Resolution 1373— September 28, 2001—reflects a willingness to face the problem of terrorism swiftly and effectively, without miring the international community in further debate over universal definitions. If the immediacy of circumstances post-9/11 prompted Resolution 1373, then its approach is justified. But years have passed since then, and no second resolution or convention has emerged to settle the question of definition that Resolution 1373 blithely avoided. The crime of global terrorism promises to be the scourge of the twenty-first century, no less than piracy was of the seventeenth. Just as the pirates' golden age resulted in the establishment of the first international crime, so too must the United Nations face the problem of terrorism squarely and give it the recognition in law it truly warrants.

Although it admittedly falls short of the sweeping aims envisioned by the General Assembly's Resolution 51/210, Resolution 1373 is nevertheless a crucial step toward the creation of an international crime of terrorism. The divergent approaches (and results) of the General Assembly and the Security Council also reflect a key aspect of international law: duality. Unlike domestic legislation, international law emerges from a variety of sources: customary law, treaties, scholarly opinions, and multinational organizations. Even within the United Nations there are distinct sources of law and distinct kinds of law. As to the latter, law may emerge from declarations, resolutions, protocols, covenants, undeclared drafts (such as the failed Resolution 51/210), bilateral or multilateral agreements between specific states, and conventions. Although the viability of enforcement varies widely between them, each serves as a precedent either for future conventions or customary law. As to the former, the debate over terrorism has produced two distinct legal documents from two distinct bodies: the General Assembly's 1997 International Convention for the Suppression of Terrorist Bombings, and the Security Council's 2001 Resolution 1373. These do not exist in conflict, but in tandem; the stated purpose of Resolution 1373 is to serve as an umbrella document for the existing terrorist conventions, mandating compliance on each.

Similarly, although the United Nations is the most widely recognized of the international legal organizations, it is not singular. The problem of organized terrorism has been addressed by a number of different multinational bodies, most particularly in the Americas and the Middle East. The Organization of American States adopted in May 2002 an Inter-American Convention against Terrorism, criminalizing a host of terrorist crimes in the Americas and facilitating extradition.[32] Even more significantly, the League of Arab States recently passed an Arab Convention for the Suppression of Terrorism that binds signatory states to a number of "preventive measures," including declining to allow terrorists to use their lands as training camps, pooling intelligence, coordinating joint efforts at capture, and heightening surveillance within their borders.[33] Once again there is a reference to *aut dedere aut judicare* obligations, but there is a significant addendum: states must also undertake to protect prosecutors, informants, and witnesses from harm. The recurring watchword of the Arab Convention is cooperation: states must cooperate with each other in establishing extradition protocols, police forces must cooperate in tracking and capturing terrorists, intelligence services must cooperate by sharing information. While the existing state of Arab relations and the burgeoning spread of terrorist activities in the region raise unfavorable comparisons between the Arab Convention and such diplomatic pipe dreams as the Kellogg-Briand Pact, its significance may lie more in precedent than enforceability. The Arab Convention elucidates: first, a recognition of the multi-layered complexity of formulating an antiterrorism response; second, a willingness—at least in theory—to create such a response. Overall, the convention is a recognition by states (even those states that continue to harbor and aid terrorist activities) that terrorism is an illegitimate use of force and that terrorists themselves are not legitimate actors on the international stage. This is but one short step from a final recognition of terrorists as *hostis humani generi* under international law.

There may be no universal definition for terrorism, but there is no shortage of attempts to furnish one. One scholar defines it as "the threat or use of violence in order to create extreme fear and anxiety in a target group so as to coerce them to meet political (or quasi-political) objectives of the perpetrators."[34] Others have attempted to break terrorism down into its component parts, concluding that the crime of terrorism consists of (1) violence, actual or threatened; (2) a loosely defined "political objective"; and (3) an intended audience. Yet even within these simple approaches, the perennial problem of distinguishing between insurgents and terrorists is apparent. At least one commentator has tried to sidestep the freedom fighter dilemma by defining terrorism as the instigation through violence of "mass fear and panic with the ostensible purpose of advancing revolutionary political goals, but often expressing a more prosaic criminal element and motivation as well."[35]

Perhaps the best definition is that suggested by Professor M. Cherif Bassiouni. Bassiouni correctly perceives terrorism as inherently international and extending to both private and government-sponsored actors; he defines it as follows:

> an ideological-motivated strategy of internationally proscribed violence designed to inspire terror within a particular segment of a given society in order to achieve a power-outcome or to propagandize a claim or grievance irrespective

of whether its perpetrators are acting for and on behalf of themselves or on behalf of a state.[36]

Terrorists are a hybrid: half revolutionary, half street thug. Their ostensibly political motives remove them from the common category of criminals that their crimes would otherwise place them, but this same faux-revolutionary status makes them a greater menace, not a lesser one. The United States incorporates an understanding of this potentiality in it own legal code, which defines terrorism as:

> An activity that involves a violent act . . . that is a violation of the criminal laws of the United States or of any State . . . and appears to be intended—(i) to intimidate or coerce a civilian population; (ii) to influence the policy of a government by intimidation or coercion; or (iii) to affect the conduct of the government by assassination or kidnapping.[37]

Yet while some scholars actively engage in the search for a universal definition, others maintain that well enough should be left alone. They regard the piecemeal status of current terrorist law as both necessary and inevitable. Terrorism, these jurists maintain, is impossible to define independent of its acts. This conclusion is based on two presumptions: first, that no universal definition could take into account the myriad acts that terrorism encompasses; second, that it is legally impossible to draw lines fine enough to distinguish between "legitimate" revolutionaries and "illegitimate" terrorists. This rather timid approach seems to owe much to another source: cultural relativism. The nemesis of all universal international law, cultural relativism is briefly defined as the belief that each law is culture specific and dependant on that culture for its legitimacy. Thus there is no absolute understanding of right or wrong, but merely divergent cultural practices. When applied to the problem of organized terrorism, the relativist approach maintains that any "universal" definition of terrorism will be inherently Western centrist in nature, and thus likely to label the legitimate political aims of revolutionary organizations as terrorist. The statement that "one man's freedom fighter is another man's terrorist" emerges from this logic. Cultural relativism also provides an ideal excuse for states sponsoring terrorism and advocating it as a quasi-legitimate means of warfare. If there is no absolute definition of terrorism, then terrorism is merely what each state declares it to be. Even if certain acts are declared to be terrorist under international law, the lack of a universal definition leaves the door open for counterarguments that (1) the terrorist act was committed as part of a legitimate revolutionary uprising or (2) state military actions such as Operation Iraqi Freedom are acts of terrorism. The inevitable result is a Babel of contradictory claims and perspectives; for anarchy and cultural relativism are blood brothers beneath the skin.

The piecemeal approach does have the virtue of flexibility; as long as there is no overall definition of terrorism to defer to—and thus the current state of terrorism never exceeds the sum of its parts—its definition can be stretched to include any act that a consensus of jurists agree upon. Yet enticing as it may be to thus avoid the problem of worldwide terrorism by continuing to define it by its acts rather than its character, the piecemeal approach owes less to efficiency than cowardice. It represents not so much the inability of states to agree upon a universal definition as their unwillingness to do so.

History shows us time and again that avoiding a problem only worsens it. So it is with terrorism: the continued survival of haphazard, disjointed terrorist law—resulting from the lack of a universal definition—has not only failed to curb terrorism but has allowed it to flourish. Advocates of the piecemeal approach exist, like terrorist law itself, in the state of legal somnolence that preceded 9/11, sharing its worldview within that comforting, illusory sphere. But the United States and its allies no longer harbor such illusions, which is why the war on terrorism has occurred thus far in a relative vacuum of international law. It is more urgent now than ever to match the energies of the United States, and those of the terrorists, with a vigorous and pragmatic international law.

With universality as our goal, there remains the problem of

approach. As I indicated earlier, scholarly arguments for a universal definition fall into two general categories: those who advocate including terrorism within existing international law, and those who seek to create a new, independent category. These divergent opinions emerge from a recognition of the most fundamental problem in terrorist law: the establishment of a successful balance between legitimacy and efficiency. Those favoring the incorporation of terrorism within existing law stress the primacy of international recognition, acceptance, and corresponding legitimacy. Defining terrorism as a war crime, crime against humanity, or genocide has the undoubted advantage of facilitating its acceptance into the rubric of international law. Terrorism *qua* genocide means, in effect, that the crime of terrorism is merely a new strain of a preexisting virus. In contrast, those who favor the creation of an independent category for terrorism argue that terrorism is a crime *sui generis*, both deserving and necessitating a new body of law. They advocate the recognition of terrorism as a violation of the law of nations and the requisite establishment of terrorism as a separate crime under the jurisdiction of the International Criminal Court.

THE FIRST APPROACH: TERRORISM AS A SPECIES OF GENOCIDE, WAR CRIMES, AND CRIMES AGAINST HUMANITY

Shortly after September 11, 2001, US Secretary of State Colin Powell termed the attacks not merely "a crime against the United States, but a crime against humanity."[38] It is not clear whether the phrase "crime against humanity" was meant to be interpreted in its legal sense—that is, as one of the enumerated crimes of Nuremberg and the ICC—or merely rhetorical. Nevertheless, at least one author has taken him at his word. James D. Fry, in his article "Terrorism as Crime against Humanity and Genocide: The Backdoor to Universal Jurisdiction," argues that the crime of terrorism may be incorporated into the jurisdiction of the ICC by means of legal analogy. His intentions are very similar to my own efforts with regard to piracy: first, allowing "large-scale acts of terrorism to be viewed in their proper light . . . when the requisite elements are present," (that is, giving terrorism a definition under the law); second, to facilitate "the prosecution of terrorists by all states because universal jurisdiction is available with crimes against humanity and genocide, whereas it is unavailable with terrorism since it lacks a universal definition."[39]

Fry employs the lawyer's popular device of an "either-or" argument. Terrorism, he writes, may be properly defined as a crime against humanity, genocide, or both. With regard to crimes against humanity, he cites 9/11 as a case in point. "The terrorist attacks of September 11," he writes, "satisfy all of the elements . . . for crime against humanity."[40] Fry raises the following in support of this proposition:

> First, the attack was part of a widespread and systematic war against the United States. These attacks were not random or isolated attacks, but were part of a coordinated assault against the United States that has continued for almost a decade. . . .
>
> Second, these attacks were against a civilian population. . . . In Bin Laden's fatwa dated February 23, 1998, he ordered all Muslims to "kill the Americans and their allies, civilian and military," and "to kill the Americans and plunder their money wherever and whenever they find it."[41]
>
> Third, Bin Laden had knowledge of the attacks in advance. . . .
>
> Fourth, a course of conduct involving the multiple commission of these types of acts was involved. The September 11 attacks involved the hijacking of four passenger planes, each of which was a catastrophic terrorist attack in and of itself. . . .
>
> Fifth, Bin Laden intended to engage in the conduct. . . .[42]

Fry makes a similar argument, although somewhat less detailed, for defining terrorism as genocide. Noting first that the requirements of genocide are similar to those for crimes against humanity, he stresses that the attacks of 9/11 were "committed with the intent to destroy a particular group in whole or in part"' and were "similar, if not greater, than the acts that led to the satisfaction of this element in previous genocide convictions in the International Criminal Tribunals."[43] Generally, he argues that the fundamental requirement for genocide that a significant number of persons are systematically eradicated with the intention of destroying the group as a whole is more than adequately met by the aims and actions of al Qaeda. Bin Laden, as its spokesman, declared in 1998: "A target, if made available to Muslims by the grace of God, is every American man. He is an enemy of ours whether he fights us directly or merely pays his taxes."[44] Fry makes the distinction between bin Laden's fatwa and conventional warfare. Bin Laden's intention is not merely to cripple the United States or to effect a change in its foreign policy, but to wipe it from the face of the earth. As such, Fry argues, his actions are removed even from those of the common terrorist to a higher plane of international genocide.

The policy arguments for adopting Fry's approach are appealing, to say the least. Classifying terrorism as genocide or a crime against humanity solves the problem of creating a universal jurisdiction—or, at least; sidesteps it. Moreover, it places terrorism within the jurisdiction of the ICC, establishing it as an international crime. For the first time, terrorists could be captured and tried not only by individual nation-states but by the world itself. Fry writes that "by providing all states with universal jurisdiction to prosecute suspected terrorists wherever they are to be found, a strong message is sent to terrorists that they are never safe from prosecution."[45] This is certainly true: the establishment of terrorism as an international crime rescinds the right of states to provide safe harbor for suspected terrorists. The significance of making terrorism a crime of universal jurisdiction cannot be overemphasized, for it would transform the manner in which terrorists are pursued, captured, and adjudicated throughout the world. Moreover, Fry argues, terming terrorism as genocide or a crime against humanity gives it its due recognition as a global menace that exceeds the harm done by individual terrorist acts. This is also incontestable. The question is not whether terrorism deserves to be classified as an international crime, but whether it can be classified as genocide/crime against humanity.

Herein lies the problem with Fry's hypothesis. His policy arguments are persuasive but merely demonstrate the need for a cohesive terrorist law, not the form that that law should take. Moreover, his reasons for relating terrorism to genocide and crimes against humanity are hindered by the fact that he bases them only on a single incident of terrorism, 9/11. While 9/11 may fit the jurisdictional requirements of a crime against humanity, legal scholars would not be hard-pressed to supply other acts of terrorism that do not. The problem of relating terrorism to either category is that the definitions of neither genocide nor crimes against humanity were designed to incorporate it. They are predicated on a very different sort of crime, committed not by private actors but by the state. Both emerge from the same historical precedent, Nazi Germany, and both reflect the implicit assumption of state action in their definitions. While one must applaud Fry for perceiving the relation between 9/11 and these crimes (indeed, this book attempts a similar comparison to piracy in chapter 4), one incident alone cannot serve as the basis for complete legal recognition. Ultimately, the admitted gains of incorporating terrorism within these existing definitions—universal jurisdiction, deterrence, international accountability—will be undermined by the inability of states to determine which acts of terrorism fit within the asynchronous definitions of genocide and crimes against humanity. It is not difficult to foresee fierce battles in the international community over whether a given act was grand enough in scope to be considered genocide, or barbarous enough to be a crime against humanity. Some will be, certainly, but a definition of terrorism must take into account not only coups de grace like 9/11 but the smaller, seamier aspects of organized terrorism as well.

There has also been an effort to define at least some forms of terrorism as war crimes. Michael Rossetti writes: "War crimes are similar in nature to acts of terrorism because of the illegitimacy of targets and types of violations. War crimes, like terrorism, can be directed at a variety of targets but the true illegitimacy of these actions is evident when the victims are civilians or their property."[46] While Rossetti does not actually advocate classifying terrorism as a war crime under ICC jurisdiction, the parallels he draws between the two are instructive in considering terrorism as a crime of universal jurisdiction. The law of nations, Rossetti writes, was recently expanded to include war crimes. This international recognition should, he argues, pave the way for a second regarding organized terrorism.[47]

THE SECOND APPROACH: TERRORISM AS A CRIME *SUI GENERIS*

As with any law, an enforceable terrorist law must reflect at least two components: it must be perceived as legitimate, and it must be perceived as just. These two requirements are not easily met, nor are they complementary. We have already seen the lengths to which some scholars will go to give the law its legitimacy; they suggest, in effect, an act of legal legerdemain by which terrorism is transmogrified into genocide, and so on. The problems with this endeavor have already been addressed. A second body of jurists, however, propose to solve the problem of terrorism under the law by focusing on its second component, justice. They advocate the creation of an entirely new body of law, and an entirely new legal definition, for organized terrorism.

The advantage to declaring terrorism an international crime *sui generis* is that this is the only method that ensures that terrorism receives its due recognition under the law. The alternatives— the "piecemeal" and (as I term it) "pack-and-stuff" approaches —leave significant gaps in the law and, by failing to give terrorism a universal definition unto itself, likewise fail to provide a commensurate legal response. Advocates of a universal definition stress that the menace of terrorism and its unique hybrid character mandate recognition as a distinct legal entity. The realities of contemporary terrorism, discussed above, lend credence to this conviction. But the problems raised by the universal approach are no less serious than those of its counterpart. In fact, they are inverse; the creation of a terrorist law *de novo* would require international consensus on a definition *without* any legal precedent bolstering it (excepting the hodgepodge of existing terrorist conventions), thus raising the same obstacles of legitimacy and consensus that the first approach avoided.

The basic position of the universalists could be summarized as follows: Terrorism has become a crime of international proportions, affecting not merely the commerce and security of one state or a group of states but all states; accordingly, the international community understands terrorism to be a violation of the law of nations; this understanding, although tacit, has no expression in written law; such law must be drafted, and it must include (1) a universal definition of terrorism; (2) recognition of terrorism as a crime of universal jurisdiction; (3) adequate provisions for pursuing, capturing, and adjudicating terrorists; and (4) demarcation of venue, which may include domestic courts, ad hoc tribunals, permanent tribunals, and/or the ICC.[48]

Advocates of the *sui generis* approach unanimously concede the necessities of a universal definition and appropriate venue for terrorism, but that is the limit of their consensus. Debates rage over which definition to adopt and which courts should have jurisdiction.

Although the proposed universal definitions of terrorism are far too numerous to list, most fall within two basic categories. These may be termed, for convenience, "loose" and "rigid" definitions. The loose definition attempts to paint the crime of terrorism in broad strokes, leaving room for ad hoc judicial decisions and unforeseen contingencies. This school of thought, says Michael Rossetti, "espouses a single unambiguous standard which incorporates the principles of just means and just cause in defining terrorist activity. The thrust of this argument is that whatever form an insurgency takes, the critical elements are whether or not the activity had sufficient justification and, if so, whether the means to carry it out were legitimate."[49] The virtue of this definition is its adaptability; adjudicators have the prerogative to determine acts of terrorism on a case-by-case basis, guided by a simple legal test of legitimacy in ends and means. But such judicial laissez-faire also grants judges enormous latitude in distinguishing between "legitimate" insurgency and "illegitimate" terrorism, without much guidance on how to do so. "It is asserted," Rossetti writes, "that it would be difficult to find support in the international community for an illegitimate insurgency or even a valid one effectuated through the use of violence against civilian targets."[50]

The rigid approach criticizes its counterpart for vagary and suggests that such a definition would be little removed from "knowing terrorism when we see it." By defining the crime in such broad terms, terrorism would have no real definition whatsoever. Vague definitions, they argue, "perpetuate the failure to mold international law to insure the effective administration of justice."[51] Instead, proponents of the rigid approach argue that any definition for terrorism must include a list of enumerated acts that comprise the offense. Rossetti writes: "This approach to defining terrorism seeks to include the condemned activities while also providing for any new forms of terrorism that may emerge. This approach provides a more rigid mechanism for enforcing claims against terrorists because it removes the ambiguities inherent in a general approach."[52]

While the rigid approach solves the problem of vagary, it raises many of the same doubts as the piecemeal approach discussed earlier. If terrorism is reduced to a list of offenses, the likelihood that an incident will eventually come to challenge that list is almost certain. The response of its advocates is that the list may be expanded for "any new forms of terrorism that may emerge," but again, this would be little different from the passage of yet another convention under the current system. To use an old expression, this would be like closing the barn doors after the horses escape.

If the former approach fails to provide a universal definition of terrorism by defining it too broadly, the latter fails by defining it too narrowly. The loose approach gives terrorism its due recognition but does not adequately enumerate its components; the rigid approach emphasizes those components at the expense of due recognition. The problems encountered here are those which every nation faces when drafting its criminal code: striking balance between broad principles and practical realities to achieve a just law in result. And, as each nation has discovered, the answer lies in compromise. The universal definition for terrorism must give the offense its due status as a violation of the law of nations and must be sufficiently broad to encompass a variety of activities known and unknown at the time of its drafting. It must also contain some parameters of the offense beyond mere judicial determination, and these must include some kind of list of proscribed offenses. One such compromise would be to define terrorism as the advocates of the first approach suggest, follow this definition with a list of terrorist activities, and include a provision that this list is not exclusive of new realities, about which judges may employ their discretion under the guidance of existing international law.

As I have argued, placing terrorism within the legal definition of piracy adequately addresses all of these problems by giving terrorism a definition under the law, a history of precedent, a list of offenses, and the potential for expanding to include new forms of terrorism should the need arise. The legitimacy test will thus be construed as whether the accused acted as part of a justifiable insurgency—that is, "quasi state" status as I have defined it previously—or privately, in which case he becomes a pirate under the law. Similarly, as the list of piratical offenses is virtually synonymous with those ascribed to terrorism, a legal construction of terrorism as a species of piracy provides it with parameters that not only meet contemporary realities but draw from hundreds of years of legal precedent as their source.

The recognition of terrorism as an international crime subject to universal jurisdiction is meaningless without the correlating establishment of a venue for such crimes to be adjudicated. There are some who favor the creation of a special international court with sole purview of terrorist crimes, but the impracticality of its creation and the unlikelihood of achieving international consensus render this possibility remote at best. Most scholarly debate centers instead on whether the new terrorist law be adjudicated by domestic courts acting under international legal standards (an approach similar to that of the 1999 Working Group for Uniformity of the Law of Piracy), by states enforcing the principle of *aut dedere aut judicare* by traditional techniques of shaming or sanctioning states that harbor terrorists or by establishing terrorism as a distinct offense under the jurisdiction of the ICC. The idea of incorporating new terrorist law into domestic legislation is best expressed by Michael Rossetti. The Alien Torts Claims Act (ATCA) of the United States has been employed to allow aliens to bring civil actions for tort claims against other aliens when there is no traditional nexus between the actors, the tort and the forum state.[53] A comparatively obscure provision of the US Code, it was invoked successfully only twice between 1789 and 1979. In the case of *Filartiga v. Pena-Irala* in 1980, however, the US Second Circuit declared that torture, as a violation of international human rights, was legitimate grounds for an ATCA tort action if the accused was served in the United States. The door was thus opened for a series of cases under the ATCA against both individuals and governments, including those of the Philippines, Guatemala, Ethiopia, and Argentina. The second landmark case, also decided by the Second Circuit of the US Federal Court, was *Kadic v. Karadic*. Previously, cases involving torture and other violations of the law of nations could only be brought against states or agents acting on behalf of states. *Kadic*, however, extended jurisdiction to private individuals acting without state authority in cases where there was "sufficient international accord that the torts alleged were in violation of the law of nations." This decision, says Rossetti, clears a path for the civil actions against terrorists under the ATCA.

His argument rests on a very specific understanding of international terrorism. As was noted earlier, Rossetti draws the link between terrorism and war crimes, which are universally recognized as violations of the law of nations. If terrorist acts are akin to war crimes, they are similar violations and judicable under the ATCA. Thus, he says, the United States might avoid the dubious task of deferring to international law to supply a definition for terrorism, especially as no concrete definition currently exists. *Filartiga* and *Kadic* provide precedents under existing domestic law for the adjudication of terrorists in the US civil courts, even in cases where neither the plaintiff nor defendant are US citizens.

The argument for adjudicating terrorism in domestic courts is attractive, but it is scarcely adequate to address the realities of twenty-first-century terrorism. First, nearly all domestic courts have some form of terrorism legislation already, either in the form of comprehensive antiterrorist laws (which are usually both recent and comparatively rare) and criminal statutes covering most, if not all, known terrorist activities. Second, the function of an international terrorist law will be to create an international standard for defining acts of terrorism, to recognize terrorism as a violation of the law of nations, and to standardize an international legal response to terrorism through universal means of definition, capture, and adjudication. Domestic legislation cannot do any of this. Third, the invocation of the ATCA applies only to civil litigation; even accepting its availability, the problem of criminal jurisdiction is still to be faced. While Professor Rossetti's arguments are persuasive, the course he proposes can go only so far, and not far enough. In his defense, this article was written in 1997, and the world has changed considerably since then.

Professor Rossetti is not alone in his fears over a successful resolution to the debate over terrorism's definition. Alfred P. Rubin sees grave problems in the recognition of terrorism as a crime in international law, most particularly the possibility of including it within the jurisdiction of the ICC. First, he writes, is the problem of lawyers "ruling the world according to their own versions of the law, in disregard of the notions of law held by those who disagree with them."[54] He goes on to dispute the entire concept of an international criminal court:

> I am reminded of Plato's Republic, in which rule by "guardians" is proposed. It is pointed out that those selected by whatever means to be guardians, if they are truly fit for the role, will certainly refuse it. . . . Yet I know of few international lawyers who would refuse selection to positions in the international court or its prosecutorial arm. They would all like to rule the world according to their notions of "law"; but since lawyers notoriously disagree about written, let alone unwritten, law, the anticipation that the members of the tribunal and its prosecutorial arm would share the same liberal values seem unduly optimistic. It also begs the famous question: "Who guards the guardians?"[55]

Although the title of his article is "Legal Response to Terror: An International Criminal Court?" it is perfectly clear that Professor Rubin questions not only the efficacy of giving ICC jurisdiction to terrorism but also the ICC itself. "An international criminal court," he writes, "seems fundamentally inconsistent with democratic processes."[56] The argument here is that the prosecution of individual criminals acting as leaders or agents of a government is an unwarranted intrusion on state sovereignty, subjects these persons to the will of the fickle and perhaps hostile international community, and fails to bring justice to the victims. In an extraordinary passage that could have been drawn verbatim from the defendants' arguments at Nuremberg, Rubin declares:

> All the [ICC] does is have foreigners do what the domestic order would rather not, for fear of provoking an unfavorable reaction by its citizenry. . . . For foreigners to question the governmental acts of any government seems to involve necessarily an intrusion into the internal affairs of the acting state. A large populace might support a repressive regime, as Germany as a whole probably supported Hitler in the late 1930's. . . . To

attach criminal liability to the persons elected or selected to represent that large populace seems to blame a single person or
small group for the default of a very large group.[57]

The principle of individual accountability by leaders or
agents of the state for criminal acts committed by that state was
established in 1945, and has remained—despite Professor
Rubin's objections—the governing principle of international
criminal law ever since. Moreover, his argument that lawyers
are inherently unfit to govern the law seems not unlike Groucho
Marx's crack that he would never belong to a club that would
take him for a member.

THE THIRD APPROACH: TERRORISM WITHIN EXISTING ICC JURISDICTION

The third and most sensible solution to the promulgation of a
new international terrorist law is the inclusion of terrorism
within the jurisdiction of the ICC. Professor Rubin's objections
on this point seem directed more at the ICC itself than the efficacy of granting it jurisdiction over terrorism. Furthermore,
they rely on concepts of state sovereignty and immunity that are
not only erroneous since 1945 but irrelevant. If adopted, terrorism would in fact be the only judicable crime in the ICC that
would not require a nexus to the state.

The possibility of incorporating terrorism within one of the
four crimes under current ICC jurisdiction has already been discussed. The alternative, creation of terrorism as a fifth offense,
has been the subject of considerable debate. Recognizing the
problem of a legal vacuum in the United States' war on terror,
Todd Sailer sees ICC jurisdiction as the answer: "A better
solution to international terrorism is to lessen the need for
nations to respond to terrorists and other international criminals with force. Instead, the international legal system needs to
be strengthened and made more effective in bringing the world's
villains to justice."[58]

Some scholars maintain that the ICC was never intended to deal with nonstate crimes like terrorism. This, as Sailer points out, is not the case. As early as 1937, the Convention against Terrorism of the League of Nations undertook to create an international criminal court to prosecute terrorist crimes. The issue of terrorism was again raised in connection with international justice in the 1980s, when the Soviet Union—which had previously been opposed to the creation of the ICC—reversed its position on the grounds that an international criminal court would be ideal for prosecuting terrorist crimes. Even in the United States, the efficacy of ICC terrorist jurisdiction has found supporters. Senator Arlen Specter stated before Congress that "if we could have a convention that lists specific terrorist offences, each with proper elements, and establish an international . . . criminal court to prosecute these offences, it would actually assist in the battle against terrorism."[59] Terrorism's noninclusion in the ICC does not denote that it has no place there, but rather that no consensus has yet been achieved on its definition. Sailer offers his own:

> A simple definition is readily available which would effectively resolve the ambiguities inherent in the term "terrorism." This would involve drawing the line between an impermissible terrorist act and a political offence according to the victim or target of the act in question. If violence is intentionally directed at civilians or civilian property, then the act should be labeled as terrorism.[60]

There are many reasons, as Sailer points out, for favoring the ICC over strictly domestic jurisdiction for terrorism. First, ICC jurisdiction would prevent incidents such as the Lockerbie dispute, where Libya resisted extradition of suspected terrorists on political grounds. If terrorism is classed as an international crime, states could no longer harbor suspected terrorists; if the ICC had jurisdiction, states could not hamper the extradition process. "The ICC could avert situations like the Lockerbie affair if it had jurisdiction over terrorism," says Sailer.

Either the Security Council, a member state, or an independent prosecutor could refer such cases to the ICC. . . . The ICC is designed to complement national judicial systems in situations, such as the Lockerbie case, where a national judicial system is either unable or unwilling to carry out investigation or prosecution. *The ICC could thus be very effective in eliminating safe havens for terrorists.*[61]

Second, the ICC would act as a more impartial body than an individual state court situated—as is often the case—in the country where the terrorist act occurred. This would also remove the defense of states harboring terrorists that they fear biased adjudication if extradition were granted. The horrific nature of terrorism, says Sailer, renders it a difficult crime to judge impartially if the court sits in the affected state. For terrorism, like treason, is a crime imputed against all the citizens of a country; thus, in effect, terrorist trials in victim states are being adjudicated by the terror victims themselves. A converse problem occurs where the requested state—that is, the state that has been asked to extradite the suspected terrorist—chooses instead to prosecute itself. Such a decision would likely reflect a political motive other than the desire to do justice and might ensure unwarranted leniency for the defendants. "These types of problems could be easily circumvented by referring cases of international terrorism to the impartial body of the ICC," Sailer argues. "Resolving international matters before such judges would greatly enhance objectivity and impartiality, which would result in greater fairness to all parties involved."[62]

The idea of an impartial and international body adjudicating terrorism is appealing, for it reflects an understanding of terrorism as a truly international crime meriting an international response. Not only will ICC jurisdiction ensure greater impartiality for the accused and the accuser, it will also "be an important step toward reducing animosity and distrust among the diverse peoples of the world."[63] The fundamental problem of domestic jurisdiction is its limited scope; no matter how inclusive a state's laws may be, no state can force extradition of a defendant from another unwilling state.

There are two solutions to this problem. One is to overcome by force all states that refuse extradition, an approach that seems to have been followed in Afghanistan and Iraq. The second is to cede jurisdiction to an international court with the understanding that, under the principles of *aut dedere aut judicare*, states that refuse to grant extradition to this impartial body are committing an offense not merely against the aggrieved victim state but the international community as a whole. The problem of achieving international consensus, disastrously unsuccessful in the recent war with Iraq, may thus be avoided. Moreover, ICC jurisdiction would prevent the spark of conflict from arising between states over the terrorists' nationality. The ICC, Sailer writes, "would . . . enable victims to assign blame to specific individuals rather than to the nation or group to which the criminal or terrorist belongs."[64] This would also reflect a correct interpretation of terrorism as distinct from state actions such as genocide, and closer to other forms of international private malfeasance, such as piracy.

The final reason for granting ICC jurisdiction over terrorism lies in the familiar problem encountered earlier in our discussion of piracy law, of political terrorism. Most extradition treaties contain a political offense exception: an exception to extradition for crimes committed in furtherance of a legitimate political purpose. The reason for this exception is twofold; first, it prevents states from seeking extradition solely on the grounds of political benefit to themselves, rather than the occurrence of an actual crime; second, it recognizes the right of people to rebel against their governments without fear of international reprisal. This is also known as the right to self-determination and is a fundamental tenet of international law. The problem with extradition is that there is no uniform standard among states as to what constitutes a political act. The United States and Great Britain employ an "incidence test," meaning that the alleged political act must be in furtherance of a political uprising. Mere declaration of political motives does not hold weight, any more than in the "political" piracy exception discussed previously.

Sailer sees the danger of heterogeneous political offense exceptions as possibly "eroding the people's right to self-determination embodied in Article I of the UN charter."[65] He points out that the opportunity for states to declare any act of rebellion as "terrorism" is great and posits that even the American Revolution of 1776 might be termed thus under the currently vague international standards. "There is a much better solution," he writes, "that could resolve most of the difficulties with extradition and the political offence exception that have been outlined."

> This solution would be able to provide impartiality, uniformity, and could also be tailored in such a way as to preserve the people's right to self-determination, while simultaneously fulfilling states' goals of reducing incidents of terrorism more effectively. This solution consists of granting the ICC jurisdiction over terrorist acts.[66]

The concept of the ICC as an impartial, apolitical alternative to extradition has even greater merit considering the refusal of the United States to submit itself to ICC jurisdiction. Under the current circumstances, the ICC might well become an impartial and apolitical alternative to US courts. This would then put pressure on the United States: first, to ensure that it conducts its prosecutions fairly, consistent with those of its international counterpart; second, to reconsider its refusal to join, since as a member it would be in a better position to arrange for the extradition and prosecution of a far greater number of terrorists than its own laws and treaties would otherwise allow. Conversely, states that feel justified in refusing extradition to the United States might not be able to muster the same arguments for extradition to an impartial, international criminal court. In a backhanded manner, this would also aid the United States: the net result would be a greater number of terrorist prosecutions.

The preceding arguments make a strong case for ICC terrorist jurisdiction, but two questions still remain: (1) on what basis should jurisdiction be granted? and (2) should terrorism be given its own category? As to the first, William Schabas argues force-fully that terrorism has no place in the ICC, as the intended pur-pose of the court is to deal solely with government-related crimes.[67] As I noted earlier, this is inaccurate. Professor Daniel Prefontaine notes that there is nothing in the Rome statute that explicitly restricts international crimes to state actors; he believes, conversely, that the loose definition of crimes against humanity is broad enough to encompass a plethora of terrorist acts.[68] Todd Sailer agrees that the ICC mandate is broad enough to include ter-rorism, but disagrees that it should be incorporated within crimes against humanity. The Rome statute, he notes, states that the ICC "shall have the power to exercise its jurisdiction over persons for the most serious crimes of international concern."[69]

Since 9/11, it would be difficult to argue that terrorism fails to meet this standard. Even prior to the attacks, terrorism was recognized as an international menace. Speaking before the UN General Assembly on September 21, 1998, President Clinton declared that states should "put the fight against terrorism at the top of our agenda,"[70] a statement that was underscored with deadly force almost exactly three years later.

CONCLUSION

This chapter has raised a number of problems surrounding the international legal response to organized terrorism. The most important are: (1) should terrorism be handled primarily in domestic or international courts and (2) should it be a distinct legal category, or incorporated into the existing law?

The first question is made paramount by the United States' refusal to join the ICC. Without American participation, one might argue, international terrorist law would be a paper tiger; a situation easily analogous to the efforts of the League of Nations, which also lacked US support. The question has both an idealistic and a pragmatic response. The idealist would prob-ably regard the ICC as the ideal seat of jurisdiction for terrorist crimes, citing all the reasons given above. Clearly, the international scale of terrorism and the pattern of response by such countries as the United States both cry aloud for an international legal framework to address the problem. It would be hoped, as noted above, that the creation of the ICC as an alternative jurisdiction would compel the United States to reconsider membership or, at the least, provide a counterbalance to American efforts to pursue, capture, and adjudicate terrorists.

However, under the existing state of things, a pragmatist would argue that a domestic response has the virtue of being more immediately effective. Recognition of terrorism as a crime *sui generis* under American law would, as Professor Rossetti argues, allow for a much more concerted and effective response to terrorist acts against American targets around the globe. It can certainly be argued that the most efficient means of combating the threat of organized terrorism is to focus on the state whose laws and courts will have the greatest role in adjudicating it. In addition, creation of domestic terrorist law is a far easier matter than its international counterpart, for it does not require the same degree of consensus on definition. The American Congress might simply agree upon a definition that best suits the circumstances and enact it into law accordingly.

Hence, another advantage of the domestic approach is *speed*. The threat of terrorism has increased exponentially over the last five years, with no sign of abatement in the near future. The impetus has never been greater for American jurists to respond to this new and potent menace with a coherent, consistent body of law. Numerous criminal statutes notwithstanding, that law exists neither domestically nor internationally. While the domestic approach may not be the most ideal solution over the long term, it is a necessary first step.

Yet even if domestic legislation is warranted, this should not and does not preclude the necessity for an international terrorist law. Domestic and international law are not in competition, but symbiosis. Even without an American presence in the ICC (or, as some might argue, *because* of that fact), the burden is still on the international community to create an effective global response to a truly global problem. Recent events have proved that even attacks launched against the United States do not always occur on US soil; while there have been only two notable attacks in the United States itself (both against the World Trade Center, in 1993 and 2001), terrorists have struck against US citizens in Yemen, Bali, Nigeria, Israel, and elsewhere. The ICC could claim jurisdiction over any and all of these offenses, assuming that the locus state was a member. The purpose would not be to preempt US jurisdiction, but to act in accord with it under the principle of *aut dedere aut judicare*; states that refused extradition to the United States on political grounds could not offer the same argument to the ICC. The ICC would thus be a powerful addition to the war on terror, asserting its jurisdiction over a greater number of suspected terrorists than could otherwise be prosecuted.

As to the second question of incorporation versus categorization in international law, I believe piracy provides the solution to the dilemma. Terrorism is a distinct crime; it merits a distinct classification. But those who favor incorporation recognize the near impossibility of finding consensus on this classification, as definitions are widely divergent and fail to resolve the crucial question of political motive. Here piracy is immensely useful, for it provides us with the example of a crime that has likewise struggled with the political question, and answered it by distinguishing between state or state-sponsored acts of piracy and "private motives."

This distinction can be easily applied to the question of terrorism versus insurgency, for the central inquiry is precisely the same: is this act committed on behalf of a recognized state or quasi state actor? If it is, then it is political. Acts that are committed by legitimate state/quasi state actors may still be violations of international law, but they would then fall into the prescribed categories of existing ICC jurisdiction. The function of melding piracy and terrorism law is to provide universal jurisdiction for private actors whose offenses rise to the level of international atrocities but cannot be prosecuted as agents of the state. Pirates are currently the only private criminals recognized by international law, under the twin doctrines of *hostis humani generi* and universal jurisdiction. An extension of these principles to terrorism not only provides definition and precedent to the crime but poses a counterexample to the dichotomy between legitimate insurgency and illegitimate terrorism.

This last point requires some explication. Political insurgency has a legal definition, but its inverse—terrorism—does not. The political offense exception defines legitimate insurgency as acting with the intention of overthrowing an existing government. Terrorism is defined as an act that does not meet this criteria. This is equivalent to an equation in which A has a positive definition, and B is defined as not being A. Piracy provides the other half of the equation, defining terrorists as *hostis humani generi*: private individuals committing international atrocities for personal motives, subject to universal jurisdiction.

In sum, the melding of terrorism and piracy in international law solves many of the problems encountered herein. First, it need not favor domestic or international solutions; ideally, *both* the American piracy laws (which defer on definition to the law of nations) *and* international law can be sources for this reform. Domestic legislation provides a swift means for recognition of terrorists as *hostis humani generi* in American law and correspondingly the basis for a new criminal code for the crime of organized terrorism. The ICC, in contrast, provides the opportunity for recognizing terrorism as an offense against the law of nations and of terrorists as international criminals subject to universal jurisdiction. Moreover, in absence of an American presence in the ICC, it provides an alternative jurisdiction for accused terrorists whose states would not allow extradition to the United States, as well as providing a model for American courts to follow in their adjudication of terrorists. Second, it avoids problems of legitimacy and definition in the ICC. Terrorism as piracy will not be seen as new law; rather, it will be seen as the most contemporary manifestation of the first international crime. Thus, the category of terrorism will not lack for legitimacy, nor definition.

NOTES

1. *Hamdan v. Rumsfeld*, 548 US 557 (2006).
2. *USA Today*, "Scalia Calls Europe 'Hypocritical' on Gitmo," March 23, 2006.
3. *Ex parte Quirin*, 317 US 1 (1941).
4. US Congress Joint Resolution of 18 September 2001, 115 Stat. 221 (2001).
5. President George W. Bush, Military Order of 13 November 2001, 66 FR 57833 (2001).
6. For a full account of the *Hamdan* trials, see Jonathan Mahler, *The Challenge:* Hamdan v. Rumsfeld *and the Fight over Presidential Power* (New York: Farrar, Straus & Giroux, 2008).
7. Ibid., p. 267.
8. Ibid., p. 269.
9. Ibid., p. 272.
10. Quoted in ibid., p. 284.
11. Ben Saul, *Defining Terrorism in International Law* (Oxford: Oxford University Press, 2008), p. 3.
12. Ibid., p. 1.
13. Third International Conference for the Unification of Criminal Law, Final Commission Proposal, n. 240.
14. Alfred Rubin, "Legal Response to Terror: An International Criminal Court?" *Harvard International Law Journal* 43, no. 1 (Winter 2002): 67.
15. Saul, *Defining Terrorism*, p. 6.
16. James Fry, "Terrorism as Crime against Humanity and Genocide: The Backdoor to Universal Jurisdiction," *UCLA Journal of International Law & Foreign Affairs* 7, no. 1 (2007): 169.
17. Todd Sailer, "The International Criminal Court: An Argument to Extend Jurisdiction to Terrorism and a Dismissal of US Objections," *Temple International and Comparative Law Journal* 13 (1999): 311.
18. Ibid., p. 326.
19. Ibid., p. 337.

20. Ibid., p. 327.

21. Fry, "Terrorism as Crime against Humanity," p. 179.

22. Jennifer Trahan, "Terrorism Conventions: Existing Gaps and Different Approaches," *New England International & Comparative Law Annual* 8 (2002): 216.

23. Ibid.

24. Ibid., p. 218.

25. Ibid., p. 219.

26. Ibid., p. 221.

27. Ibid., p. 222.

28. International Convention for the Suppressions of the Financing of Terrorism (1999), art. 14.

29. Ad Hoc Committee Report of Committee Established by General Assembly Resolution 5 11210, December 17, 1996, 6th sess., UN Doc. Al57137.

30. Trahan, "Terrorism Conventions," p. 239.

31. Security Council Resolution 1373 (September 28, 2001).

32. Fry, "Terrorism as Crime against Humanity," p. 180.

33. Arab Convention for the Suppression of Terrorism, art. 3.I–4.III.

34. Fry, "Terrorism as Crime against Humanity," p. 182.

35. Ibid.

36. Quoted in Sailer, "The International Criminal Court," p. 320.

37. Quoted in Fry, "Terrorism as Crime against Humanity," p. 183.

38. Quoted in ibid., p. 169.

39. Ibid., p. 198.

40. Ibid., p. 190.

41. It is worth noting in passing the startling correlation between bin Laden's instructions to his followers, particularly with regard to "killing and plundering the Americans wherever and whenever they are found," and the universal aspects of the crime of piracy.

42. Fry, "Terrorism as Crime against Humanity," p. 190.

43. Ibid., p. 193.

44. Quoted in ibid.

45. Ibid., p. 197.

46. Michael Rossetti, "Terrorism as a Violation of the Law of Nations after *Kadic v. Karadzic*," *St. John's Journal of Legal Commentary* 12 (1996–97): 585.

47. Ibid., p. 590.

48. See, generally, Sailer, "International Criminal Court."

49. Rossetti, "Terrorism as a Violation of the Law of Nations," p. 587.

50. Ibid.

51. Ibid., p. 588.

52. Ibid.

53. Rossetti, "Terrorism as a Violation of the Law of Nations," p. 565.

54. Rubin, "Legal Response to Terror," p. 68.

55. Ibid.

56. Ibid.

57. Ibid., p. 69.

58. Sailer, "The International Criminal Court," p. 312.

59. Quoted in ibid., p. 320.

60. Ibid., p. 328.

61. Ibid.

62. Ibid., p. 330.

63. Ibid.

64. Ibid., p. 331.

65. Ibid., p. 337.

66. Ibid., p. 339.

67. William Schabas, "The ICC: The Secret of Its Success," unpublished article.

68. Daniel Prefontaine, "Under International Law Is There a Category of Prisoner in Armed Conflicts Known as an 'Unlawful or Unprivileged or Enemy Combatant'?" *Canadian Council on International Law Conference* (October 2002): 4.

69. Sailer, "The International Criminal Court," p. 318.

70. Quoted in ibid., p. 323.

Chapter 6
A NEW TERRORIST LAW

ow that we have considered the efficacy of piracy law for terrorism, the need for such a law, and its proper venue, only one task remains: providing a definition.

In determining the necessity of an international terrorist law, one must consider the dual purpose of every criminal law. First, by proscribing certain conduct, it terms that conduct anathema to society and deters it through punishment. Second, by delineating the state's role in the capture, trial, and punishment of offenders, it legitimizes the state as the just enforcer of universal social principles. International terrorist law performs both functions: first, terrorism is recognized as a crime *sui generis* that is contrary to the social good; second, by ceding their impunity, the United States and its allies gain legitimacy to capture, adjudicate, and punish offenders under the law. It is not enough for the United States to declare that terrorists are international criminals. For the threat of terrorism to be successfully countered, this de facto status must be accompanied with a definition *de jure*. International terrorist law will not only govern the legal parameters of jurisdiction and capture; it will also give terrorists legal status as enemies of the human race and subject them to universal jurisdiction. Terrorists will not be enemies of *one* state but of *all* states. Thus the United States' burden will be shared by every nation. The war on terrorism will become an international effort, transforming itself from personal vengeance and individual state security to international condemnation and the eradication of a global scourge. Only in this manner can the threat of global terrorism be successfully countered. Today, Americans question why we must give terrorists the benefit of international law. The answer, which I gave at the beginning of this book, is that we must do so for our own safety's sake.

I have argued that the only means of addressing the problem of terrorism in international law is through the law of piracy. Piracy is the ancestor of terrorism, sharing its essential characteristics; its history in both fact and law mirrors that of terrorism. Piracy is also terrorism's blood brother in the law, raising the same problems of definition and political exception that have frustrated recent attempts to create an international crime of terrorism. Moreover, pirates share with terrorists the unique status of individual menaces to the international order, the only such criminals existing independent of state agency or sponsorship. Based on the arguments raised in the preceding chapters, the interrelation between piracy and terrorism cannot be doubted. The question remains, however, of how best to approach this relationship in the law. This concluding chapter will address the question of formulating a new international terrorist law based on the existing law of piracy. A proposal outlining this law's definition and jurisdiction will be advanced. Finally, the events of September 11, 2001, will be used as a test case. The purpose of this test will not be to prove merely that 9/11 fits the definition of an act of piracy, but that all international acts of terrorism share certain commonalities with piracy sufficient to make them analogous under the law.

A MODEL DEFINITION FOR
THE CRIME OF TERRORISM

The first chapter of this book demonstrated the strong historical linkages between piracy and terrorism. Later, we considered the synonymous *mens rea*, *actus reus*, and *locus* of piracy and terrorism. The previous chapter has shown that there is no universal definition of terrorism to draw from, but rather a list of proscribed offenses, all of which could fit within the aforementioned definition of piracy. Now we may bring together these separate strands into a cohesive definition. Drawing from the 1982 United Nations Convention of the Law of the Sea as the most recent source of piracy law, and mindful of all the debates surrounding the question of political exemptions, piracy on land, and the problem of maritime terrorism, I recommend that the new definition of the crime of terrorism— including acts of piracy—to be defined as follows:

1) The crime of terrorism is defined as:
   a) any illegal acts of violence or detention, or any act of depredation, destruction of property, or homicide;
   b) as well conspiracy to commit such acts, membership in an organization that conspires to commit these acts, and any form of active sponsorship including financial support, refuge, or withholding knowledge of such activities from the authorities;
   c) committed by persons not acting under the color of a state, government, or revolutionary organization engaged in the replacement of an established regime within the borders of its own state;
   d) against the citizens or property of another state;
   e) with the purpose of inflicting terror on the citizens or government of that state or achieving international recognition for a private cause;
   f) none of these provisions is meant to contradict or negate the existing terrorist offenses currently pro-

scribed by convention, covenant, treaty, agreement, or customary international law.

2) Terrorists do not lose their definition under the law if they are sponsored by a state, government, or revolutionary organization acting in accordance with clause (1)(b):
   a) political exemption is only to be inferred if the terrorists act as de facto agents of that state, government, etc. by committing their acts by its direct order and in furtherance of its policy;
   b) in that event, criminal liability transfers from the terrorists as agents to the state as agency; and
   c) the state is then inferred to have committed an act of war;
   d) states that sponsor terrorist activities as outlined in clause (l)(b) are not inferred to have committed acts of war but share criminal liability with the terrorists for any acts undertaken during their sponsorship.

3) The crime of piracy is defined as sharing the definition given in sections (1) and (2), specifically for crimes committed:
   a) on the high seas, against another ship or aircraft, or against persons or property on board such ship or aircraft;
   b) against a ship, aircraft, persons, or property in a place outside the jurisdiction of any state;
   c) against persons or property within the jurisdiction of the state, where the pirates have:
      i)   descended by sea to a coastal port;
      ii) descended by air to any city or township;
   d) the crime of piracy also includes acts committed for pecuniary gain.

4) Terrorists and pirates are defined as *hostis humani generi* under the law of nations and therefore they are subject to universal jurisdiction, meaning:

a) as enemies of all nations, any state may effect the capture of a suspected offender;
b) such capture must be made in accordance with international law;
c) the capturing state must then either prosecute the offender under its own laws and in good faith, or;
d) extradite the suspect to the jurisdiction of a requesting state, or to a requesting competent international tribunal.

There are many reasons for providing a joint definition of piracy and terrorism, but the most crucial is that it solves the dilemma between political and nonpolitical acts. We have already seen how piracy law reflects a gradual shift away from the doctrine of sea robbery to one of maritime terrorism: an evolution that was delayed, but not deterred, by the events of the twentieth century. We have also seen how contemporary scholars face the same obstacle with terrorism. The political spectrum of terrorism ranges from legitimate acts of insurgency at one end to isolated, individual acts of destruction or homicide on the other. The former is protected by the right of self-determination; the latter falls within the jurisdiction of ordinary domestic criminal law. The hybrid crime of terrorism lies in the murky gulf between them. Without some precedent from which to draw, no universal definition of terrorism can ever be agreed upon: for states and lawyers will battle ceaselessly over what constitutes a legitimate insurgency on the one hand, and what is an ordinary crime on the other.

Piracy provides the way out of this conundrum, as the definition offered above indicates. In distinguishing between political and nonpolitical piracy, the consensus is that for the political exemption to apply, the pirate must have some direct and appreciable nexus to a recognized government. This, in short, is the difference between pirating and privateering. While both acts are offenses against international law, the latter criminalizes the *government* rather than the individual. The government is perceived to have committed an act of war against the victim state; moreover, the illegality of employing pirates as a fifth column suggests that the agent state may be subject to charges of war crimes as well. This is precisely the same approach that I suggest should be applied to the difference between private terrorism (including state sponsorship as outlined above) and terrorists as agents of the state. We need not become mired in the difference between state sponsorship and state agency: the former assumes only that the state aids or finances the terrorist, whereas in the latter example he or she is acting on direct orders from the state, in furtherance of state policy. In both cases the state is equally guilty, although the precise nature of the crime differs between conspiracy to commit terrorism and war crimes.

The crucial difference between them is not in the culpability of the state but of the individual: whereas a terrorist is defined above as *hostis humani generi,* persons acting under color of the state are regarded as agents of that state, and thus not individually liable for the crime of terrorism. Similarly, revolutionaries acting on the orders of a revolutionary government are likewise not terrorists if their activities are in furtherance of a regime change within their own state. Some might question how to distinguish between revolutionary regimes and terrorist organizations. I addressed this question earlier: revolutionaries seek to replace an existing regime with their own and direct their attacks toward that end, within that nation; terrorist organizations have neither these political nor geographic limitations.

A melding of piracy and terrorism settles the problem of political exemptions once and for all by removing the gray areas and reducing it to a simple question: does the suspect act as an agent of a state or revolutionary regime? If he does, then the other four offenses of the ICC govern his actions. If he does not, then he is a private actor and thus exempt from prosecution for these crimes. The central purpose of equating piracy with terrorism is to create a separate category specifically for these individuals.

SUGGESTED JURISDICTION FOR
THE CRIME OF TERRORISM

The question of appropriate jurisdiction for the crime of terrorism has been dealt with extensively in the last chapter, with considerable attention given to arguments on all sides of the issue. It has also been advanced that the law of piracy provides a solution to the legitimacy-efficiency dichotomy raised by many scholars, giving terrorism both a definition and a history of precedent.

This book argues that the combination of piracy and terrorism allows for domestic and international legal recognition, and indeed both are equally necessary to combat the threat that terrorism poses. The United States has criminalized most terrorist acts under its own laws and has provided a definition of terrorism in its code. It also, in 2001, passed the Patriot Act, which covers a range of terrorist activities and commensurate state responses, including everything from protecting the northern border to extending the permissible use of wire intercepts. Title 8, which is headed "Strengthening the Criminal Laws against Terrorism," amends the definition of domestic terrorism outlined in US Code, Section 233 1. Revealingly, the words "assassination or kidnapping" have been replaced by "mass destruction, assassination, or kidnapping." Under the definition outlined in the Patriot Act, domestic terrorism is defined thus:

5) The term *domestic terrorism* means activities that
   a) involve acts dangerous to human life that are a violation of the criminal laws of the United States, or of any state;
   b) appear to be intended
      i) to intimidate or coerce a civilian population;
      ii) to influence the policy of a government by intimidation or coercion; or
      iii) to affect the conduct of a government by mass destruction, assassination, or kidnapping; and

> c) occur primarily within the territorial jurisdiction of the United States.

Section 808 of the Patriot Act offers a list of proscribed terrorist activities, which is striking in its inclusiveness. A far cry from previous enumerated lists (as discussed in chapter 3), the act includes offenses ranging from the destruction of an energy facility to the manufacture or use of biological weapons. In sum, the Patriot Act is a significant advance in domestic terrorist legislation. Yet despite its breadth, the act does little to legitimize the crime of terrorism. The domestic definition remains largely intact, with the significant addition of mass destruction, but no linkage is made or even attempted with any other form of criminal activity, nor does the law draw from any stated precedent.

As such, it is a definition without gravitas, and has already been widely criticized for its reactionary emergence in the wake of 9/11. For the Patriot Act to gain recognition and legitimacy, it must be wedded to American piracy law. Indeed, by giving terrorism the definition and precedent of piracy, the United States will in fact be complementing both laws; a melding with terrorism and the Patriot Act gives piracy a revitalizing boost of current relevance, while piracy provides this new terrorist law with both the legitimacy and the definition it so desperately needs. This same function will be served on the international level, but it is vital in US law; the United States is the principle actor in the war on terrorism, and hence its laws are the logical locus for the first reform to occur.

It must be emphasized, however, that this is indeed the *first* reform. This book advocates a two-stage process by which piracy and terrorism are wedded in both domestic and international law. As it will be easier—given the legislative structure of the United States—to effect this change domestically, it seems preferable to begin the process with domestic laws. A bill should be introduced before Congress providing a definition along the lines of that advanced above. This will not be in conflict with any existing American criminal law. Neither the Patriot Act nor US Code, Section 233 1 contain any provisions that prohibit the marriage of piracy and terrorism; neither provide any historical precedent for the crime of terrorism at all.

Moreover, there is nothing in the US piracy laws, in definition or practice, that would preclude its alliance with terrorism. The *Harmony* decision expressly includes acts of terrorism in its definition of piracy; the legal trend of the twentieth century was unmistakably toward universal jurisdiction for these crimes. In fact, the explicit joining of piracy and terrorism would merely serve to make apparent a relationship that has existed *sub rosa* for decades.

There is no doubt that such a reform is permissible under American law. The question, however, lies in the will of the American legislature to undertake it. Why should they effect this change, when the current status of the law allows them to pursue terrorists with relative impunity? One answer, outlined above, is that the United States has the duty to grant due process to even the worst criminals. One might also argue that democratic nations have a special responsibility to make their criminal laws explicit and their punishments just. Yet neither of these reasons, I fear, would be sufficient to persuade a reluctant legislature bent on extracting its pound of flesh from international terrorists. The primary reason, then, for creating a cohesive American terrorist law must be to facilitate the pursuit, capture, extradition, and adjudication of terrorists.

All these aims would be vastly aided by a crime of terrorism that owes its source to piracy and shares its principles of universal jurisdiction and *hostis humani generi*. Under the current law, terrorists can be tried only for the crimes enumerated under Section 808 of the Patriot Act, not for the crime of terrorism itself. Thus, terrorists must either commit these acts or conspire to commit them; in any event, the focus is on the act, not the actor. The crime of terrorism, as defined above, includes liability for mere membership in a terrorist organization. This is analogous to numerous provisions in piracy law that criminalize membership in a pirate band, absent any overt piratical actions. The assumption there, as here, is that membership itself signifies a willful break from the laws and protection of society and thus classifies the culprit as an enemy of the human race.

Second, the classification of terrorists as enemies of the human race gives legal credence to almost any action undertaken to capture them, at home or abroad, under the doctrine of universal jurisdiction. It has already been remarked that the American courts recognize this principle in piracy law; a similar recognition for terrorism would mean, in effect, that the United States may capture suspected terrorists anywhere they may be found, and compel the extradition of such persons from hostile states on the grounds of *aut dedere aut judicare*. A new terrorist law would not signify that the United States could do these things when previously they could not; in fact, both have been done repeatedly already. Terror suspects such as Osama bin Laden are pursued worldwide; the United States has repeatedly demanded extradition of terrorists ranging from the *Achille Lauro* hijackers to the Lockerbie bombers, on the basis of *aut dedere aut judicare*. The difference, however, is that it would now be able to do so with the foundation of universal jurisdiction behind it.

Defining terrorists as *hostis humani generi* has no adverse affect on their capture or adjudication under the law. On the contrary, such a classification would primarily serve to justify past captures and insulate them from international liability as breaches of state sovereignty and provide a foundation of legality for similar captures undertaken in the future. It is an established principle among states that it is always better— given the choice—to act in accordance with the law rather than in absence of it. A reform of domestic law along the lines I have outlined will give the United States' war on terrorism a solid bulwark of legal legitimacy.

Domestic recognition of terrorism and piracy will aid the United States' efforts to combat terrorism worldwide, but alone it provides only part of the solution. Equally vital is a parallel recognition in international law and the demarcation of jurisdiction to an international court to try offenders for the crime. For all the reasons stated in chapter 3, I advocate the creation of a separate crime of terrorism in the ICC, with the definition stated above. The arguments of numerous scholars have already demonstrated the efficacy of ICC jurisdiction in contrast to any other alternative, yet there are also singular reasons for creating a crime of terrorism as piracy in international law, irrespective of which court should have jurisdiction. First and foremost, the function of international criminal law is to recognize certain forms of conduct that the international community abjures as threats to society itself.

Prosecution is only one aspect of this criminalization; equally important, if not more so, is the mere recognition of criminality, absent any mechanism for capture or enforcement. The primacy of the second purpose is evident from the law's history: whereas certain activities—including piracy—have been deemed crimes against the law of nations for hundreds of years, a viable and permanent international court designated to try them is still in its infancy. The problem of enforceability redolent in nearly all international law suggests that the purpose of such law is as much symbolic as actual. Thus, while there are many practical arguments for extending ICC jurisdiction to the crime of terrorism, it is just as important to remember the symbolic significance of establishing terrorism as an international crime and terrorists as *hostis humani generi.*

Yet the practical arguments cannot be overemphasized, either. Symbolic significance without actual enforcement has been the persistent bugbear of international criminal law and is the primary reason the ICC was created. The court's purpose is to provide a permanent locus of jurisdiction for crimes that transcend national borders or confound national judiciaries. Terrorism qualifies on both counts. It is, by definition, an international crime: committed by persons of one state against persons of another. It is also a considerable problem for domestic courts, as previous difficulties in extradition and political disputes aptly attest.

The mere creation of terrorism as an international crime, however, is meaningless without a cognate recognition of terrorists themselves as enemies of the human race. This is because all the crimes currently judicable by the ICC concern actions made by a state or its agent; introducing the concept of private terrorism among (or within) these definitions is fraught with difficulty. Persuasive as it may be to term terrorism as a crime against humanity (which it certainly appears to be), the hurtle of state nexus remains to be faced. I have suggested that the problems encountered in finding international consensus on terrorism's definition lie in the impossibility of reconciling the private, nonstate nature of terrorism with its overtly state-oriented criminal brethren. The debate then becomes one of sophist line-drawing between political and nonpolitical terrorism, a problem that can easily be avoided by giving terrorism the legal definition of piracy.

In sum, the best course for approaching the problem of international terrorism is to effect the creation of a new terrorist law based on the laws of piracy for both domestic and international jurisdiction. As long as the United States continues to abstain itself from the ICC, that court will serve as both a guarantor of due process for accused terrorists and an alternate source of jurisdiction for suspects for whom states including the United States fail to secure extradition. Thus the ICC will not be a competitor or drain on individual state jurisdiction, but rather a role model and—more important—complementary judicial body for cases that would be otherwise nonjudicable. Domestic and international courts will be working in tandem, prosecuting a far greater number of cases than either could achieve by itself. Overall, the recognition of terrorists as *hostis humani generi* by domestic and international law will give notice to terrorists and the states that harbor them that there is no safe haven for them anywhere on earth. Wherever they go, wherever they may hide or seek shelter, they remain fugitives not only from the nations they have attacked but from the world entire.

THE LAW IN ACTION: 9/11 AND THE
FUTURE OF INTERNATIONAL TERRORISM

The immediate necessity for an international terrorist law post-9/11 lends urgency to the debate surrounding that law, removing it from abstract academic inquiry. Thus it is not enough to merely demonstrate the close relationship between piracy and terrorism as a basis for new law; it must also be shown how that law will aid the international community in the crises ahead. The problem facing jurists is a formidable one; the rapid pace of events forestalls the dispassionate inquiry necessary for creating a just law in favor of swift action; yet swift action without the foundation of law may ultimately worsen the threat of terrorism rather than abate it. Hence, the argument for creating a new law of terrorism from the existing law of piracy must have not only academic merit but practical merit as well. It must facilitate the capture and prosecution of terrorists under the law, while still providing the parameters by which states may engage in these activities.

It is for this reason that I have chosen to examine the events of 9/11 in light of both existing piracy law and the recommended law of terrorism as piracy. It is not my intention, however, to base the entire legitimacy of this legal argument on its applicability to the specific circumstances of 9/11. As I mentioned earlier, other scholars have made this mistake in their attempt to relate 9/11 to crimes against humanity and genocide. They have done so by arguing that certain elements of those attacks—such as bin Laden's genocidal fatwa or the sheer number of people killed—have requisite commonalities with crimes under ICC jurisdiction. This may be true. But it is not enough to prove that the events of 9/11 render it definable as an act of genocide to argue that *all* terrorist attacks may be termed thus. The focus should be not on the singularities of 9/11 but on the universal elements it shares with all international terrorist attacks.

The first of these is the piratical concept of descent by sea. This provision has both singular and universal applicability to

9/11. Singularly, one could argue that the fact that the terrorists flew airliners into a port city means that the attack was analogous to the sacking of a coastal port by pirates emerging from their pirate vessel: the only difference being that the former descended from the air, while the latter descended from the sea itself. International recognition of aerial piracy negates the significance of this distinction; it has long been understood that pirate attacks may occur in the air as from the sea, on the principle that both are outside the jurisdiction of the state.

The circumstances that make 9/11 an act of descent by sea have a universal element as well. While not all terrorist attacks occur on commercial aircraft, or against port cities, the idea of international terrorism presupposes that the terrorist arrives by some means from a country other that the victim state, with the express purpose of committing a terrorist act against that state. This is equally true in cases where the terrorist attack is not against the state itself but its outlying military bases, embassies, warships, or anywhere around the world where the flag of that state is flying. In all these circumstances—but most particularly those involving attacks within the state itself—the idea of descent by sea may be inferred to mean any person (not a citizen) who arrives in the state from overseas with terrorist intentions. The reasons for this inference are provided in chapter 2. As 9/11 contains an actual descent by sea—by way of commercial aircraft—it may also be termed a legal descent by sea in that the terrorists entered the United States from abroad for the express purpose of committing an act of destruction and homicide. While the former circumstances apply to only a limited number of attacks, the latter is nearly universal.

Second, the concept of destruction and homicide absent any intention of taking is present in 9/11, nearly all acts of terrorism, and the law of piracy. The attack on the World Trade Center accomplished three objectives: it terrorized Americans, killed a significant number of them, and disrupted trade. In each of these intentions it was analogous to the pirates' war against the world, as well as to the legal elements of the crime of piracy as wanton destruction, depredation, and homicide, with or without pecuniary gain. While the scale of 9/11 may be greater, these elements are present in nearly all terrorist attacks, either singly or in combination.

The third universal aspect of piracy and terrorism reflected in 9/11 is the idea of an international crime committed by foreign nationals. Although pirates might be considered to be at war with their own state, the legal definition of pirates removes them from the legal protection of that state and renders them, in effect, stateless criminals. This is the practical meaning of *hostis humani generi*. Terrorists as *hostis humani generi* are similarly defined as international criminals, and the crime of terrorism presupposes an attack on the state by outsiders, not citizens under the aegis of its laws.

Accordingly, the definition of terrorism provided above contains the requirement that the terrorists not be citizens of the affected state. The reason for this, as I have discussed, is to distinguish between acts of legitimate rebellion or individual criminality from the crime of terrorism. Was the Oklahoma City bombing a terrorist act? Under this definition, no. The political motives and even the actions of Timothy McVeigh may mirror those of a terrorist organization, but the fact that he was a citizen of the United States must distinguish his crime, however heinous, from actual terrorism. Were it otherwise, domestic courts would have the dubious task of distinguishing homicide from acts of terrorism, which would place an intolerable burden on the legal system.

This raises the difficult question, however, of terrorist acts committed on behalf of an international terrorist organization by citizens of the affected state. While these would not, strictly speaking, be crimes of international terrorism, the nexus between the criminal and the organization—if proved—should be sufficient to make an exception in jurisdiction and allow the prosecution for crimes of terrorism to proceed. The justification for this lies in the fact that terrorists are *hostis humani generi* and consequently those citizens allying themselves with international terrorist organizations remove themselves from the protection of their state. Conversely, not every act of homicide or destruction committed by a foreign national may be termed terrorist. As evidenced by the definition above, the crime of terrorism contains a *mens rea* of deliberation to inflict terror or bring attention to a cause. This must be distinguished from other motivations for homicide, and while the distinction may not always be entirely clear, it is not beyond the abilities of justices to determine whether a suspect acted for private motives or in furtherance of a terrorist agenda.

Whereas the descent by sea and international components of 9/11 provide the basis for a correlation between piracy and terrorism for attacks against the state on its own territory, the hijacking element has applicability to acts committed not against the state per se but against its property and citizens around the world. 9/11, in fact, is almost unique in combining both these aspects—seizure of an aircraft and attack on the state—into a single act of terrorism.

Yet the seizure of a commercial aircraft in itself is an act of piracy, defined as taking by force of a commercial vessel while in transit and holding her passengers and crew captive. The menace of aerial piracy, first addressed in the 1932 Harvard Convention, has been the subject of considerable scholarly debate and is recognized as a form of terrorism in the 1963 UN Convention on Offences and Certain Other Acts Committed on Board Aircraft, the 1970 UN Convention for the Suppression of Unlawful Seizure of Aircraft, and the 1971 UN Convention for the Suppression of Unlawful Acts against the Safety of Civil Aviation. It is also closely allied to that other great menace to civilian transit, maritime terrorism. This relationship is underscored by the 1988 Convention for the Suppression of Unlawful Acts against the Safety of Maritime Navigation, which came in the wake of the 1985 *Achille Lauro* affair.

Thus 9/11 can be regarded as the most recent of a series of piratical attacks against the vessels of the United States and other countries, and the passengers aboard such vessels.

Recalling the definition of piracy as an act of depredation, destruction, or homicide against a civilian vessel, it is unquestionable that the seizure of four civilian aircraft and the deliberate murder of their crew and passengers qualify as piracy under the law.

The attacks on September 11, 2001, may, in fact, be considered as two distinct but interrelated acts of piracy. First is the seizure of said aircraft, which is a piratical taking under both international convention and international customary law of piracy. Second is the deliberate use of these aircraft as the means of destroying US property and attacking US territory. The link between them is the passengers, whose deaths may be considered in furtherance of both the piratical seizure and the attack against the World Trade Center. In either view, the applicability of piracy law to the events of 9/11 has profound implications for applying that same law to the crime of terrorism itself.

CONCLUSION

Just as events determine when a law is most needed, those same events will eventually determine what form that law will take. It is impossible to speculate on the future of international terrorist law absent the events of September 11, 2001. Likewise it is not the intention of this book to transform the law merely because of those attacks but rather to amend it so it may respond fairly and adequately to the new reality that they engendered. That reality, shortly stated, is war. The war on terrorism may lack the traditional components of state versus state conflict, but it must not be mistaken for anything else. Two regimes have already fallen in its wake; more may do so. Yet the war is not truly waged against these sponsor states but against the terrorist cells that exist in every nation, including our own. Terrorists may be of any nationality and may be found anywhere on earth. Thus this new war is not merely between the state and its enemies but the state and itself. It presents problems of definition and jurisdiction that have never been faced and lie well beyond the existing parameters of domestic and international law.

The problems posed by a war on terrorism exist not only among states but within them as well. Nations have two sets of laws: one for times of peace, another for war. Under the latter, peacetime liberties are curtailed, external restraints are imposed upon social commerce, and some freedoms are temporarily suspended. Such measures are deemed necessary to serve the greater good of protecting the nation from infiltration by its enemies, both within and without. Yet never in its history has America faced a situation such as it finds itself in today.

Unlike the experiences of the European states, whose histories are replete with Hundred Years' Wars, nor those of the Middle East and Africa, where local conflict spans millennia, armed conflict for the United States has always come in sporadic bursts. Its wars begin and end on definite dates, and it is entirely unacquainted with the idea of perpetual war. Today, however, America is in a state of *quasi bellum*, or half war, wherein the threat and the casualties are undeniable, yet the course of the conflict and even the enemy remain nebulous. We cannot know when the war on terrorism will end because we cannot use our successes and failures as a yardstick of its progress. Thus, a universal definition of the crime of terrorism is as crucial for domestic law and policy as it is for international relations.

*   *   *

The task before all states, but most particularly the United States of America, is to formulate a new law to govern the pattern of this new and nebulous conflict. The pervasive, ubiquitous nature of international terrorism mandates that this law address problems not only affecting interstate relations but intrastate criminal matters as well. To do so, terrorist law must effect a combination unique in our history: a melding of traditional concepts of individual criminality with traditional concepts of international conflict. The key problem centers on a class of international criminals whose actions and allegiances raise them above the status of mere criminals, yet who lack the legitimacy given to hostile states. If terrorist law does not take into account this unique hybrid status—halfway between criminal and revolutionary—then it will certainly fail to address the reality of twenty-first-century terrorism.

Historically, there has been only one class of private, nonstate-oriented international criminals, and that is pirates. Thus it is not merely advantageous to base the definition of a terrorist on that of a pirate; it is essential. Classification of terrorism as a crime against humanity or genocide may address the horrendous nature of the act, but it fails to account for the singular status of the actor. Both crimes, as with all international crimes excepting piracy, presume that only states or their agents can be held responsible.

Hence international criminal law, and the ICC itself, are extensions of the historical presumption that just as conflict can exist only within or between states, international crimes can occur only during and in furtherance of these conflicts. The war on terrorism stands in stark contrast to this presumption, requiring an entirely new perspective on the nature of not only international relations but also international law. The transformation of the former has already begun and will emerge by natural process as the United States continues its pursuit of terrorists across the globe. But the transformation of the latter must be effected by a positive act; it cannot rely on events to bring it to fruition, for the law emerges not from events but in response to them, and is thus a profoundly artificial and manmade creation.

That positive act must be the creation of a new terrorist law, based on the law of piracy.

Conclusion
RULE OF LAW

When taking on a book of this kind, the author must ask what his or her goals are. For most of us, especially those in academia, these goals are prescribed along narrow lines: recognition for one's work, the respect of one's peers, perhaps a column or two of restrained praise in a scholarly journal. At best, academics can only hope to—as one of my first professors termed it—"place their small brick in the great edifice of scholarship."

That was never my intention with this book. While recognition of the idea is crucial, recognition alone is insufficient. My purpose is not merely to present the linkages between piracy and terrorism but to offer them as a way out of the woods: a means of reconceptualizing the fight against terrorism, placing it within recognized, legitimate legal parameters and, most important, seeing it through to ultimate success.

Indeed, the most disturbing aspect of this ongoing war is that almost no one speaks of a conclusion any more. In the past nine years we have become conditioned to perpetual stalemate, an endless prolonging of the next 9/11. We accept "orange alerts" and heightened security at airports as part of our daily lives, and without surprise we hear of plots to destroy our most sacred landmarks, contaminate our air or water supplies, even incinerate our cities. Moreover, we have come to regard President George W. Bush's early prognostications of "victory" with jaded skepticism. Osama bin Laden still lives. His followers still plan attacks against us and other nations. The nine years that have passed since the last successful attack on American soil do not signify, in our minds, that the war against terrorism is over. We know that it is not, and even in our relative composure we dread the next assault and anticipate it. Americans are not accustomed to living in fear. Yet today we do.

Fear does not always mean a constant state of panic. More often it is a resignation, an acceptance of circumstances that allows us to function normally, yet with the dull thrum of anxiety ever present in the background. Hearing my fellow New Yorkers declare that a recent threat against the subways would not deter them from going out and living their daily lives, I was reminded of Londoners during the blitz cheerfully strolling among the rubble, placing placards in shattered shop windows reading "Business As Usual." For us the lengths between bombings may be long, yet we still scan the skies for danger.

It was this perpetual threat that led me to ask the seemingly obvious question: *why*? Why can this war never end? Why can we not even conceive "total victory" much less work toward it? Why have we accepted that states must forever remain under siege by terrorist organizations?

As Shakespeare would say, the fault lies not in our stars, but in our selves. The United States has never willingly defined this war. Definition means deference to a code of conduct, of law. But in our haste and panic, confronted with a menace virtually unique in our history, we chose instead to ignore the law and keep our options fluid. Did it work? Some would say it has: there have been no further successful attacks against the United States. Could we have achieved this result without suspending habeas corpus, trampling international agreements, ostracizing our allies, wiretapping our citizens, and engaging in two full-scale ground wars? We cannot know, and it will be left to historians to decide. What matters now is not whether these aims were justified, or even conscionable, but where we go from here.

The question is not an idle one. President Barack Obama has indicated a willingness to work within the law, closing down Guantanamo and rebuilding alliances frayed and in some cases shattered by the previous administration. He has opened channels of communication with nations formerly (and even still) hostile to American interests, especially in the Middle East. Most important, he has scaled back the occupation of Iraq and shored up the American presence in Afghanistan, where the al Qaeda presence is arguably the strongest. All these initiatives reflect a sincere desire to reset the dialogue on the war against terrorism, placing it within its proper context as a war shared by all states, and recovering some of the post-9/11 goodwill that we squandered so soon thereafter.

Yet while these initial measures are positive, there is still a discernible sense that he, too, regards this war as perpetual. The military commissions established under President Bush, and rejected in part by the Supreme Court, remain in force. Terrorists are still regarded as "unlawful enemy combatants," with nothing done to define the term. Most disturbing is the fact that the impetus to define the nature of this conflict seems to have faded. Aside from a directive to alter its terminology from a "war on terror" to a "fight against terrorism," little has changed since 2001.

I do not believe this reflects a willful disregard of the law, or even indifference to it, but rather uncertainty. Attempts to define terrorism, both nationally and internationally, have met with universal failure. While we recognize that the abuses of the previous administration occurred largely because of a vacuum of law, most commentators have simply blamed the Bush administration's unwillingness to bind itself, rather than attempted to explore the deeper causes of this legal quagmire.

The first step must be to define our terms. The war on terror cannot be an unknown but rather must be incorporated within an existing body of precedent. This precedent operates on two levels. First, it must be legally viable, providing the framework for conceptualizing the war. This has proved a major obstacle, as the United States has thus far been forced to choose between either limiting itself to domestic criminal law or international laws of war. It has chosen both, and neither. The results speak for themselves.

Second, the precedent must also be comprehensible on a general level. This means that when we define terrorism, that definition cannot be culture specific or open to misinterpretation. The most difficult problem for the United States has thus far been in distinguishing its fight against terrorism from other military and political endeavors. Hence the war on terror is conceived of as an American war brought about in response to the events of 9/11. But this is inaccurate and, worse, counterproductive. If it remains a US action, however that is defined, then states have no obligation to assist. Yet experience has shown us that without international cooperation, no real progress is possible. Thus it follows that however one defines this conflict, it is unquestionably an international one.

This book has gone to great lengths to demonstrate the linkages between piracy and terrorism, as well as the applicability of the former's law to the latter. Having examined the matter from both historical and legal angles, I believe these linkages are beyond dispute. But this is more than just an academic recognition of shared aspects. Piracy offers a way for us to understand the war we are fighting as an international police action against an international scourge. It offers a way, too, to understand terrorism free from subjective political, social, or religious aspects: a "war against the world entire" waged by persons who willingly divorce themselves from their nation-states, band together in extraterritorial enclaves, and employ acts of homicide and destruction to weaken states and pursue private agendas.

Most of all, terrorism as piracy offers a means for the United States to willingly bind itself within a system of laws, and thus gain legitimacy from so doing, while still reaping enormous benefits. Terrorism as piracy means that terrorists exist outside the pale of the law and states are justified in capturing them wherever they may be found. This does not excuse renditions, but it reclassifies them. The United States would still not be permitted to violate the sovereignty of another state in order to capture a terrorist suspect, but if it is willing to present evidence demonstrating that the suspect is guilty of crimes or is a member of a terrorist organization, the issue of state sovereignty would be effectively waived. Thus terrorist law would fulfill the double purpose of all laws: binding the state within a framework of certain rules yet awarding it the legitimacy and prerogative to capture and prosecute criminals.

Such potentialities are certainly far off from present circumstances, and there are those who would question whether the United States will ever gain the international cooperation needed to remove terrorist safe havens once and for all. My response is to look to the history. It took many centuries for states to band together to defeat piracy, but mostly what it took was a shared recognition that pirates were anathema, not merely to one nation, but to all. From that understanding came concerted action, just as we have seen off the coast of Somalia in the present day. Neither piracy nor terrorism may ever disappear entirely, but with the cooperation of states we can insure that when such threats surface, they can be quickly and effectively put down.

I close this book with a personal appeal to the US president, members of Congress, and all those committed to seeing an end to the fight against terrorism. Victory is possible. Indeed it is certain, once we are willing to recognize the nature of what we are fighting. But first we must cede our impunity so that we may more than gain it back in legitimacy. We must define our terms. We must see this fight not in terms of ordinary crime or ordinary war but as a hybrid of both that has only one precedent in known history.

Piracy.

Appendix
SIGNIFICANT INCIDENTS OF PIRACY & MARITIME TERRORISM, 1961–2010

1961   Hijacking of the Portuguese cruise ship *Santa Maria* by Portuguese rebels in the Caribbean Sea

1981–82   Attacks on Irish coastal shipping by members of the IRA

1985   Hijacking of the Italian cruise ship *Achille Lauro* by Palestinian terrorists in the Mediterranean Sea

1992   Hijacking of the *Nagasaki Spirit* in the Malacca Strait, resulting in collision with second vessel and numerous fatalities

1992–94   Hijacking and sinking of four Nile cruise vessels by Egyptian terrorists

1996   Hijacking of a Turkish ferry by Chechen rebels in the Black Sea

1998   Hijacking of the cargo vessel *Chang Song* by Chinese pirates in the South China Sea

2000   Suicide bombing of the USS *Cole* by al Qaeda at Aden, Yemen

2002   Suicide bombing of the tanker MV *Limburg* by al Qaeda at Yemen

2003   Hijacking of the tanker MV *Penrider* by GAM, Indonesian terrorists, off the coast of Singapore

2003   Hijacking of the supertanker *Dewi Madrim* by pirates in the Malacca Strait

2004   Attempted conversion of *Abu Hassan*, fishing trawler, to maritime attack vessel for Hezbollah

2004   Attacks on Khawr Al-Amaya and Al-Basrah port oil terminals by Zodiac craft (similar to the USS *Cole* incident) by al Qaeda

2004   Bombing and destruction of the Philippine *Superferry 14* by Abu Sayyaf Group and Rajah Revolutionary Movement

2005   Attack on the American cruise vessel *Seabourne Spirit* by Somali pirates

2007   Hijacking of the North Korean cargo vessel MV *Dai Hong Dan* by Somali pirates

2007   Hijacking of the tanker *Nepline Delima* by Indonesian pirates in the Malacca Strait

2008   Hijacking of the French luxury yacht *Le Ponant* by Somali pirates

2008   Hijacking of the Ukrainian arms vessel MV *Faina* by Somali pirates

2008   Hijacking of the Saudi supertanker MV *Sirius Star* by Somali pirates off the coast of Kenya

2008   Attack on the American cruise ship MS *Nautica* by Somali pirates

2008   Planned al Qaeda operation against Caribbean cruise ships uncovered by British Intelligence MI6

2009   Hijacking of the MV *Maersk Alabama* by Somali pirates and subsequent rescue of Capt. Richard Philips by the US Navy

2009   Attempted attack on Suez Canal infrastructure by al Qaeda

2009   Attack on the Italian cruise ship MSC *Melody* by Somali pirates

2009   Capture of the British yacht *Lynn Rival* by Somali pirates; owners and crew held for ransom

2010   Attack on the USS *Nicholas*, an Oliver Hazard Perry class frigate, by Somali pirates

2010   Capture of the South Korean supertanker *Samho Dream* by Somali pirates

GLOSSARY

Note: As many of the definitions discussed in this book are contentious, this glossary is intended merely to provide the reader with the basic distinctions between certain legal and political terms of art.

actus reus: the act or acts constituting a crime under common law

aerial piracy: the hijacking of a flying airplane

aut dedere aut judicare: "either extradite or prosecute," the legal principle under the law of nations that requires states to act in good faith to prosecute suspected violators

belligerent: belonging to, or recognized as, a state at war and protected by and subject to the laws of war

brigand: one who lives by plunder, usually as a member of a band

causus belli: legitimate causes for defensive war

corsair: a privateer of the Barbary Coast

extremism: advocacy of extreme and reactionary political measures or views

felon: one who has committed a crime for which the punishment in federal law may be death or imprisonment for more than one year

hijacking: to commandeer a moving vessel by coercion

hostis humani generi: "enemies of the human race," referring to international criminals perceived to have renounced their citizenship through their crimes and who may be seized by any party under universal jurisdiction

insurgent passenger: a legal term of the nineteenth century, referring to a civilian passenger attempting to seize control of a commercial vessel through coercion

jure gentium: laws that fall within the purview of the law of nations

jus cogens: international law gained through custom, common usage or shared understanding

law of nations: the body of laws governing relations between nations

letters of marque (*licentia marcandi*): commissions granted by the state during wartime sanctioning maritime acts of deprivation and destruction against the vessels of an enemy state

locus in quo: in the common law, the place where a crime occurs

maritime terrorism: the undertaking of terrorist acts and activities within the maritime environment, using or against vessels or fixed platforms at sea or in port, or against any one of their passengers or personnel, against coastal facilities or settlements, including tourist resorts, port areas, and port towns or cities

mens rea: in the common law, the mental state of a criminal at the time of the act

military combatant: a member of the armed forces of the state with which another state is at war

mutiny: concerted revolt of a naval crew against discipline or a superior officer

petit treason: in early modern England, the crime of killing a person to whom the offender owed duty or subjection

pirate: one who has committed piracy, as defined by the law of nations

privateer: an armed private ship licensed by a state to attack enemy shipping, and a sailor on such a ship

rendition: the extrajudicial transfer of a criminal suspect from one state to another

terrorist: one who employs the systematic use of terror as a means of coercion

terrorist organization: a political movement that uses terror as a weapon to achieve its goals

traitor: one who commits the offense of attempting by overt acts to overthrow the government of the state to which the offender owes allegiance or to kill or personally injure the sovereign or the sovereign's family

universal jurisdiction: a principle in public international law whereby states claim criminal jurisdiction over persons whose alleged crimes were committed outside the boundaries of the prosecuting state, notwithstanding extradition or any other treaty

unlawful enemy combatant: according to the Bush administration, a person who has engaged in hostilities or who has purposefully and materially supported hostilities against the United States or its cobelligerents who is not a lawful enemy combatant (under the Obama administration the term has been altered to "unlawful enemy belligerent," but the definition has not changed)

BIBLIOGRAPHY

Allen, David. *In English Ways: The Movement of Societies and the Transferal of English Local Law and Custom to Massachusetts Bay in the Seventeenth Century*. Chapel Hill: University of North Carolina Press, 1981.

Amussen, Susan. "Punishment, Discipline and Power: The Social Meaning of Violence in Early Modern England." *Journal of British Studies* 34, no. 1 (1995): 32.

Andrews, Charles. *Vice-Admiralty Courts in the Colonies*. Washington, DC: American Historical Association, 1936.

Andrews, Kenneth. *Drake's Voyages: A Reassessment of Their Place in Elizabethan Maritime Expansion*. London: Weidenfeld & Nicholson, 1967.

———. *Elizabethan Privateering*. Cambridge: Cambridge University Press, 1964.

Appleton, Marguerite. "Rhode Island's First Court of Admiralty." *New England Quarterly* 5, no. 1 (1932): 158.

Aravamudan, Srinivas. *Tropicopolitans: Colonialism and Agency, 1688–1804*. Durham, NC: Duke University Press, 1999.

Armitage, David, and Michael Braddock. *The British Atlantic World, 1500–1800*. New York: Palgrave, 2002.

Barrett, Andrew, and Christopher Harrison. *Crime and Punishment in England*. London: UCL Press, 1999.

Beattie, J. M. *Crime and the Courts in England, 1600–1800.* Princeton, NJ: Princeton University Press, 1986.

Beccaria, Cesare. *An Essay on Crimes and Punishment.* Brookline, MA: Branden, 1992 (1819).

Beier, A. L. *Masterless Men: The Vagrancy Problem in England, 1560–1640.* New York: Methuen, 1985.

Bentley, Jerry, Renate Bridenthal, and Karen Wigen, eds. *Seascapes: Maritime Histories, Littoral Cultures, and Transoceanic Exchanges.* Honolulu: University of Hawaii Press, 2007.

Benton, Lauren. *Law and Colonial Cultures.* Cambridge: Cambridge University Press, 2002.

———. "Legal Spaces of Empire: Piracy and the Origins of Ocean Regionalism." *Comparative Studies in Society and History* 47, no. 4 (2005): 700–24.

Blackstone, William. *Commentaries on the Law of England.* Boston: Beacon Press, 1962.

Botein, Stephen. *Early American Law and Society.* New York: Knopf, 1983.

Botting, Douglas. *The Pirates.* Alexandria, VA: Time-Life Books, 1978.

Boyer, Allan, ed. *Law, Liberty and Parliament: Selected Essays on the Writings of Sir Edward Coke.* Indianapolis: Liberty Fund, 2004.

Bradford, Alfred S. *Flying the Black Flag: A Brief History of Piracy.* Westport, CT: Praeger, 1999.

Brewer, John. *The Sinews of Power: War, Money and the English State, 1688–1783.* New York: Knopf, 1989.

Bridenbaugh, Carl, and Roberta Bridenbaugh. *No Peace beyond the Line: The English in the Caribbean 1624–1690.* New York: Oxford University Press, 1972.

Brierly, P. R. *The Law of Nations.* Oxford: Oxford University Press, 1928.

Brooks, Graham, ed. *The Trial of Captain Kidd.* London: William Hodge, 1930.

Buhler, Phillip. "New Struggle with an Old Menace: Towards a Revised Definition of Maritime Piracy." *Currents International Trade Law Journal* 8 (1999).

Burg, B. R. "Legitimacy and Authority: A Case Study of Pirate Commanders in the Seventeenth and Eighteenth Centuries." *The American Neptune* 37 (1977): 40–49.

Burgess, Douglas R. *The Pirates' Pact: The Secret Alliances between History's Most Notorious Buccaneers and Colonial America.* New York: McGraw-Hill, 2008.

Carse, Robert. *The Age of Piracy.* New York: Rinehart, 1957.

Chapin, Howard. *Privateer Ships and Sailors.* Toulon: Imprimerie G. Mouton, 1926.

Clark, Grover. "The English Practice Regarding Reprisals." *American Journal of International Law* 14 (1933): 690–723.

Cockburn, J. S., ed. *Crime in England 1550–1800.* Princeton, NJ: Princeton University Press, 1977.

Cockburn, J. S., and Thomas Green. *Twelve Good Men and True.* Princeton, NJ: Princeton University Press, 1988.

Coke, Sir Edward, *Institutes of the Laws of England; Concerning High Treason, and Other Pleas of the Crown and Criminal Causes.* London: E & R Brooke, 1794 (1628).

Conley, J. M., and William O'Barr. *Just Words: Law, Language and Power.* Chicago: University of Chicago Press, 1998.

Corbett, Percy. *Law in Diplomacy.* Princeton, NJ: Princeton University Press, 1959.

Cordingly, David. *Under the Black Flag.* New York: Harcourt Brace, 1995.

Cruikshank, E. A. *Life of Sir Henry Morgan.* Toronto: Macmillan, 1935.

Crump, Helen. *Admiralty Jurisdiction in the Seventeenth Century.* London: Longmans, 1931.

Defoe, Daniel. *A General History of the Pyrates.* Mineola, NY: Dover Publications, 1999.

———. *The Life, Adventures and Pyracies of the Famous Captain Singleton.* Oxford: Oxford University Press, 1990.

DiMaggio, Paul, ed. *The Twenty-First-Century Firm: Changing Economic Organization in International Perspective.* Princeton, NJ: Princeton University Press, 2001.

Dubner, Barry. *The Law of International Sea Piracy.* Boston: Martinus Nijhoff, 1980.

Earle, Peter. *Corsairs of Malta and Barbary.* New York: Sidgwick & Jackson, 1970.

———. *The Pirate Wars.* London: Methuen, 2003.

———. *The Sack of Panama.* New York: Thomas Dunn, 2007.

Ehrmann, Henry. *Comparative Legal Cultures.* Englewood Cliffs, NJ: Prentice-Hall, 1977.

Ellen, Eric, ed. *Piracy at Sea*. Paris: ICC Publishing,1989.

Evans, Peter, Deitrich Rueschemeyer, and Theda Skocpol, eds. *Bringing the State Back In*. Cambridge: Cambridge University Press, 1985.

An Exact Narrative of the Tryals of the Pyrats George Cusack, Henry Lovewell, et al. . . . held at the Old Bailey on Thursday and Saturday the 7th and 9th of January, 1674. London: 1675.

Forbes, Rosita. *Admiral Sir Henry Morgan, King of the Buccaneers*. Gretna, LA: Pelican, 2005.

Fry, James. "Terrorism as Crime against Humanity and Genocide: The Backdoor to Universal Jurisdiction." *UCLA Journal of International Law & Foreign Affairs* 7, no. 1 (2002).

Gould, Eliga. "Zones of Law, Zones of Violence: The Legal Geography of the British Atlantic, circa 1772." *William & Mary Quarterly* 60, no. 3 (July 2003): 471–510.

The Grand Pirate, or the Life and Death of Captain George Cusack. London: 1675.

Greenberg, Michael, et al. *Maritime Terrorism: Risk and Liability*. New York: Rand, 2008.

Hale, Sir Matthew. *Pleas of the Crown*. London: Richard Tonson, 1678.

Hanna, Mark. "The Pirate Nest: The Impact of Piracy on Newport, Rhode Island and Charles Town, South Carolina, 1670–1740." PhD diss., Harvard University, 2006.

Hebb, David. *Piracy and the English Government, 1616–1642*. Aldershot, UK: Scholar Press, 1994.

Heyman, Josiah, ed. *States and Illegal Practices*. New York: Berg, 1999.

Ho, Joshua, et al. *The Best of Times, The Worst of Times: Maritime Security in the Asia-Pacific*. Singapore: Scientific World, 2005.

ICC International Maritime Bureau. Piracy and Armed Robbery against Ships Annual Report, 1 January–31 December 2003.

———. Piracy and Armed Robbery against Ships Annual Report, 1 January–31 December 2006.

Jenkins, Brian. *Future Trends in International Terrorism*. New York: Parrit, 1986.

Johnson, D. H. N. "Piracy in Modern International Law." *Grotius Society Transactions* 43 (1957).

Konig, David. *Law and Society in Puritan Massachusetts: Essex County, 1629–1692*. Chapel Hill: University of North Carolina Press, 1987.

Langbein, John. "The Criminal Trial before the Lawyers." *University of Chicago Law Review* 45 (1978): 263–316.

Laslett, Peter. "John Locke, the Great Recoinage, and the Origins of the Board of Trade: 1695–1698." *William & Mary Quarterly* 3, no. 14 (1957): 370–402.

Lawson, Philip, ed. *Parliament and the Atlantic Empire*. Edinburgh: Edinburgh University Press, 1995.

Lewis, William, ed. *The Oxford History of the British Empire*. Oxford: Oxford University Press, 1998.

Mahler, Jonathan. *The Challenge:* Hamdan v. Rumsfeld *and the Fight over Presidential Power*. New York: Farrar, Straus & Giroux, 2008.

Marcedo, Stephen, ed. *Universal Jurisdiction: National Courts and the Prosecution of Serious Crimes under International Law*. Philadelphia: University of Pennsylvania Press, 2004.

Meyer, W. R. "English Privateering in the War of 1688 to 1697." *Mariner's Mirror* 67 (1981): 259–72.

Morgan, Gwenda, and Peter Rushton. *Eighteenth-Century Criminal Transportations: The Formation of a Criminal Atlantic*. New York: Palgrave Macmillan, 2004.

Nelson, William. *The Americanization of the Common Law*. Cambridge, MA: Harvard University Press, 1975.

Nordquist, Myron, et al. *Legal Challenges to Maritime Security*. Boston: Martinus Nijhoff, 2008.

Ormerod, Henry. *Piracy in the Ancient World: An Essay in Mediterranean History*. Baltimore: Johns Hopkins University Press, 1997.

Parker, John. "Pirates or Terrorists? BIMCO Links the Two Together in an Effort to Increase Ocean Shipping Security." *Traffic World* 31 (December 3, 2001).

Pennell, C. R., ed. *Bandits at Sea*. New York: New York University Press, 2001.

Pestana, Carla. *The English Atlantic in the Age of Revolution, 1640–1661*. Cambridge, MA: Harvard University Press, 2004.

Prefontaine, Daniel. "Under International Law Is There a Category of Prisoner in Armed Conflicts Known as an 'Unlawful or Unprivileged or Enemy Combatant'?" *Canadian Council on International Law Conference* (October 2002).

Rankin, Hugh. *The Golden Age of Piracy*. New York: Henry Holt, 1969.

Rediker, Marcus. *Between the Devil and the Deep Blue Sea: Merchant Seamen, Pirates and the Anglo-American World 1700–1750.* Cambridge: Cambridge University Press, 1987.

———. "Pirates and the Imperial State." *Reviews in American History* 16 (1988): 351–57.

———. "Under the Banner of King Death: The Social World of Anglo-American Pirates, 1716 to 1726." *William & Mary Quarterly* 38, no. 2 (1981): 203–27.

———. *Villains of All Nations: Atlantic Pirates in the Golden Age.* Boston: Beacon Press, 2004.

Ritchie, Robert. *Captain Kidd and the War against the Pirates.* Cambridge, MA: Harvard University Press, 1986.

Roger, N. A. M. "The Naval Service of the Cinque Ports." *English Historical Review* 111, no. 442 (1996): 623–49.

Rome Convention for the Suppression of Unlawful Acts against the Safety of Maritime Navigation, 27 ILM 672 (1988).

Ronald, Susan. *The Pirate Queen.* New York: HarperCollins, 2007.

Ronzitti, Natalino. *Maritime Terrorism and International Law.* Boston: Martinus Nijhoff, 1990.

Rossetti, Michael. "Terrorism as a Violation of the Law of Nations after *Kadic v. Karadzic.*" *St. John's Journal of Legal Commentary* 12 (1996–97).

Rubin, Alfred. *The Law of Piracy.* New York: Transnational Publishers, 1998.

———. "Legal Response to Terror: An International Criminal Court?" *Harvard International Law Journal* 43, no. 1 (Winter 2002).

Sailer, Todd. "The International Criminal Court: An Argument to Extend Jurisdiction to Terrorism and a Dismissal of US Objections." *Temple International & Comparative Law Journal* 13 (1999).

Sassen, Saskia. *Territory, Authority, Rights: From Medieval to Global Assemblages.* Princeton, NJ: Princeton University Press, 2006.

Saul, Ben. *Defining Terrorism in International Law.* Oxford: Oxford University Press, 2008.

Senior, C. M. *A Nation of Pirates.* New York: Crane, Russak, 1976.

Sharpe, Buchanan, and Mark Fissel. *Law and Authority in Early Modern England.* New York: Rosemont, 2007.

Sharpe, J. A. *Crime in Early Modern England 1550–1750.* London: Longman, 1984.

Starkey, David. *Pirates and Privateers: New Perspectives on the War of Trade in the Eighteenth and Nineteenth Centuries.* Exeter, UK: Exeter University Press, 1997.

Sundberg, John. "Piracy: Air and Sea." *De Pauw Law Review* 20 (1970): 338–56.

Tanaka, Takeo. "Japan's Relations with Overseas Countries." In *Japan in the Muromachi Age,* edited by John Whitney Hall and Toyoda Takeshi. Berkeley: University of California Press, 1977.

Thompson, Janice. *Mercenaries, Pirates and Sovereigns: State-Building and Extraterritorial Violence in Early Modern Europe.* Princeton, NJ: Princeton University Press, 1994.

Trahan, Jennifer. "Terrorism Conventions: Existing Gaps and Different Approaches." *New England International & Comparative Law Annual* 8 (2002): 215–43.

Trial of Major Stede Bonnet at the Court of Vice Admiralty, 5 George I. 1718, 1234–37.

Trials of Joseph Dawson, et al. at the Old Bailey, Oct. 31, 1696. London: John Everingham, 1697.

United Nations Convention on the Law of the Sea, Montego Bay, ILM 21 (December 10, 1982).

Villiers, Alan. *Men, Ships and the Sea.* Washington, DC: National Geographic Survey, 1973.

White, Stephen. *Sir Edward Coke and the Grievances of the Commonwealth, 1621–1628.* Chapel Hill: University of North Carolina Press, 1979.

Williams, Lloyd. *Pirates of Colonial Virginia.* Richmond, VA: Dietz Press, 1937.

INDEX

283

Significant Incidents of Piracy & Maritime Terrorism, 1961–2010

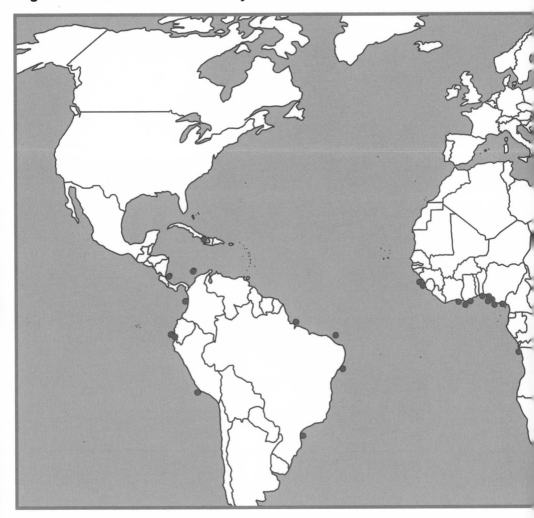

1961	Hijacking of the Portuguese cruise ship *Santa Maria* by Portuguese rebels in the Caribbean Sea	**2000**	Suicide bombing of the USS *Cole* by al Qaeda at Aden, Yemen
1981–82	Attacks on Irish coastal shipping by members of the IRA	**2002**	Suicide bombing of the tanker MV *Limburg* by al Qaeda at Yemen
1985	Hijacking of the Italian cruise ship *Achille Lauro* by Palestinian terrorists in the Mediterranean Sea	**2003**	Hijacking of the tanker MV *Penrider* by GAM, Indonesian terrorists, off the coast of Singapore
1992	Hijacking of the *Nagasaki Spirit* in the Malacca Strait, resulting in collision with second vessel and numerous fatalities	**2003**	Hijacking of the supertanker *Dewi Madrim* by pirates in the Malacca Strait
1992–94	Hijacking and sinking of four Nile cruise vessels by Egyptian terrorists	**2004**	Attempted conversion of *Abu Hassan*, fishing trawler, to maritime attack vessel for Hezbollah
1996	Hijacking of a Turkish ferry by Chechen rebels in the Black Sea	**2004**	Attacks on Khawr Al-Amaya and Al-Basrah port oil terminals by Zodiac craft (similar to the USS *Cole* incident) by al Qaeda
1998	Hijacking of the cargo vessel *Chang Song* by Chinese pirates in the South China Sea	**2004**	Bombing and destruction of the Philippine *Superferry 14* by Abu Sayyaf Group and Rajah Revolutionary Movement